Hiking
Mount Rainier
National Park

Heidi Schneider and Mary Skjelset

FALCON®

HELENA, MONTANA

A FALCON GUIDE ®

Falcon® Publishing is continually expanding its list of guidebooks. All books include detailed descriptions, accurate maps, and all the information necessary for enjoyable trips. You can order extra copies of this book and get information and prices for other Falcon books by writing Falcon, P.O. Box 1718, Helena, MT 59624 or calling toll free 1-800-582-2665. Also, please ask for a free copy of our current catalog. Visit our website at www.FalconOutdoors.com or contact us by e-mail at Falcon@falcon.com

©1999 by Falcon® Publishing, Inc., Helena, Montana

2 3 4 5 6 7 8 9 0 MG 05 04 03 02 01 00

Falcon and FalconGuide are registered trademarks of Falcon® Publishing, Inc.

Printed in the United States of America.

Cataloging-in-Publication Data

Schneider, Heidi, 1978-
    Hiking Mount Rainier National Park/Heidi Schneider and Mary Skjelset.
        p.   cm. — (A Falcon guide)
        Includes index.
        ISBN 1-56044-698-6 (pbk.)
        1. Hiking—Washington (State)—Mount Rainier National Park—Guidebooks.
    2. Trails—Washington (State)—Mount Rainier National Park (Wash.)—Guide-
    books. 3. Mount Rainier National Park (Wash.)—Guidebooks. I. Skjelset,
    Mary, 1978- . II. Title. III. Series.
    GV199.42.W22M6862 1999
    917.97'7820443--DC21   99-17420
                                              CIP

CAUTION

Outdoor recreational activities are by their very nature potentially hazardous. All participants in such activities must assume the responsibility for their own actions and safety. The information contained in this guidebook cannot replace sound judgment and good decision-making skills, which help reduce risk exposure, nor does the scope of this book allow for disclosure of all the potential hazards and risks involved in such activities.

Learn as much as possible about the outdoor recreational activities in which you participate, prepare for the unexpected, and be cautious. The reward will be a safer and more enjoyable experience.

♻ Text pages printed on recycled paper.

For John V. with love and thanks.

Contents

Acknowledgments vii

USGS Maps viii

Overview Map ix

Legend x

Introduction: The Mountain 1

How to Use This Guide 4

Planning Your Trip 6

Being Prepared 11

Seasons and Weather 18

Zero Impact 21

Trail Finder 23

The Hikes:

Longmire 27

   1. Klapatche Park 27

   2. Emerald Ridge 32

   3. Gobbler's Knob 35

   4. Indian Henry's Hunting Ground 39

   5. Rampart Ridge 43

   6. Van Trump Park 46

   7. Eagle Peak 50

   8. Narada Falls 52

   9. Comet Falls 56

  10. Trail of the Shadows 59

  11. West Wonderland 62

Paradise 70

  12. Nisqually Vista 70

  13. Alta Vista Summit 73

  14. Camp Muir 75

  15. Lakes Trail 80

  16. Dead Horse Creek 83

  17. High Lakes Trail 85

  18. Pinnacle Peak Saddle 88

  19. Skyline Trail 91

  20. Paradise Glacier 94

  21. Snow Lake 98

  22. Stevens Canyon 101

  23. Stevens Creek 105

  24. Box Canyon 106

Ohanapecosh **109**

  25. Silver Falls 109

  26. Grove of the Patriarchs 112

  27. Three Lakes 115

  28. Pacific Crest Trail 118

  29. Shriner Peak 122

  30. Ohanapecosh Park 125

Sunrise **130**

  31. Owyhigh Lakes 130

  32. Naches Peak 134

  33. Crystal Lakes 136

  34. Palisades Lakes 139

  35. Dege Peak 142

  36. Sourdough Ridge Nature Trail 145

  37. Silver Forest 147

  38. Emmons Moraine 149

  39. Mount Fremont Lookout 152

  40. Forest Lake 154

  41. Berkeley Park 157

  42. Grand Park 159

  43. Burroughs Mountain 162

  44. Glacier Basin 164

  45. Northern Loop 166

  46. Lake Eleanor 173

  47. Summerland 176

  48. Indian Bar 178

  49. Sunrise Rim 182

Carbon River **186**

  50. Windy Gap 186

  51. Carbon Glacier and Moraine 190

  52. Mystic Lake 193

  53. Green Lake 197

  54. Paul Peak Trail 199

  55. Tolmie Peak 202

  56. Mother Mountain 205

  57. Yellowstone Cliffs 209

  58. Spray Park 212

  59. Spray Falls 214

The Wonderland Trail **218**

  60. Wonderland Trail 219

Appendix A. For More Information **233**
Appendix B. Further Reading **236**
Appendix C. Hiker's Checklist **238**

About the Authors **240**

Acknowledgments

First and foremost, we want to thank the rangers and staff of Mount Rainier National Park. National Park Service employees spent many hours poring over this manuscript to ensure its accuracy. Special thanks to John Wilcox for coordinating the editorial efforts and to his coworkers, Debbie Brenchley and Rick Kirschner. Their expertise was invaluable to the formation of a quality hiking guide to Mount Rainier National Park.

We would also like to thank those people who offered their time, energy, companionship, and sometimes vehicles to help us hike the more than 300 miles of maintained trails in Mount Rainier National Park: Denise Peterson, Bill and Margaret Schneider, Marika Engelhardt, Stefan Durham, and Adela Soliz. Special thanks to John Caldwell and Bill Schneider for contributing photography.

On the home front, we would like to thank many people for their love and support. Thanks to Nikki Wallin, Alexandra Folias, Miles Norton, Miriam Aronoff, Alison Madsen, and our housemates, Esther Harlow and Daphne Stanford. We love you and appreciate you all.

USGS Maps

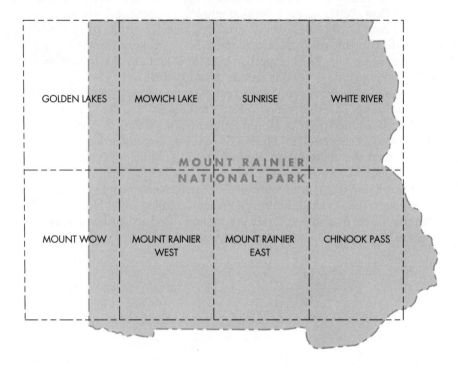

GOLDEN LAKES | MOWICH LAKE | SUNRISE | WHITE RIVER

MOUNT RAINIER
NATIONAL PARK

MOUNT WOW | MOUNT RAINIER WEST | MOUNT RAINIER EAST | CHINOOK PASS

Overview Map

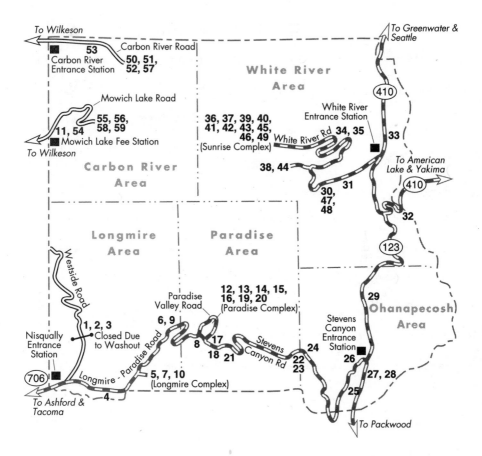

Legend

Interstate	26	Campground	▲
US Highway	17	Auto Camp	△
State or Other Principal Road	66 690	Bridge	
Forest Service Road	708	Cabins/Buildings	■
Interstate Highway		Elevation	3,294 ft. ✗
Paved Road		Gate	•—•
Gravel Road		Mine Site	✗
Unimproved Road	========⟫	Overlook/Point of Interest	◘
Trailhead/Parking	◯ Ⓟ	Restricted Area	
Starting Point	◯	National Volcanic Monument Boundary	
One Way Road	One Way →	Map Orientation	N
Railroad	+++++++++++++	Scale	0 0.5 1 Miles
Described trail			
Secondary Trail			
River/Creek/Falls		Mount Rainier National Park Locator	
Lake/Pond			
Marsh/Swamp			
Boardwalk	▮▮▮▮▮▮▮▮▮▮▮		

Introduction: The Mountain

Mount Rainier is, above all else, eclectic. Rising from the Cascade foothills, the mountain's broad shoulders carry steep-sloped forests, meadowed parks, U-shaped river valleys, jagged ridges, and a deceptively smooth-looking cap of ice and snow. This varied terrain harbors an array of habitats, from extensive montane and subalpine forests to bands of tundra and swatches of temperate rain forest. At higher elevations, glaciers and permanent snowfields exist in an Arctic environment just 40 miles from the mild, humid shores of Puget Sound.

Although its stature and majesty seem exceptional, Mount Rainier is only one of more than 400 volcanoes that constitute the "Ring of Fire" around the Pacific Ocean. The collision of oceanic and continental plates created this string of volcanoes. Almost a million years ago, Mount Rainier rose from a weak spot between the Juan de Fuca plate and the North America continental plate. By then, the rugged Cascades, including the Tatoosh Range, had already been created by carving rivers.

The Pleistocene Age, the ice age that began 3 million years ago and continued until 10,000 years ago, bore Mount Rainier. The first eruption sent massive amounts of lava cascading over a 15-mile radius around the small cone. Lava filled the streambeds and canyons of yesteryear, only to be carved again by new streams into the jutting ridges surrounding Mount Rainier. Ensuing smaller eruptions slowly built the cone to heights far above present calculations. Considerable erosion from glaciation, explosion, collapse, and the creation of riverbeds reduced Mount Rainier to its present zenith, 14,411 feet above sea level.

Mount Rainier was not undergoing these drastic changes alone. Mount St. Helens, Mount Adams, and Mount Baker were also in the process of formation. In fact, much of the pumice and ash found on Mount Rainier did not originate from its own volcanic eruptions, but from those of neighboring mountains, including Mount Mazama (home now to Crater Lake) and Mount St. Helens. These materials, although deadly and scorching to extant fauna and wildlife, create a fecund landscape for successive organisms. Below timberline, in areas temperate enough for plant growth, vegetation prospered. As a result of dramatic elevation and climatic disparities on Mount Rainier, an incredible variety of species developed in four distinct ecological zones: temperate rain forest, silver fir forest, subalpine forest, and the alpine zone.

As you hike the trails that traverse such a diverse land, keep in mind the dynamics of the past. The National Park Service has preserved this culmination of millions of years of evolution for the public to enjoy. Please, obey park regulations while you delight in this marvel of nature.

THE HUMAN PRESENCE ON MOUNT RAINIER

While becoming familiar with the geography of Mount Rainier National Park, you may notice the distinctive blend of cultural influences on place names. The human history of Mount Rainier divides into two discrete periods: pre– and post–Manifest Destiny. Before the arrival of Europeans, the ten surrounding Native American tribes revered the mountain, using its abundant resources only as a means of sustenance. Subsequent English and American explorers found Mount Rainier a challenge. Hence, those features with English titles were named after prominent summit-climbers, while Native American names bear witness to the spiritual veneration held for Rainier by local peoples.

Most of the tribes near Mount Rainier knew it as *Tahoma*, or a similar derivation. This word has been translated variously as "The Great Snow" or "The Great Snowy Peak," but these dry translations do not portray the reverence with which the word was spoken. The original name for the south flank of Mount Rainier, *Saghalie Illahe*, or "Land of Peace," designated a place of armistice. Today, we call this area Paradise. All tribal wars or skirmishes of all kinds ended when Paradise was entered.

Carbon dating indicates Native American presence on the mountain for 6,000 years. Never were these settlements permanent nor was the use damaging. With the summer melt-off, coastal and plains tribes alike set out for the high mountain meadows in pursuit of berries and game. The mountain provided an abundance of resources, which the plains tribes east of Mount Rainier depended upon for survival.

After the discovery of Mount Rainier by Captain George Vancouver, sustainable use gave way to commercialization, and concerns about survival arose only on the ascent to the summit. With the exception of Rear Admiral Peter Rainier, a little-known English naval officer who fought against the United States in the American Revolution, the names of features are those of summit-climbers. James Longmire, a prominent local who advocated the use of Mount Rainier's hot springs as a panacea, led the first two climbers to scale the entirety of the mountain to what is now called Sluiskin Falls. From this point on August 17, 1870, General Hazard Stevens and Philemon Van Trump completed the first ascent to the summit of Mount Rainier.

With the publicity of later summit attempts and the building of Longmire Paradise and Paradise Valley roads, the popularity of Mount Rainier grew. The need for the preservation of Mount Rainier and its surrounding area became evident, advocated by conservationists such as John Muir. With wide popular support, President McKinley signed into law the act declaring Mount Rainier the fifth national park on March 2, 1899.

Attempting to keep up with the mountain's increasing inundation of visitors, the management of Mount Rainier is in a constant state of flux. Lenient regulations of the past led to activities as damaging, dangerous, and frivolous as a ski-race from Camp Muir to Paradise Valley. The ski lift is now gone, as are the motorcycle track and the boat rentals, yet their legacies remain. Some of the earth was nearly irreparably scarred.

Aurora Lake. BILL SCHNEIDER *PHOTO.*

The recent implementation of the fee system should assuage some of the financial difficulties related to trail reparation. Some of the money might be allotted to replace all of the mileage signs. An attempt to convert all of the mileage signs to kilometers a few years ago resulted in major discrepancies in what the signs read and mislabeled, unlabeled and incorrect mileages. The National Park Service is now in the process of returning all of the distance readings to miles. The mileages that we have compiled came directly from the National Park Service's database and should reflect the most accurate numbers. The National Park Service has begun implementing various and reservation systems in order to find the one that best suits Mount Rainier National Park. Fees, permits, and regulations are apt to change, so call ahead for the most recent information on these systems. Appreciate the conservation attempts of the National Park Service, and preserve Mount Rainier National Park accordingly.

How to Use this Guide

To use this book effectively, please note the following items.

TYPES OF TRAILS

Suggested hikes have been split into the following categories:

Loop—Starts and finishes at the same trailhead, with no (or very little) retracing of your steps. Sometimes the definition of loop is stretched to include "lollipops" and trips that involve a short walk on a road at the end of the hike to get back to your vehicle.

Shuttle—A point-to-point trip that requires two vehicles (one left at the other end of the trail) or a prearranged pickup at a designated time and place. One good way to manage the logistical problems of shuttles is to arrange for another party to start at the other end of the trail. The two parties meet at a predetermined point and then trade keys. When finished, they drive each other's vehicles home.

Out-and-back—Traveling to a specific destination, then retracing your steps back to the trailhead.

RATINGS

To help you plan your trip, trails are rated as to difficulty. However, difficulty ratings for trails serve as a general guide only, not the final word. What is difficult to one hiker may be easy to the next. In this guidebook, difficulty ratings consider both how long and how strenuous the route is. Here are general definitions of the ratings.

Easy—Suitable for any hiker, including children or elderly persons, without serious elevation gain, hazardous sections, or places where the trail is faint.

Moderate—Suitable for hikers who have some experience and at least an average fitness level. Probably not suitable for children or the elderly unless they have an above-average level of fitness. The hike may have some short sections where the trail is difficult to follow, and often includes some hills.

Strenuous—Suitable for experienced hikers with an above-average fitness level, often with sections of the trail that are difficult to follow or even some off-trail sections that could require knowledge of route-finding with topographic map and compass, sometimes with serious elevation gain, and possibly some hazardous conditions.

DISTANCES

The distances we used in this book are derived from the National Park Service's database. Currently the National Park Service is correcting the mileage on all signs in the park to correspond to distances listed in the database. Keep this in mind when trail signs do not correlate with the numbers listed in this guide.

Our distances are current and accurate, although they are rounded to the nearest 0.1 mile.

MAPS

The maps in this book serve as a general guide only. It is wise to take a better map with you on your hike. The maps here are for general reference and do not have enough detail or cover enough territory to help much if you get disoriented.

There are a variety of maps for Mount Rainier, but in preparing this book we used Trails Illustrated Maps, Earthwalk Press Maps, or the USGS quadrangles. You can get these maps at park visitor centers or sport stores around the park. This list includes all the USGS quads that cover trails in Mount Rainier National Park.

USGS QUADS:
1. Golden Lakes
2. Mowich Lake
3. Sunrise
4. White River
5. Mount Wow
6. Mount Rainier West
7. Mount Rainier East
8. Chinook Pass

ELEVATION CHARTS

Most—but not all—hike descriptions include elevation charts. These charts do not give a detailed picture of elevation gain and loss on a hike, but they do provide a general idea of how much climbing or descending you face on a trail. Hikes without elevation charts are either very short hikes or hikes without more than 500 feet of elevation gain or loss.

Planning Your Trip

It is amazing how pleasant and stress-free your hiking trip to Mount Rainier can be when it is well planned. The following information should help you plan your trip.

GETTING TO MOUNT RAINIER

Mount Rainier is located in west-central Washington and has four entrance stations—one at each corner of the park. The southwest entrance, Nisqually Entrance Station, is open year-round, but the other three, Carbon River Entrance Station (NW), Stevens Canyon Entrance Station (SE), and White River Entrance Station (NE), are generally open mid-to late June or early July. It is an easy drive from Seattle, Tacoma, or Portland to any of the four entrance stations. It is also possible to fly into either Portland or the Seattle/Tacoma airport, where you can rent a car, take a shuttle, or ride a bus into the park.

Here is detailed information on how to reach each entrance station by car:

Stevens Canyon Entrance Station: From the north (Seattle or Tacoma), go south on Interstate 5 until you reach Washington Highway 512, which originates in Tacoma. Go east on WA 512 to WA 410. Get on WA 410 heading east. The park entrance is 33 miles from Enumclaw. After entering Mount Rainier National Park, continue traveling east to the junction with WA 123, 8.9 miles later. Go right (south) onto WA 123 for 11.2 miles to Stevens Canyon Road. Turn right (west) onto Stevens Canyon Road and the Stevens Canyon Entrance Station is directly in front of you.

From the south (Portland), go about 80 miles north on I-5 to U.S. Highway 12. Go east on US 12 through Packwood (the last town—and gas, camping supplies, etc.—before entering the park) and continue 7 miles to WA 123. Go left (north) on WA 123 and in 3 miles enter Mount Rainier National Park. In another mile, go left (west) on Stevens Canyon Road and the entrance station is directly in front of you.

From the east (Yakima), drive west on WA 410. The park boundary is 13 miles past the hamlet of American River. From the park boundary, continue 3.6 miles west on WA 410 and turn left (south) on WA 123. Drive 11.2 miles, turn right (west) onto Stevens Canyon Road, and the entrance station is directly in front of you.

Nisqually Entrance Station: From the north (Seattle or Tacoma), go south on Interstate 5 to WA 512, just south of Tacoma. Drive 2 miles east on WA 512 and turn south on WA 7. Drive 31 miles south to Elbe and go east on WA 706. Continue 13 miles to the park boundary. The last town before entering the park is Ashford, so be sure to stock up on supplies. The Nisqually Entrance Station is 5 miles east of Ashford, where WA 706 turns into the Longmire-Paradise Road.

From the south (Portland), drive about 80 miles north on I-5 to US 12. Go 30 miles east on US 12, then turn north on WA 7. Drive 17 miles north to Elbe and turn east on WA 706. Drive 13 miles to the park boundary. The last town before entering the park is Ashford, so be sure to stock up on supplies. The Nisqually Entrance Station is 5 miles east of Ashford.

From the East (Yakima), drive west on US 12 to WA 123. Turn right (north) on WA 123 and drive 3 miles to the park entrance. Turn left (west) on Stevens Canyon Road. Pay the entrance fee at the Stevens Canyon Entrance Station and continue west on Stevens Canyon Road, which eventually becomes Longmire-Paradise Road. The Nisqually Entrance Station is 6.7 miles west of the Longmire complex.

Carbon River Entrance Station: Whether you are coming from the north or south, the best route starts from Tacoma. From Tacoma, go east on WA 512 to WA 410. Go about 16 miles east on WA 410 to WA 165 in the town of Buckley. Go right (south) on WA 165, through Wilkeson, and continue 9 miles to where the road forks. Go to the left (east) onto Carbon River Road. Continue 8 miles to the Carbon River Entrance Station.

From the east (Yakima), drive west on WA 410 to Buckley. The junction with WA 165 is in the middle of Buckley. Turn left and drive south on WA 165, through Wilkeson, and continue 9 miles to where the road forks. Go to the left (east) onto Carbon River Road. Continue 8 miles to the Carbon River Entrance Station.

White River Entrance Station: From the north (Seattle or Tacoma), go south on I-5 to WA 512, which originates right out of Tacoma. Drive east on WA 512 until you reach WA 410. Go east to WA 410, which goes east and

Mount Rainier from Silver Forest Trail.

bends south as it nears the park. The road enters Mount Rainier National Park and continues 4.5 miles to White River Road. Turn right (west) and go 1.5 miles to the White River Entrance Station.

From the south (Portland), drive about 80 miles north on I-5 to US 12. Go 72 miles east on US 12 and turn left (north) onto WA 123, 7 miles east of Packwood. Be sure to get gas in Packwood because there is no gas available in the park. Continue 14.2 miles north on WA 123 and go left (west) on WA 410. Drive 1.9 miles and turn left (west) onto White River Road. Continue 1.5 miles to the White River Entrance Station.

From the east (Yakima), drive west on WA 410. The park boundary is 13 miles past the hamlet of American River. From the park boundary, continue west on WA 410 3.6 miles to the junction with WA 123. Stay on WA 410 to the right, and drive 1.9 miles to White River Road. Turn left (west) onto White River Road and drive 1.5 miles to the White River Entrance Station.

All of these entrance stations require an entrance fee depending on your party and your stay. Fortunately, most of the money goes to improving the park. It is a $10 fee for a single, private, noncommercial vehicle, and the fee covers all persons in that vehicle. The pass is valid for seven consecutive days. If you plan to return to the park, consider buying an annual pass for $20. Additional fee information can be obtained by calling 360-569-2211 ext. 2390.

Here are a few additional services that provide transportation to and from Mount Rainier:

Grayline Bus Services
800-426-7532; 206-626-5208
Bus service from downtown Seattle. Call for rates and reservations.

Rainier Overland
360-569-0851
Operates shuttles by reservations between Sea-Tac Airport, Ashford, and points within Mount Rainier National Park. Call for rates and reservations.

Rainier Shuttle
360-569-2331

The roads to the park are well maintained, but all are winding two-lanes and are often crowded with traffic, including slow-moving vehicles. If you drive during the day, don't be in a hurry. Also, remember that driving off any park road is prohibited.

BACKCOUNTRY CAMPING PERMITS

In Mount Rainier, you must have a permit for any overnight stay in the backcountry. Under the Fee Demonstration Project, authorized by Congress, the National Park Service began charging a fee for park visitors using backcountry camps in 1998, the year this book was compiled. The fees fund services and projects that directly benefit both the visiting public and park resources.

The fee system, new to Mount Rainier National Park, is undergoing some changes to better accommodate visitors. Specifically, the National Park Service is exploring alternative ways to manage the fee system. It is possible that it may be eliminated altogether. Check out the Mount Rainier website or call ahead to find out details of the current fee system. (See Appendix A for phone numbers and websites.)

Here is a list of regulations to help you obtain your backcountry permit.

- All permits are made on a first-come, first-served basis.
- The number of permits is limited.
- No more than five persons are allowed to stay at an individual site. If you have more than five persons, you will have to obtain a group permit. A group permit follows the same conditions/regulations as individual sites, but allows 6 to 12 persons. Mount Rainier has 21 backcountry group sites.
- Permits must be picked up in person no more than 24 hours in advance, but the park service is currently considering a reservation system. Check out the website or call ahead to find out. (See Appendix A.)
- If a trail or campsite is closed for resource protection or safety reasons, park service rangers will try to help you plan a similar trip.

The table on the next page will help you obtain your permit in the fastest, easiest way possible by directing you to the wilderness information center or ranger station closest to the hike you plan to take. (See Appendix A for the locations and phone numbers of these offices.)

CLOSEST WILDERNESS INFORMATION CENTER OR RANGER	HIKE
Longmire Wilderness Information Center	1 Klapatche Park
	2 Emerald Ridge
	3 Gobbler's Knob
	8 Narada Falls
	11 West Wonderland
Wilkeson Wilderness Information Center	51 Carbon Glacier and Moraine
	52 Mystic Lake
	54 Paul Peak
	56 Mother Mountain
	57 Yellowstone Cliffs
	58 Spray Park
	59 Spray Falls
Paradise Ranger Station	14 Camp Muir
	21 Snow Lake
	22 Stevens Canyon Shuttle
	30 Ohanapecosh Park
White River Wilderness Information Center	31 Owyhigh Lakes
	33 Crystal Lakes
	34 Palisades Lakes
	40 Forest Lake
	41 Berkeley Park
	42 Grand Park
	44 Glacier Basin
	45 Northern Loop
	46 Lake Eleanor
	47 Summerland
	48 Indian Bar
	49 Sunrise Rim
	50 Windy Gap
Ohanapecosh Wilderness Information Center	27 Three Lakes
	28 Pacific Crest Trail
	29 Shriner Peak

Being Prepared

BACKCOUNTRY SAFETY AND HAZARDS

Boy Scouts and Girl Scouts have been guided for decades by what is perhaps the best single piece of safety advice—Be Prepared! For starters, this means carrying survival and first-aid materials, proper clothing, compass, and topographic map—and knowing how to use them.

Perhaps the second-best piece of safety advice is to tell somebody where you're going and when you plan to return. Pilots must file flight plans before every trip, and anybody venturing into a blank spot on the map should do the same. File your "flight plan" with a friend or relative before taking off.

Close behind filing your flight plan and being prepared with proper equipment is physical conditioning. Being fit not only makes wilderness travel more fun, it makes it safer. To whet your appetite for more knowledge of wilderness safety and preparedness, here are a few tips.

- Check the weather forecast. Be careful not to get caught at high altitude by a bad storm or along a stream in a flash flood. Watch cloud formations closely, so you do not get stranded on a ridgeline during a lightning storm. Avoid traveling during prolonged periods of cold weather.
- Avoid traveling alone in the wilderness.
- Keep your party together.
- Study basic survival and first aid before leaving home.
- Do not eat wild plants unless you have positively identified them.
- Before you leave for the trailhead, find out as much as you can about the route, especially any potential hazards.
- Do not exhaust yourself or other members of your party by traveling too far or too fast. Let the slowest person set the pace.
- Do not wait until you're confused to look at your maps. Follow them as you go along, from the moment you start moving up the trail, so you have a continual fix on your location.
- If you get lost, do not panic. Sit down and relax for a few minutes while you carefully check your topographic map and take a reading with your compass. Confidently plan your next move. It is often smart to retrace your steps until you find familiar ground, even if you think it might lengthen your trip. Lots of people get temporarily lost in the wilderness and survive—usually by calmly and rationally dealing with the situation.
- Stay clear of all wild animals.
- Take a first-aid kit that includes, at a minimum, the following items: sewing needle, snake-bite kit, aspirin, antibacterial ointment, two antiseptic swabs, two butterfly bandages, adhesive tape, four adhesive strips, four gauze pads, two triangular bandages, codeine tablets, two inflatable splints, Moleskin or Second Skin for blisters, one roll of 3-inch gauze, CPR shield, rubber gloves, and lightweight first-aid instructions.

- Take a survival kit that includes, at a minimum, the following items: compass, whistle, matches in a waterproof container, cigarette lighter, candle, signal mirror, flashlight, fire starter, aluminum foil, water purification tablets, space blanket, and flare.
- Last but not least, do not forget that the best defense against unexpected hazards is knowledge. Read up on the latest in wilderness safety information in the recently published *Wild Country Companion*. (See Appendix B for ordering information.)

HYPOTHERMIA: THE SILENT KILLER

Be aware of the danger of hypothermia—a condition in which the body's internal temperature drops below normal. It can lead to mental and physical collapse and death.

Hypothermia is caused by exposure to cold and is aggravated by wetness, wind, and exhaustion. The moment you begin to lose heat faster than your body produces it, you're suffering from exposure. Your body starts involuntary exercise, such as shivering, to stay warm and makes involuntary adjustments to preserve normal temperature in vital organs, restricting bloodflow in the extremities. Both responses drain your energy reserves. The only way to stop the drain is to reduce the degree of exposure.

With full-blown hypothermia, as energy reserves are exhausted, cold reaches the brain, depriving you of good judgment and reasoning power. You will not be aware that this is happening. You lose control of your hands.

Mount Rainier from atop Tolmie Peak.

Your internal temperature slides downward. Without treatment, this slide leads to stupor, collapse, and death.

To defend against hypothermia, stay dry. When clothes get wet, they lose about 90 percent of their insulating value. Wool loses relatively less heat; cotton, down, and some synthetics lose more. Choose rain clothes that cover the head, neck, body, and legs and provide good protection against wind-driven rain. Most hypothermia cases develop in air temperatures between 30 and 50 degrees, but hypothermia can develop in warmer temperatures.

If your party is exposed to wind, cold, and wet, think hypothermia. Watch yourself and others for these symptoms: uncontrollable fits of shivering; vague, slow, slurred speech; memory lapses; incoherence; immobile, fumbling hands; frequent stumbling or a lurching gait; drowsiness (to sleep is to die); apparent exhaustion; and inability to get up after a rest. When a member of your party has hypothermia, he or she may deny any problem. Believe the symptoms, not the victim. Even mild symptoms demand treatment, as follows:

- Get the victim out of the wind and rain.
- Strip off all wet clothes.
- Dress the victim in warm clothes and a warm sleeping bag. Place well-wrapped water bottles filled with heated water close to the victim. If the victim is only mildly impaired, give him or her warm drinks.
- If the victim is badly impaired, attempt to keep him or her awake. Put the victim in a sleeping bag with another person—both naked. If you have a double bag, put two warm people in with the victim.

COUGAR SAFETY

Although there has never been a reported cougar attack in Mount Rainier National Park, there have been sightings. It is important to be prepared for an encounter. The most important safety element for recreation in cougar country is simply recognizing their habitat. Deer are the primary prey of cougar, and these ungulates are a key element in cougar habitat. If you are not experienced at observing deer or at recognizing their tracks or feces, talk to locals, park rangers, or state wildlife biologists. Fish and wildlife agencies usually have good information about deer distribution from population surveys and hunting results.

Deer tracks can be found easily on dirt roads and trails. If you are not familiar with identifying deer tracks, seek the advice of someone knowledgeable, or refer to a book on animal tracks such as Falcon's *Scats and Tracks* series.

Safety guidelines for traveling in cougar country.

1. Travel with a friend or group.

2. Keep small children close.

3. Do not let pets run unleashed.

4. Try to minimize your recreation during dawn and dusk—the times cougars are most active.

5. Watch for warning signs of cougar activity.

6. Know how to behave if you encounter a cougar (see below).

What to do if you encounter a cougar.

In the vast majority of cougar encounters, these animals exhibit avoidance, indifference, or curiosity that never results in human injury. But it is natural to be alarmed if you have an encounter of any kind. Try to keep your cool and consider the following:

1. Recognize threatening cougar behavior.
There are a few cues that may help you gauge the risk of attack. If a cougar is more than 50 yards away and it directs its attention to you, it may be only curious. This situation represents only a slight risk for adults, but a more serious risk to unaccompanied children. At this point, you should move away, while keeping the animal in your peripheral vision. Also, look for rocks, sticks, or something to use as a weapon, just in case.

If a cougar is crouched and staring intensely at you less than 50 yards away, it may be assessing the chances of a successful attack. If this behavior continues, the risk of attack may be high.

2. Do not approach a cougar; give the animal the opportunity to move on.
Slowly back away, but maintain eye contact if close. Cougars are not known to attack humans to defend young or a kill, but they have been reported to "charge" in rare instances. Best choose another route or time to venture through the area.

3. Do not run from a cougar. Running may stimulate a predatory response.

4. If you encounter a cougar, be vocal and talk or yell loudly and regularly. Try not to panic: Shout in a way that others in the area may understand to make them aware of the situation.

5. Maintain eye contact. Eye contact presents a challenge to the cougar, showing you are aware of its presence. Eye contact also helps you know where it is. However, if the behavior of the cougar is not threatening (if it is, for example, grooming or periodically looking away), maintain visual contact through your peripheral vision and move away.

6. Appear larger than you are. Raise your arms above your head and make steady waving motions. Raise your jacket or another object above your head. Do not bend over as this will make you appear smaller and more "preylike."

7. If you are with small children, pick them up. First bring children close to you, maintain eye contact with the cougar, and pull the children up without bending over. If you are with other children or adults, band together.

8. Be prepared to defend yourself and fight back, if attacked. Try to remain standing. Do not feign death. Pick up a branch or rock, pull out a knife, pepper spray, or other deterrent device. Remember, everything is a potential weapon, and individuals have fended off cougars with blows from rocks, tree limbs, and even cameras.

9. Defend your friends or children, but not your pet. In past attacks on children, adults have successfully stopped attacks. However, it is very dangerous and risky, and physically defending a pet is not recommended.

10. Respect any warning signs posted by agencies.

11. Teach others in your group how to behave in case of a cougar encounter. Anyone who starts running could bring on an attack.

12. If you have an encounter with a cougar, record your location and the details of the encounter, and notify the nearest park official, landowner, or other appropriate agency. The land management agency (federal, state, or county) may want to visit the site and, if appropriate, post education/warning signs. Fish and wildlife agencies should also be notified because they record and track such encounters.

If physical injury occurs, it is important to leave the area and not disturb the site of attack. Cougars that have attacked people must be killed, and an undisturbed site is critical for effectively locating the dangerous animal.

See Falcon Publishing's *Mountain Lion Alert* for more details and tips for safe outdoor recreation in cougar country. (Ordering information is available in Appendix B.)

GEOLOGICAL HAZARDS

Since Mount Rainier is considered an active volcano, it is important to be aware of geological hazards. Eruption is the most severe and most obvious hazard, but others are debris flows, glacial outburst floods, and rockfall. Eruptions are most commonly preceded by earthquakes, but all of the other phenomena can occur without warning.

You are more at risk to geological hazards when you are camping due to longer exposure and greater reaction/evacuation time. The National Park Service considers the danger of geological incidents to be relatively low, but you personally must assume the risk of staying overnight at any backcountry campsite or any automobile campground.

The park also advises that if anytime you are near a river and notice a rapid rise in water level or hear a roaring sound coming from upvalley—often described as sounding similar to a fast-moving train—move quickly to higher ground. The National Park Service suggests moving to a location 160 feet or more above river level to remove yourself from the path of a glacial outburst flood.

In Mount Rainier National Park, the South Mowich River, Kautz Creek, Carbon River, and West Fork White River continually experience glacial outburst floods. Footbridges across these waters are frequently washed out. The National Park Service does not advise fording glacial rivers due to the high concentration of debris in them. Large glacial boulders are always a potential hazard. If you must cross, the National Park Service recommends crossing early in the day and using any fallen logs. Also, always wear your hiking boots to protect yourself from any debris suspended in the river, but you might want to take your socks off before crossing to keep them dry.

If you would like additional information about geological activity in Mount

Rainier National Park, detailed information is available from the USGS Cascades Volcano Observatory.

USGS Cascades Volcano Observatory
5400 MacArthur Blvd.
Vancouver, WA 98661
Website: www.vulcan.wr.usgs.gov/

SPRINGTIME HIKING

Snow is found on most trails through June and lingers on some trails throughout summer. If you are planning to hike in the spring or on higher elevation trails, you should anticipate the hazards of hiking in snow and take the necessary precautions. Here is a list of safety tips to assist you.

- Snow-covered trails are harder to follow. Hikers must have a reliable map and compass skills to travel through many areas of the park. Known problem areas: Panhandle Gap, Spray Park, Seattle Park, St. Andrew's Park, and Ipsut Pass.
- Avoid crossing steep, snow-covered slopes where a fall could be disastrous. Turn around instead. Comet Falls and Pinnacle Peak trails have hazardous slopes during spring.
- Falling through thin snowbridges is a hazard anywhere streams remain snow covered. Stay alert for the muffled sound of running water.
- Falling into snow moats around trees and adjacent to logs and rocks can cause injury. Avoid getting too close.
- Avoid stepping on wet, slippery rocks, especially those near rivers and waterfalls. Common hazard areas: Narada Falls and Silver Falls.
- Avoid stepping onto snow cornices as they may collapse under your weight.
- Stop by a wilderness information center or park visitor center for details about current trail conditions, or visit the park website: www.nps.gov/mora.
- Be prepared for wet, cold weather at any time; snow can fall during any month of the year.

BE BEAR AWARE

Bears are wild animals and you should treat them as such. Never feed a bear; it is detrimental to the animal's survival skills. Also, a fed bear is more likely to be aggressive, thus increasing dangerous encounters.

Nobody likes surprises, and bears dislike them, too. The majority of human/bear conflicts occur when a hiker surprises a bear. Therefore, it is vital to do everything possible to avoid these surprise meetings. Perhaps the best way is to know the five-part system. Follow these five rules to reduce the chance of a close encounter with a bear to the slimmest possible margin.

- Be alert.
- Don't hike alone.
- Stay on the trail.

- Don't hike in the late evening or early morning.
- Make lots of noise. Singing, whistling, and hand-clapping work well.

If you do see a bear, freeze and begin to slowly back away. Let the bear know you are there by clapping or talking to it in a loud voice. Never run from a bear, since it might consider you prey. Nine times out of ten, the bear will take action to avoid you.

Currently, the National Park Service is in the process of establishing food storage poles at every backcountry camp. Park regulations require that you hang your food at night. Remember to keep a clean camp and use a minimum of odorous food to avoid attracting bears. If you desire any additional information on how to be bear aware and camp in bear country, Falcon publishes an excellent book, *Bear Aware*. (See Appendix B for ordering information.)

Seasons and Weather

The most severe weather on Mount Rainier occurs in the winter months. An immense elevated mass, Mount Rainier stands in the midst of a temperate lowland forest. The surrounding area receives massive amounts of rain in the winter months, while the nature of the mountain's situation leads to incredible amounts of snow. Moisture-laden air from the Pacific Ocean bombards Mount Rainier. As the air is pushed above the mountain, it cools, and the moisture falls as snow. The western flank of the mountain, Paradise in particular, receives record level snowfalls yearly. In 1971–1972, Paradise saw the most inches of snowfall ever recorded: 1,122 inches.

This book, however, is targeted at those who visit Mount Rainier National Park in the summer months. Compared to the winter, the weather at this time is relatively mild. The heavier rainfall in early summer abates by mid-July. In July and August, Mount Rainier sees many nice, clear days. That is not to say that you will not encounter fog. Many visitors of Mount Rainier never actually see the mountain. If lenticular clouds, those which form a saucer-like disc on the summit, do not obscure the peak, thick blankets of fog that rise from the humid lower levels may. You can experience the beauty of Mount Rainier National Park on such days: crashing waterfalls, subalpine fields of flowers, wildlife, and mountain lakes. If you seek views of the mountains or the surrounding forests, however, hope for a clear day.

The below list gives an idea of the time of year trails become snow-free or nearly snow-free. As weather is both immutable and unpredictable, these times may change. For a general idea of when trails open, however, look below.

May:
10 Trail of the Shadows
23 Stevens Creek
24 Box Canyon
25 Silver Falls
26 Grove of the Patriarchs
53 Green Lake
54 Paul Peak Trail

June:
 5 Rampart Ridge
22 Stevens Canyon

Early July:
 8 Narada Falls
 9 Comet Falls
12 Nisqually Vista

13 Alta Vista Summit
16 Dead Horse Creek
29 Shriner Peak
38 Emmons Moraine
44 Glacier Basin
59 Spray Falls

Mid-July:
 1 Klapatche Park
 2 Emerald Ridge
 3 Gobbler's Knob
 4 Indian Henry's Hunting Ground
 6 Van Trump Park
 7 Eagle Peak
15 Lakes Trail
17 High Lakes Trail
19 Skyline Trail
20 Paradise Glacier
21 Snow Lake
27 Three Lakes
31 Owyhigh Lakes
33 Crystal Lakes
34 Palisades Lakes
35 Dege Peak
36 Sourdough Ridge Nature Trail
37 Silver Forest
41 Berkeley Park
42 Grand Park
45 Northern Loop
46 Lake Eleanor
47 Summerland
50 Windy Gap
51 Carbon Glacier and Moraine
52 Mystic Lake
55 Tolmie Peak
57 Yellowstone Cliffs

Late July:
11 West Wonderland
14 Camp Muir
18 Pinnacle Peak Saddle
28 Pacific Crest Trail
30 Ohanapecosh Park
32 Naches Peak
39 Mount Fremont Lookout
40 Forest Lake
43 Burroughs Mountain

48 Indian Bar
56 Mother Mountain
58 Spray Park
60 Wonderland Trail

August:
43 Burroughs Mountain
49 Sunrise Rim

BACKCOUNTRY REGULATIONS

Backcountry use regulations are not intended to complicate your life. They help preserve the natural landscape and protect park visitors. The following backcountry use regulations for Mount Rainier National Park are distributed to hikers when they obtain their permits.

- Have a permit for all overnight use of the backcountry.
- Camp in designated campsites.
- Carry out all trash. If you can pack it in, you can pack it out.
- Fish by hook and line only. This is permitted without a license, but some waters are closed. Check with a ranger to be certain.
- Do not feed, touch, tease, frighten, or intentionally disturb wildlife.
- Do not take pets into the backcountry (except on the Pacific Crest Trail, which allows dogs if they are on a leash).
- Do not possess or operate a motorized vehicle, bicycle, wheeled vehicle, skateboard, roller skates, or cart in any undeveloped area or on any backcountry trail.
- Do not drive off any park road.
- Do not pick wildflowers.
- Do not destroy, injure, deface, remove, dig, or disturb from its natu ral state any plant, rock, animal, mineral, cultural, or archaeologi cal resource.
- Do not violate a closure, designation, use or activity restriction or condition, schedule of visiting hours, or public use limit.
- Do not use or possess weapons.
- Do not pollute or contaminate any water source (with soap, waste, etc.).
- Never shortcut on any trail.
- Do not dispose of waste within 100 feet of water or within sight of trail.
- Do not camp within 100 feet of water except in a designated camp site.

Zero Impact

Going into a national park such as Mount Rainier is like visiting a famous museum. You obviously do not want to leave your mark on an art treasure in the museum. If everybody going through the museum left one little mark, the piece of art would be quickly destroyed—and of what value is a big building full of trashed art? The same goes for a pristine wilderness such as Mount Rainier, which is as magnificent as any masterpiece by any artist. If we all left just one little mark on the landscape, the wilderness would soon be despoiled.

A wilderness can accommodate human use as long as everybody behaves, but a few thoughtless or uninformed visitors can ruin it for everybody who follows. All wilderness users have a responsibility to know and follow the rules of no trace camping. An important source of these guidelines, including the most updated research, can be found in the book *Leave No Trace*. (Ordering information is in Appendix B.)

Nowadays most wilderness users want to walk softly, but some are not aware that they have poor manners. Often their actions are dictated by the outdated habits of a past generation of campers who cut green boughs for evening shelters, built campfires with fire rings, and dug trenches around tents. In the 1950s, these "camping rules" may have been acceptable. But they leave long-lasting scars, and today such behavior is absolutely unacceptable. The wilderness is shrinking, and the number of users is mushrooming. More and more camping areas show unsightly signs of heavy use.

Consequently, a new code of ethics is growing out of the necessity of coping with the unending waves of people who want an enjoyable wilderness experience. Today, we all must leave no clues that we have gone before. Canoeists can look behind the canoe and see no trace of their passing. Hikers, mountain bikers, and four-wheelers should have the same goal. Enjoy the wildness, but leave no trace of your visit.

THREE FALCON PRINCIPLES

- Leave with everything you brought in.
- Leave no sign of your visit.
- Leave the landscape as you found it.

Most of us know better than to litter—in or out of the wilderness. Be sure you leave nothing, regardless of how small it is, along the trail or at the campsite. This means you should pack out everything, including orange peels, flip tops, cigarette butts, and gum wrappers. Also, pick up any trash that others leave behind.

- Follow the main trail. Avoid cutting switchbacks and walking on vegetation beside the trail.

Mount Rainier from a meadow near Mystic Lake.

- Do not pick up "souvenirs," such as rocks, antlers, or wildflowers. The next person wants to see them, too, and collecting such souvenirs violates park regulations.
- Avoid making loud noises that may disturb others. Remember, sound travels easily to the other side of lakes. Be courteous.
- Carry a lightweight trowel to bury human waste 6 to 8 inches deep and pack out used toilet paper. Keep human waste at least 300 feet from any water source.
- Finally, and perhaps most importantly, strictly follow the pack-in/pack-out rule. If you carry something into the backcountry, consume it or carry it out.

Zero impact—and put your ear to the ground in the wilderness and listen carefully. Thousands of people coming behind you are thanking you for your courtesy and good sense.

Trail Finder

	EASY	MODERATE	STRENUOUS
Mountain Lakes	17 High Lakes Trail 21 Snow Lake 32 Naches Peak 53 Green Lake	3 Gobbler's Knob 34 Palisades Lake 46 Lake Eleanor 40 Forest Lake 27 Three Lakes 31 Owyhigh Lakes 33 Crystal Lakes 28 Pacific Crest Trail 55 Tolmie Peak	11 West Wonderland 50 Windy Gap 1 Klapatche Park 60 Wonderland Trail 52 Mystic Lake
Waterfalls	8 Narada Falls 53 Green Lake 59 Spray Falls 9 Comet Falls 25 Silver Falls 23 Stevens Creek	19 Skyline Trail 22 Stevens Canyon 6 Van Trump Park	30 Ohanapecosh Park 60 Wonderland Trail 48 Indian Bar
Alpine Country	39 Mount Fremont Lookout	43 Burroughs Mountain 47 Summerland 48 Indian Bar 19 Skyline Trail 20 Paradise Glacier	30 Ohanapecosh Park 60 Wonderland Trail 14 Camp Muir
Peaks	18 Pinnacle Peak Saddle 39 Mount Fremont Lookout	3 Gobbler's Knob 55 Tolmie Peak	29 Shriner Peak 7 Eagle Peak
Overnight Backpacking Trips		46 Lake Eleanor 28 Pacific Crest Trail	56 Mother Mountain 11 West Wonderland 60 Wonderland Trail 30 Ohanapecosh Park 45 Northern Loop 1 Klapatche Park 48 Indian Bar

Trail Finder

	EASY	MODERATE	STRENUOUS
Trails to Avoid If You Don't Want to See Lots of People	39 Mount Fremont Lookout 36 Sourdough Ridge Nature Trail 59 Spray Falls 49 Sunrise Rim 32 Naches Peak 26 Grove of the Patriarchs 24 Box Canyon 8 Narada Falls 55 Tolmie Peak 10 Trail of the Shadows 35 Dege Peak	58 Spray Park	
Glaciers		19 Skyline Trail 51 Carbon Glacier and Moraine 20 Paradise Glacier	2 Emerald Ridge 45 Northern Loop 60 Wonderland Trail 11 West Wonderland 14 Camp Muir 30 Ohanapecosh Park 52 Mystic Lake 48 Indian Bar
Trails That Allow Pets * Pets are allowed on the portion of the Naches Peak loop that leaves the park.	32 Naches Peak*	28 Pacific Crest Trail	
Wildflowers (in season)	40 Forest Lake 21 Snow Lake 37 Silver Forest	46 Lake Eleanor 31 Owyhigh Lakes 33 Crystal Lakes 58 Spray Park 42 Grand Park 3 Gobbler's Knob 41 Berkeley Park	11 West Wonderland 60 Wonderland Trail 29 Shriner Peak 2 Emerald Ridge 1 Klapatche Park 30 Ohanapecosh Park 56 Mother Mountain 45 Northern Loop

Trail Finder

	EASY	MODERATE	STRENUOUS
Wildflowers (in season)		55 Tolmie Peak	4 Indian Henry's Hunting Ground 48 Indian Bar
Great Views of Mount Rainier	18 Pinnacle Peak Saddle	42 Grand Park 19 Skyline Trail 58 Spray Park 55 Tolmie Peak	2 Emerald Ridge 29 Shriner Peak 56 Mother Mountain 1 Klapatche Park 14 Camp Muir 11 West Wonderland 60 Wonderland Trail 30 Ohanapecosh Park 4 Indian Henry's Hunting Ground 48 Indian Bar
For a Good Chance of Seeing a Bear		48 Indian Bar 2 Emerald Ridge 42 Grand Park 46 Lake Eleanor 51 Carbon Glacier and Moraine	30 Ohanapecosh Park 45 Northern Loop 60 Wonderland Trail 11 West Wonderland 29 Shriner Peak 52 Mystic Lake
For a Long, Hard Day Hike			1 Klapatche Park 48 Indian Bar 29 Shriner Peak 2 Emerald Ridge 46 Lake Eleanor 52 Mystic Lake 50 Windy Gap 57 Yellowstone Cliffs

Ranger Falls.

Longmire

The area now named Longmire was originally the home of a hot springs resort founded by James Longmire. The resort no longer operates, but is now the home of the Longmire Museum, the Longmire Wilderness Information Center, and the National Park Inn. Because of its variety of services and attractions, the Longmire complex continues to be a popular place for people to visit, whether they plan to day hike or begin the renowned Wonderland Trail.

The backcountry in the Longmire area is unique. Kautz Creek and Tahoma Creek constantly reroute themselves due to glacial outburst floods caused by geological activity. The area has experienced more washouts of this kind than any other area of the park, but fortunately the National Park Service responds quickly to restore the bridges. In contrast to the pebbly valleys these rivers flow through, a multitude of gorgeous flower filled meadows are in the Longmire backcountry, namely Sunset Peak, Indian Henry's Hunting Ground, St. Andrew's Park, Emerald Ridge and Klapache Park.

1   Klapatche Park

Type of hike:	Loop or out-and-back; one- or three-night backpack.
Total distance:	19.6 miles (31.4 kilometers).
Difficulty:	Strenuous.
Elevation gain:	2,960 feet.
Best months:	Mid-July–September.
Maps:	USGS Mount Wow; Trails Illustrated Mount Rainier National Park; Astronaut's Vista: Mount Rainier National Park, Washington; Earthwalk Press Hiking Map & Guide.
Starting point:	Westside Road closure.

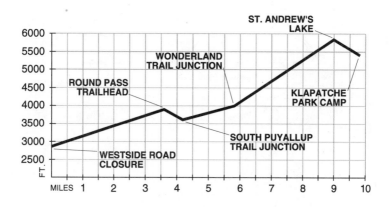

Klapatche Park

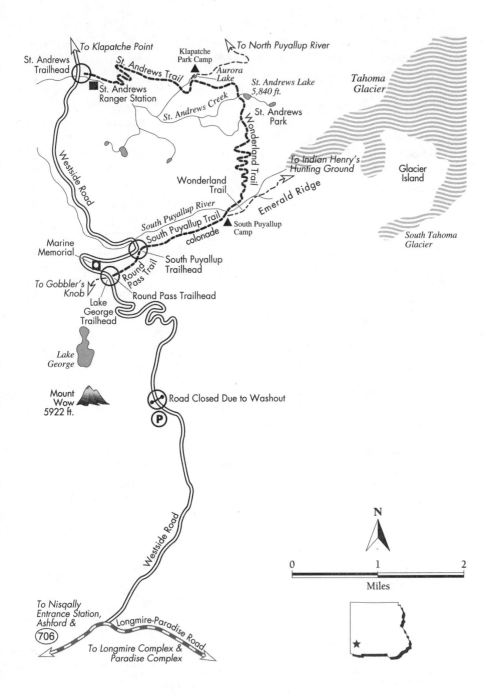

To Klapatche Point

St. Andrews Trailhead

St. Andrews Ranger Station

St. Andrews Trail

Klapatche Park Camp

To North Puyallup River

Aurora Lake

St. Andrews Lake 5,840 ft.

Tahoma Glacier

St. Andrews Creek

St. Andrews Park

Wonderland Trail

Westside Road

To Indian Henry's Hunting Ground

Glacier Island

Wonderland Trail

Emerald Ridge

South Puyallup River

South Puyallup Trail

colonade

South Puyallup Camp

South Tahoma Glacier

Marine Memorial

Round Pass Trail

South Puyallup Trailhead

To Gobbler's Knob

Round Pass Trailhead

Lake George Trailhead

Lake George

Mount Wow 5922 ft.

Road Closed Due to Washout

P

Westside Road

N

0   1   2
Miles

To Nisqally Entrance Station, Ashford &

706

Longmire-Paradise Road

To Longmire Complex & Paradise Complex

Aurora Lake. PHOTO BY BILL SCHNEIDER

General description: A long but rewarding climb, passing through St. Andrews Park, by St. Andrews Lake, to the scenic meadows of Klapatche Park.

Finding the trailhead: From the Nisqually Entrance Station, drive east on Longmire-Paradise Road 1 mile to the Westside Road. Turn left (north) onto Westside Road and drive 3.3 miles to the road closure.

The National Park Service originally closed the road in 1967 due to a glacial outburst flood that washed out pieces of the road. The road reopened, but was closed again due to a washout in 1987. Every three years a geologist evaluates the road to determine if it is safe to reopen. The road has remained closed since the 1987 washout, but if it is open when you arrive, continue up the road for 7.8 miles to the St. Andrews Trailhead.

Parking & trailhead facilities: Directly before the Westside Road closure, there is a gravel parking lot that often fills up in the summer. There is also an outhouse here.

If Westside Road is open, park in the parking lot to the left of the Lake George Trailhead. Bike racks are present at the trailhead. Since Westside Road has been closed, it has become a popular route to bike up, but remember that bikes are not allowed on any of the backcountry trails of Mount Rainier National Park.

Key points:
3.6 (5.8) Round Pass Trailhead.
4.2 (6.7) Junction with South Puyallup Trail.

5.8	(9.3)	Wonderland Trail junction.
9.0	(14.4)	St. Andrews Lake.
9.8	(15.5)	Klapatche Park Camp.

The hike: If Westside Road has been reopened, start your hike at the St. Andrews Trailhead. Klapatche Park is less than 2.6 miles from the trailhead, but the trail is all steep switchbacks. Another option is to bicycle to the St. Andrews Trailhead, 11.4 miles from the road closure.

From the Westside Road closure, you will have to hike up the road 3.6 miles to reach the trailhead. It is all uphill, but at a nice grade and easy to follow. Be aware that cougars are often seen along Westside Road. Make sure to look at the cougar safety section before venturing up the road.

The Round Pass Trailhead is located between the Lake George Trailhead and the Marine Memorial. This memorial, dedicated to the 32 U.S. Marines killed in a plane crash on the South Tahoma Glacier in 1946, offers a great view of the glacier.

Hike 0.6 mile northeast on the Round Pass Trail to the junction with the South Puyallup Trail. The Round Pass Trail continues left, heading west. Go to the right and take the South Puyallup Trail, which continues northeast. Hike up this trail for just under one mile to the South Puyallup Camp.

About 0.2 mile shy of the camp, look for some peculiar rock formations on the right. The formations are called *colonade*, columnar pieces of andesite rock. The columns were formed thousands of years ago during the cooling process after hot lava flowed through this area.

After you pass the South Puyallup Camp, you come to the Wonderland Trail. Go left (north) onto the Wonderland Trail and cross the South Puyallup River. The trail is all steep switchbacks up a ridge covered in brush for the next 2 miles. Once you reach St. Andrews Park, the trail levels out a bit and the scenery takes your mind off the uphill. In July, alpine lilies fill the meadows of St. Andrews Park, and Mount Rainier towers majestically above all these natural wonders.

You reach St. Andrews Lake 3.2 miles from the junction with the Wonderland Trail, 9 miles into your hike. Previous hikers have greatly impacted the lake by creating numerous social trails along the fragile banks of this subalpine lake. Minimize your impact by admiring the lake from the designated trail. You can also see a west-side climbing route that many climbers have used to attempt the summit. Fortunately, the trails do not entirely take away from the deep blue waters of St. Andrews Lake.

Klapatche Park Camp is a little over 0.7 mile from St. Andrews Lake, and the trail slopes downhill the rest of the way. Beautiful wildflowers fill the meadows of Klapatche Park and surround Aurora Lake in mid-July. Aurora Lake is only a shallow pool of snowmelt, but looks astonishing with Mount Rainier towering above it and surrounded by colorful wildflowers. If you are staying at Klapatche Park Camp, it is located at the west end of the lake.

On the return trip, you can either head back the way you came or take the St. Andrews Trail to Westside Road and hike all the way to your car on a gravel road. Because the return trip is almost entirely downhill, either option will be hard on your knees. The Westside Road option offers a change of scenery and will likely take less time, but it also features an 800-foot elevation gain up to Round Pass. Keep in mind that the Westside Road option is much less of a wilderness experience.

Options: Take a side trip to Emerald Ridge by turning right (east) at the junction with the Wonderland Trail. It will make your trip 3.4 miles longer, but the emerald green meadow, with close-up views of the South Tahoma Glacier, is worth it.

Camping & services: Depending on how many miles you want to travel per day and your skill level, this hike can be either a one-night or three-night backpack. If you only go for one night, you will stay at Klapatche Park and hike almost 10 miles per day. If you spread it out over three nights, you can stay at South Puyallup Camp the first and third nights and hike about 5 miles per day.

Fires are prohibited in backcountry camps and Klapatche Park is no exception. Bring a stove for cooking. The Klapatche Park Camp is amazing, by far our favorite campground in Rainier. If you can, stay in site 1. Mount Rainier is visible from site 1 and it overlooks the lake, but all of the sites have an enjoyable view. Sites 3 and 4 have a nice view of the north side of Klapatche Ridge. All of the sites are relatively close together, and Klapatche Park Camp has both an outhouse and a food storage pole. Aurora Lake is the water source, but keep in mind that it usually dries up by mid- to late September.

South Puyallup Camp has four individual sites and one group site. Number 1 is probably the best campsite. It is private, with a close water source. Be forewarned that the toilet is a 0.1-mile hike from all the campsites. Site 2 also has its own water source with good tent sites. Sites 3 and 4 have just been improved, and if seclusion is your primary concern, site four is your best bet.

Some groceries and supplies can be obtained at the Longmire General Store located in the National Park Inn, but this store stocks limited backpacking supplies; it is best to bring everything you need with you. The nearest place to obtain gas and extensive supplies is the town of Ashford on Washington Highway 706, about 5 miles west of the park boundary.

For more information: Contact the Longmire Wilderness Information Center or the Longmire Museum (see Appendix A).

2 Emerald Ridge

Type of hike: Out-and-back; day hike or overnighter.
Total distance: 15 miles (24 kilometers).
Difficulty: Strenuous.
Elevation gain: 3,060 feet.
Best months: Mid-July–September.
Maps: USGS Mount Rainier West; Trails Illustrated Mount Rainier National Park; Astronaut's Vista: Mount Rainier National Park, Washington; Earthwalk Press Hiking Map & Guide.
Starting point: Westside Road closure.

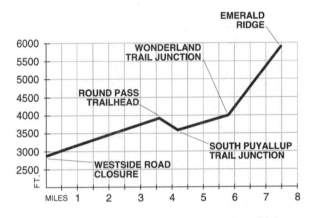

General description: A long and meandering hike past the Colonades to an emerald green meadow where you have a close-up view of the South Tahoma Glacier and Glacier Island.

Finding the trailhead: From the Nisqually Entrance Station, drive east on Longmire-Paradise Road 1 mile to Westside Road. (See Planning Your Trip for directions to the Nisqually Entrance Station.) Turn left (north) onto Westside Road and drive 3.3 miles to the road closure.

The National Park Service originally closed the road in 1967 due to a glacial outburst flood that washed out pieces of the road. The road reopened, but was closed again due to a washout in 1987. Every three years a geologist evaluates the road to determine if it is safe to reopen. The road has remained closed since the 1987 washout, but if it is open when you arrive, continue up the road for 3.6 miles to the Round Pass Trailhead.

Parking & trailhead facilities: Directly before the Westside Road closure, there is a gravel parking lot that often fills up in the summer. There is also an outhouse here.

If Westside Road is open, park in the parking lot to the left of the Lake George Trailhead. Bike racks are present at the trailhead. Since Westside

Emerald Ridge

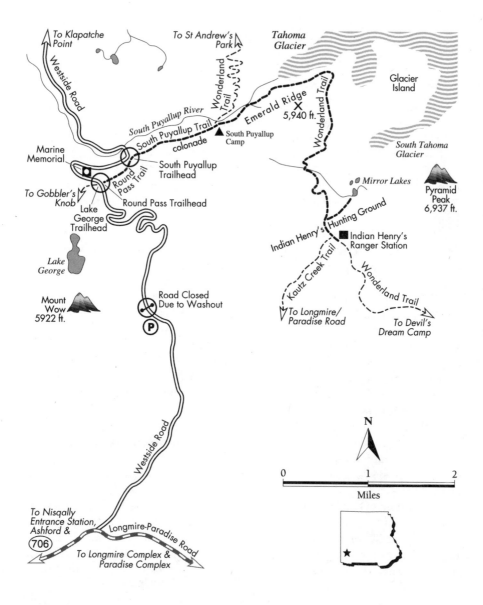

To Klapatche Point

To St Andrew's Park

Tahoma Glacier

Westside Road

Wonderland Trail

Glacier Island

South Puyallup River

South Puyallup Trail

Emerald Ridge
X
5,940 ft.

Wonderland Trail

colonade

South Puyallup Camp

South Tahoma Glacier

Marine Memorial

Round Pass Trail

South Puyallup Trailhead

Mirror Lakes

Pyramid Peak 6,937 ft.

To Gobbler's Knob

Round Pass Trailhead

Lake George Trailhead

Indian Henry's Hunting Ground

Indian Henry's Ranger Station

Lake George

Kautz Creek Trail

Wonderland Trail

Mount Wow 5922 ft.

Road Closed Due to Washout

P

To Longmire/ Paradise Road

To Devil's Dream Camp

Westside Road

N

0   1   2
Miles

To Nisqally Entrance Station, Ashford &

Longmire-Paradise Road

706

To Longmire Complex & Paradise Complex

★

Road has been closed, it has become a popular route to bike up, but remember that bikes are not allowed on any of the backcountry trails of Mount Rainier National Park.

Key points:
3.6	(5.8)	Round Pass Trailhead.
4.2	(6.7)	Junction with South Puyallup Trail.
5.7	(9.1)	South Puyallup Camp.
5.8	(9.3)	Wonderland Trail junction.
7.5	(12.0)	Emerald Ridge.

The hike: If Westside Road has been reopened, start your hike directly at the Round Pass Trailhead, 3.6 miles from the Westside Road closure. Another option is to bicycle from the road closure to the Round Pass Trailhead.

From the Westside Road closure, you will have to hike up the road 3.6 miles to reach the Round Pass Trailhead. It is all uphill, but at a nice grade and easy to follow. Be aware that cougars are often seen along Westside Road. Make sure to look at the cougar safety section before venturing up the road.

The Round Pass Trailhead is located between the Lake George Trailhead and the Marine Memorial. This memorial, dedicated to the 32 marines killed in a plane crash on the South Tahoma Glacier in 1946, offers a great view of the glacier.

Hike northeast on the Round Pass Trail 0.6 mile to South Puyallup Trail. The Round Pass Trail continues left, heading west. Go to the right and take the South Puyallup Trail, which continues northeast. Hike another mile to the South Puyallup Camp. About 0.2 mile shy of the camp, look for peculiar rock formations on the right. The formations are called *colonade*, columnar pieces of andesite rock. The columns were formed thousands of years ago during the cooling process after hot lava flowed through this area.

After you pass the South Puyallup Camp, you will come to the Wonderland Trail. Go right (east) toward Emerald Ridge. From here it is 1.7 miles to the top of Emerald Ridge, 7.5 miles into your hike. The trail along the north side of Emerald Ridge has washed out many times and lines a steep, unstable ledge. Be very careful. Take the new trail that crosses diagonally across the ridge.

The Tahoma Glacier and its moraine is to your left (north). If you look up at Mount Rainier, you will see the top of the Tahoma Glacier, accompanied by the South Tahoma Glacier to the right. Between the two glaciers is Glacier Island. Mountain goats are often seen grazing on Glacier Island, a green haven in a sea of glaciers; if you look closely, you can see fields of lupine there.

The top of Emerald Ridge is an emerald green meadow that is filled with wildflowers, especially subalpine lupine in mid-July. Tons of hoary marmots live in the meadows and are definitely not shy. Do not feed these wild animals; they need to be self-sufficient to survive in their natural habitat. Also, it is illegal to feed the wildlife in Mount Rainier National Park.

Options: If you decide to stay at South Puyallup Camp, you might want to take an additional day hike. Klapatche Park is amazing, as is actually geting there. You pass through St. Andrews Park and by St. Andrews Lake, two natural wonders guaranteed to take your breath away. Klapatche Park is 4 miles away from the South Puyallup Camp, making it an 8-mile day hike. You might consider making this trip a two- or three-night backpack trip in order to stay at Klapatche Park. (See Hike 1: Klapatche Park.)

Camping & services: Fires are prohibited in the backcountry and the South Puyallup Camp is no exception. Bring a stove for cooking. There are four individual sites at South Puyallup Camp and one group site. Number 1 is probably the best campsite. It is private, with a close water source. Be forewarned that the toilet is more than 0.1 mile from all the campsites. Site 2 also has its own water source with good tent sites. Sites 3 and 4 have just been improved, and if seclusion is your primary concern, site 4 is your best bet.

You can also stay at Sunshine Point Campground if you wish to day hike and car camp. Campfires are allowed. Some groceries and supplies can be obtained at the Longmire General Store located in the National Park Inn, but this store stocks limited backpacking supplies; it is best to bring everything you need with you. The nearest place to obtain gas and extensive supplies is Ashford, 5 miles west from the park boundary on Washington Highway 706.

For more information: Contact the Longmire Wilderness Information Center or the Longmire Museum (see Appendix A).

3 Gobbler's Knob

        Type of hike: Out-and-back; day hike or overnighter.
     Total distance: 12 miles (19.2 kilometers).
         Difficulty: Moderate.
  Elevation gain: 2,605 feet.
     Best months: Mid-July–September.
            Maps: USGS Mount Wow; Trails Illustrated Mount Rainier National Park; Astronaut's Vista: Mount Rainier National Park, Washington; Earthwalk Press Hiking Map & Guide.
  Starting point: Westside Road closure.

General description: A short hike past a clear lake up to a peak with great views of Mount St. Helens, the Goat Rocks, the North Cascades, and Mount Rainier.

Finding the trailhead: From the Nisqually Entrance Station, drive 1 mile east on Longmire-Paradise Road to Westside Road. Turn left (north) onto Westside Road and drive 3.3 miles to the road closure.

Gobbler's Knob

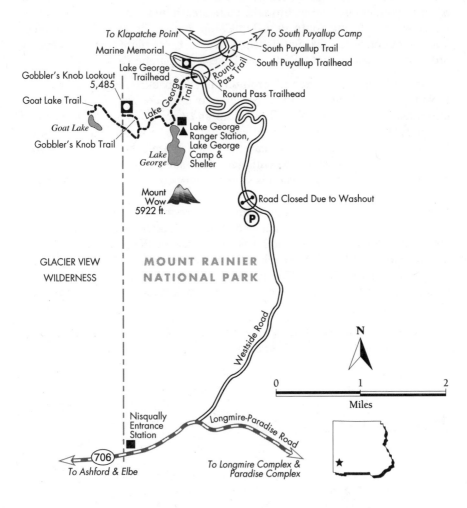

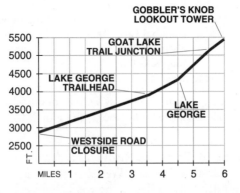

Mount Rainier from Gobbler's Knob.

The National Park Service originally closed the road in 1967 due to a glacial outburst flood that washed out pieces of the road. The road reopened, but was closed again due to a washout in 1987. Every three years a geologist evaluates the road to determine if it is safe to reopen. The road has remained closed since the 1987 washout, but if it is open when you arrive, continue up the road 3.6 miles to the Lake George Trailhead.

Parking & trailhead facilities: Directly before the Westside Road closure, there is a gravel parking lot that often fills up in the summer. There is also an outhouse here.

If Westside Road is open, park in the parking lot to the left of the Lake George Trailhead. Bike racks are present at the trailhead. Since Westside Road has been closed, it has become a popular route to bike up, but remember that bikes are not allowed on any of the backcountry trails of Mount Rainier National Park.

Key points:
3.6	(5.8)	Lake George Trailhead.
4.5	(7.2)	Lake George.
5.6	(9.0)	Goat Lake Trail.
6.0	(9.6)	Gobbler's Knob lookout tower.

The hike: If Westside Road is not closed, you can immediately start hiking up the Lake George Trail. Another option is to bicycle up Westside Road from the road closure, a 3.6-mile ride.

If Westside Road is closed, you will have to hike up the road for 3.6 miles to reach the Lake George Trailhead. It is all uphill, but at a nice grade and easy to follow. Although hiking up a dirt road can seem long and uneventful, the view from Gobbler's Knob is definitely worth it. Cougars are often seen along Westside Road. Make sure to look at the cougar safety section before venturing up this road.

The first section of the trail to Lake George is less than 0.9 mile and all uphill, but not too steep. You can steal a couple glimpses of Mount Rainier along the way. Take a break at Lake George, especially if you fish. The fish were rising like crazy the last time we were here. For the next 1.5 miles to Gobbler's Knob, the trail ascends a steep hill. After hiking for 1.1 miles up the hill, 5.6 miles into your hike, you encounter the Goat Lake Trail. Go right (north) and stay on the Lake George Trail. The Goat Lake Trail leaves the park and continues on to Goat Lake.

After the junction, you travel through several meadows filled with beautiful wildflowers. In July, lupine, magenta paintbrush, and an occasional Columbia lily color these meadows. From the last meadow, you clearly see the huge rock that makes up Gobbler's Knob, your destination.

From the lookout tower atop the knob, a variety of landmarks ring the horizon. Refer to your map to identify them. If it is a clear day, you can see Mount St. Helens to the southwest, the Goat Rocks to the southeast, the Cascades to the north, and magnificent Mount Rainier to the northeast. There is also a fabulous view of Lake George and Mount Wow, which is directly above Lake George.

When you have had your fill of natural wonders, head back the way you came. If you have the time and energy, take the option to Goat Lake.

Options: Take a side trip to Goat Lake. This side trip will add 3.8 miles to your hike. You will experience a little taste of the Glacier View Wilderness, just west of the park. From the junction with the Goat Lake Trail, head west on the Goat Lake Trail. You travel uphill for just a couple of steps and then go downhill all the way to Goat Lake. The descent is relatively steep and has only a few switchbacks. The ledge of the trail drops off rather abruptly in places; watch where you step. At Goat Lake, you can enjoy the tranquillity of the lake or take your chances fishing the banks.

Camping & services: Lake George has five individual campsites and one group site. Number 5 is closest to the lake, but has semi-slanted tent sites. The rest of the campsites are along the ridge and require a short hike to water and the bathroom. If possible, avoid site 4, which lacks a good tent site. Campsite number 3 is as flat as a board and has a view of Mount Rainier. The group site is to the east of the individual sites on its own hill and has at least one good tent site, maybe two.

You can also stay at Sunshine Point Campground if you wish to day hike and car camp. Campfires are allowed. Some groceries and supplies can be obtained at the Longmire General Store located in the National Park Inn, but this store stocks limited backpacking supplies; it is best to bring every-thing you need with you. The nearest place to obtain gas and extensive supplies is Ashford on Washington Highway 706, about 5 miles west from the park boundary.

For more information: Contact the Longmire Wilderness Information Center or the Longmire Museum (see Appendix A).

4 Indian Henry's Hunting Ground

Type of hike:	Out-and-back; day hike.
Total distance:	11.4 miles (18.2 kilometers).
Difficulty:	Strenuous.
Elevation gain:	3,200 feet.
Best months:	Mid-July–September.
Maps:	USGS Mount Rainier West; Trails Illustrated Mount Rainier National Park; Astronaut's Vista: Mount Rainier National Park, Washington; Earthwalk Press Hiking Map & Guide.
Starting point:	Kautz Creek Trailhead.

General description: A long day hike with some steep uphill to beautiful meadows and great views of Mount Rainier.

Indian Henry's Hunting Ground

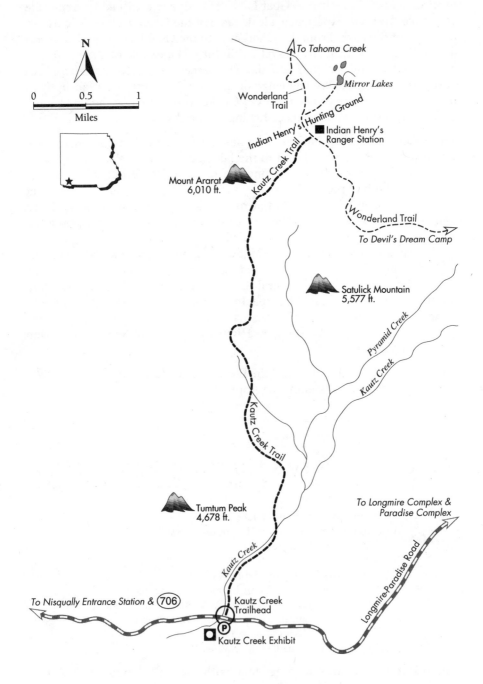

N

0   0.5   1
Miles

To Tahoma Creek

Mirror Lakes

Wonderland Trail

Indian Henry's Hunting Ground

Indian Henry's Ranger Station

Mount Ararat
6,010 ft.

Kautz Creek Trail

Wonderland Trail

To Devil's Dream Camp

Satulick Mountain
5,577 ft.

Pyramid Creek

Kautz Creek

Kautz Creek Trail

Tumtum Peak
4,678 ft.

To Longmire Complex &
Paradise Complex

Kautz Creek

Longmire-Paradise Road

To Nisqually Entrance Station & 706

Kautz Creek
Trailhead

Kautz Creek Exhibit

Kautz Creek.

Finding the trailhead: From the Nisqually Entrance Station, drive east on Longmire-Paradise Road 3.5 miles to the Kautz Creek Picnic Area. Park there and walk across the street to the trailhead.

Parking & trailhead facilities: There is a paved parking lot at the Kautz Creek Picnic Area and Exhibit, but it is often full in the summer. If it is full, you might have to find an alternate hike. Bathrooms are available here.

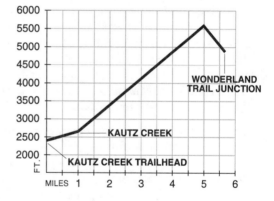

Key points:

1.0	(1.6)	Kautz Creek.
5.0	(8.0)	Beginning of Indian Henry's Hunting Ground.
5.7	(9.1)	Junction with Wonderland Trail.

The hike: This hike gives you a large dosage of uphill for those who really want a workout. The trail takes you to the beautiful meadows named Indian Henry's Hunting Ground. Mount Rainier is visible from the meadows, as well as Copper and Iron Mountains. The first mile of this trail is deceiving, since it is so flat and the rest of the hike is so steep.

The trailhead is across the street from the Kautz Creek Picnic Area. Cross Longmire-Paradise Road to the wooden boardwalk. The sign for the Kautz Creek Trail is to your right. The boardwalk to your left was constructed by volunteers in 1994 and leads to a viewpoint of the Kautz Creek Mudflow. Unless you want to check out the viewpoint first, take the Kautz Creek Trail heading north.

The first mile of the trail takes you through the remnants of the Kautz Creek Mudflow. In October 1947, a glacial outburst flood wiped out the forest all around Kautz Creek. Another glacial outburst flood in 1969 almost took out the road bridge over Kautz Creek. The forest growing around you is a virgin forest.

After you cross Kautz Creek, 1 mile into your hike, the trail turns into steep switchbacks that last for almost 4 miles. At first the trail takes you through mature forest. Much later on, this forest disappears to reveal beautiful meadows with scenic views of Mount Ararat on the left and Satulick Mountain on the right.

The last 0.7 mile of the hike is slightly downhill and quite a relief after all that uphill. At this point, you have reached Indian Henry's Hunting Ground, which is probably obvious by the showcase of flowers. You can hike all the way to the junction with the Wonderland Trail and then head back the way you came, or take the Mirror Lakes option.

Options: You can take a side trip to Mirror Lakes, adding 1.8 miles to your hike. Before you take this option, be aware the lakes that make up Mirror Lakes are not very big. But it is a very enjoyable side trip through flower-filled meadows. Go left (north) at the junction with the Wonderland Trail and go 0.2 mile to the Mirror Lakes Trail. Go right (northeast) 0.6 mile to the lakes. Follow the Mirror Lakes Trail to its end where there is a great view of Pyramid Peak and Mount Rainier.

Camping & services: You can stay at Sunshine Point Campground if you want to day hike and car camp (campfires are allowed). You can also stay at the National Park Inn, which is open year-round and located right next to the Longmire Museum.

Some groceries and supplies can be obtained at the Longmire General Store located in the National Park Inn, but supplies are limited. The nearest place to obtain gas and extensive supplies is Ashford on Washington Highway 706, about 5 miles west from the park boundary.

For more information: Contact the Longmire Wilderness Information Center or the Longmire Museum (see Appendix A).

5 Rampart Ridge

Type of hike: Loop; day hike.
Total distance: 4.8 miles (7.7 kilometers).
Difficulty: Moderate.
Elevation gain: 1,280 feet.
Best months: June–September.
Maps: USGS Mount Rainier West; Trails Illustrated Mount Rainier National Park; Astronaut's Vista: Mount Rainier National Park, Washington; Earthwalk Press Hiking Map & Guide.
Starting point: Longmire complex.

General description: A short but steep day hike up Rampart Ridge to a viewpoint overlooking Eagle Peak, the Nisqually River, and Mount Rainier.

Finding the trailhead: From Nisqually River Entrance Station, drive 6.7 miles east on the Longmire-Paradise Road to the Longmire complex. Then turn right (southeast) into the parking lot. Park here and walk on one of the two crosswalks to the Rampart Ridge Trailhead, across the street from the National Park Inn.

Parking & trailhead facilities: Park in one of the parking lots around Longmire Wilderness Information Center, the Longmire Museum, and the National Park Inn. Parking is a potential problem on sunny weekends and you might have to choose an alternate hike. There are pay phones and bathrooms next to the Longmire Museum.

Key points:
0.1 (0.2) Junction with Rampart Ridge Trailhead.
1.8 (2.9) Spur trail to viewpoint.
3.0 (4.8) Junction with Wonderland Trail.
3.2 (5.1) Junction with Van Trump Park Trail.
4.6 (7.3) Longmire-Paradise Road.
4.8 (7.6) Longmire complex.

The Hike: This hike is great for those who want a workout, great scenery, and a hike that is snow-free in June. In less than 2 miles the trail takes you up 1,200 feet and allows you to peer into the valley you just ventured from and then into the valley on the other side of Rampart Ridge. The switchbacks are steep, but definitely bearable. Remember to bring plenty of water because this hike has no water sources.

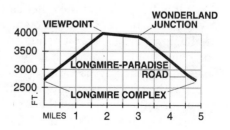

Rampart Ridge

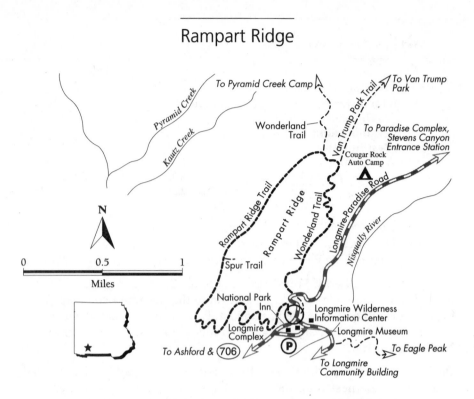

Stay to your left (west) after crossing the street. The first 0.1 mile of the trail is also part of the Trail of the Shadows until the Rampart Ridge Trail veers off to the left. The Trail of the Shadows is a self-guided hike that takes you around a field of mineral springs.

At the junction with the Rampart Ridge Trail, go left (north). For the next 1.7 miles, there are relatively steep switchbacks, although they level out at the end just before the viewpoint. This part of the trail is mainly in the trees, but at one point you catch a glimpse of Tumtum Peak to the west. After hiking a total of 1.8 miles, you reach a spur trail that goes to a viewpoint. Take a break and enjoy the scenery from the viewpoint. On a clear day, you can see Eagle Peak, the Nisqually River, the Longmire complex, and Mount Rainier.

The next 1.2 miles along the ridge are flat and very pleasant. You can see down into the valley on the other side of Rampart Ridge along this section. A glimpse of Kautz Creek can be had 0.2 mile after the viewpoint. You hit the Rampart Ridge Trail junction after traveling 1.2 miles from the viewpoint and 3 miles into your hike. Go right (south) at this junction. This turn takes you off the Rampart Ridge Trail and onto the Wonderland Trail. From then on, the trail loses elevation all the way back to the Longmire complex. About 0.2 mile after joining the Wonderland Trail, you will come to the Van Trump Trail splitting off to the left. Stay to the right (south) here and continue down the Wonderland Trail. At 4.6 miles, cross Longmire-Paradise

Rampart Ridge Viewpoint.

Road and continue hiking on the Wonderland Trail all the way to the Longmire complex. There are many signs to point the way on this last stretch.

Options: You can walk up to Indian Henry's Hunting Ground from the Wonderland Trail junction. This scenic area is 4.8 miles from the junction, adding 9.6 miles to your hike. From Indian Henry's Hunting Ground, there are fabulous views of Mount Rainier, beautiful meadows filled with lupine, and views of Copper and Iron Mountains. If you choose to take this option, at the junction go left (north) up the Wonderland Trail.

Camping & services: You can stay at Sunshine Point Campground if you wish to day hike and car camp (campfires are allowed). You can also stay at the National Park Inn located next to the Longmire Museum.

Some groceries and supplies can be obtained at the Longmire General Store located in the National Park Inn, but backpacking supplies are limited. The nearest place to obtain gas and extensive supplies is Ashford on Washington Highway 706, about 5 miles west from the park boundary.

For more information: Contact the Longmire Wilderness Information Center or the Longmire Museum (see Appendix A).

6 Van Trump Park

Type of hike:	Out-and-back; day hike.
Total distance:	5.8 miles (9.3 kilometers).
Difficulty:	Moderate.
Elevation gain:	2,160 feet.
Best months:	Mid-July–September.
Maps:	USGS Mount Rainier West; Trails Illustrated Mount Rainier National Park; Astronaut's Vista: Mount Rainier National Park, Washington; Earthwalk Press Hiking Map & Guide.
Starting point:	Van Trump Park Trailhead (sometimes referred to as Comet Falls Trailhead).

General description: This hike takes you by Comet Falls and up to Van Trump Park, a series of beautiful flower-filled meadows with great views of the Tatoosh Range and Mount Rainier.

Finding the trailhead: From the Nisqually Entrance Station, drive 10.7 miles east on Longmire-Paradise Road. The parking lot is on your left.

Parking & trailhead facilities: The parking lot at the Van Trump Park Trailhead is often overcrowded on sunny weekends. If you cannot find a space in the parking lot or in the few spaces across the street, you might have to find an alternate hike.

Key points:
1.9 (3.0) Comet Falls.
2.6 (4.3) Junction with spur trail up Van Trump Park.
2.9 (4.6) End of maintained trail.

The hike: Van Trump Park is a great place to view the Tatoosh Range and magnificent Mount Rainier, as long as you have a clear day. When we were there, the fog hid Mount Rainier from us, but the hike was still very enjoyable. You travel through forest, through flower-filled meadows, and by several waterfalls.

From the Van Trump Park parking lot, travel north up the Van Trump Park Trail. In less than 0.3 mile you come to a bridge over a beautiful falls, the top of Christine Falls. The trail stays mainly in the forest all the way, but it opens up right before Comet Falls. At that point, you can relish Van Trump Creek on your left and the bushes of salmonberries to your right.

You come to a bridge before you reach Comet Falls. The trail seems to fork before the bridge, but stay to the left (north). The trail to the right (east) is a small spur trail that wraps around the bend to the foot of an unnamed falls. You also have a nice view of the falls from the bridge.

When you reach your first view of Comet Falls, 1.7 miles from the beginning of your hike, several viewing areas await. The white waters of Comet Falls resemble the tail of a comet, the inspiration for its name. The

Van Trump Park

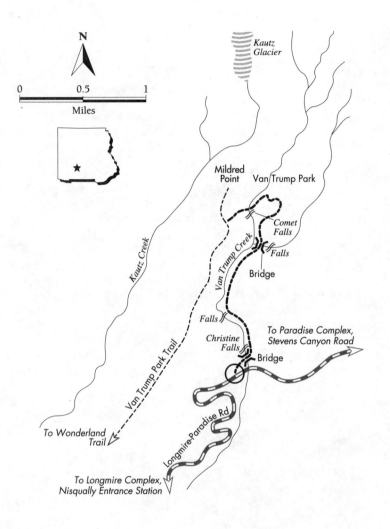

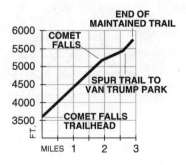

Comet Falls.

spectacular falls are visible from the bottom of the switchbacks, but you have to travel 0.2 mile up the steep switchbacks adjacent to the falls to receive a close-up view. You might even get a little wet!

The switchbacks continue to ascend steeply, and the grade stays that way for the remainder of the trip to Van Trump Park. The trail affords a clear view of the Tatoosh Range to the southeast, and this part of the trail is often lined with wildflowers in mid- to late summer. Travel up the switchbacks for the next 0.7 mile, 2.6 miles total into your hike, until you reach a spur trail that goes up to Van Trump Park. At the junction, go right (north) up to Van Trump Park. If you are taking the spectacular option to Mildred Point, stay to the left. (See Options.)

The maintained spur trail continues for only 0.3 mile. After this point the trail is unmaintained and you travel at your own risk; be careful to only cause minimal impact. The unmaintained trail leads to a ridge with an excellent view of Mount Rainier.

Options: The side trip to Mildred Point is a must-do. The trail is extremely steep and not very well maintained, but the view is spectacular. Deer are also common along this trail, grazing in the adjacent grassy meadows. The knoll up to Mildred Point is filled with an array of wildflowers, from lupine to Columbia lilies. The top of Mildred Point provides a great view of the Kautz Glacier and Mount Rainier.

Camping & services: You can stay at Sunshine Point Campground or Cougar Rock Campground if you wish to day hike and car camp (campfires are allowed). If you want to stay at a hotel, the National Park Inn is located in the Longmire complex, next to the Longmire Museum, and is open year-round.

Some groceries and supplies can be obtained at the Longmire General Store located in the National Park Inn, but supplies are limited. The nearest place to obtain gas and extensive supplies is Ashford on Washington Highway 706, about 5 miles west from the park boundary.

For more information: Contact the Longmire Wilderness Information Center or the Longmire Museum (see Appendix A).

7 Eagle Peak

Type of hike: Out-and-back; day hike.
Total distance: 7.2 miles (12.0 kilometers).
Difficulty: Strenuous.
Elevation gain: 2,955 feet to the saddle; 3,158 feet to the summit.
Best months: Mid July–September.
Maps: USGS Mount Rainier East; Trails Illustrated: Mount Rainier National Park; Astronaut's Vista: Mount Rainier National Park, Washington; Earthwalk Press Hiking Map & Guide.
Starting point: Eagle Peak Trailhead.

General description: A constant and strenuous ascent through varied terrain, ending with a spectacular view in the saddle between two peaks. The hike takes nearly four hours, so be prepared to spend that much time in the woods.

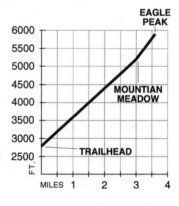

Finding the trailhead: From the Nisqually Entrance Station, drive 6.7 miles east along Longmire-Paradise Road to the Longmire complex on the right. Take the second turn right (east) into the complex. Stay on this road beyond the parking lots and employee housing. The road narrows and curves right (south). Cross the bridge over the Nisqually

Eagle Peak

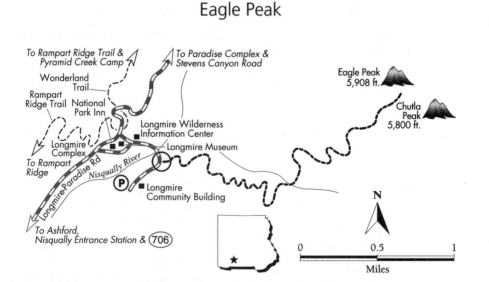

River and in less than 0.1 mile look for the trailhead on the left (east). Drive a little farther down the road and park in one of the spaces in front of the Longmire Community Building.

Parking & trailhead facilities: If the parking lot opposite the Longmire Community Building is full, you should be able to find a spot somewhere in the Longmire area, and follow the same directions to the trailhead. The Longmire complex has toilets, a grocery store, a museum, a restaurant, and the National Park Inn.

Key points:
    3.0   (5.0)   Mountain meadow.
    3.6   (6.0)   Eagle Peak saddle.

The hike: One of the most interesting attributes of this hike is the variety in the surroundings. You begin in dense virgin forest and end in subalpine rocky terrain. The trail itself, however, changes little, holding to a steady climb.

For the first 2 miles, the trail makes a moderate to steep ascent by means of long switchbacks. On the north end of most of the switchbacks, you can catch an obscured glimpse of an unnamed tributary to the Nisqually River below. A full view of this tributary will come 2 miles into the hike as you cross over the wooden bridge just past the halfway point.

Another mile of hiking in forest suddenly ends as the trees are exchanged for a mountain meadow and subalpine fields of wildflowers. After 0.5 mile of very steep hiking along a rocky face, you reach the saddle of Eagle Peak.

For the sake of aesthetics, hope for a clear day. The Eagle Peak saddle provides a fantastic view of the Nisqually Valley, the Nisqually Glacier, the Tatoosh Range, Mount St. Helens, and Mount Rainier.

Options: If you feel the need to conquer the peak, the climb to the summit is a scramble up a rocky face. You should have some climbing experience before attempting the summit. This option adds about 0.5 mile to your hike, raising the total miles hiked round trip to 8.

Camping & services: The National Park Inn is located next to the Longmire Museum. You can also stay at Cougar Rock Campground for $10 per night. Groceries and limited supplies can be obtained at the Longmire General Store located in the National Park Inn. The nearest place to obtain gas and extensive supplies is Ashford on Washington Highway 706, about 5 miles west from the park boundary.

For more information: Contact the Longmire Wilderness Information Center or the Longmire Museum (see Appendix A).

8 Narada Falls

Type of hike: One-way, with a vehicle shuttle; day hike or overnighter.

Total distance: 4.5 miles (7.2 kilometers).

Difficulty: Easy.

Elevation loss: 2,044 feet.

Best months: Early July–September.

Maps: USGS Mount Rainier West and Mount Rainier East; Trails Illustrated Mount Rainier National Park; Astronaut's Vista: Mount Rainier National Park, Washington; Earthwalk Press Hiking Map & Guide.

Starting point: Narada Falls.

General description: A completely downhill hike (with a vehicle shuttle) that passes three waterfalls and runs along the Paradise and Nisqually Rivers.

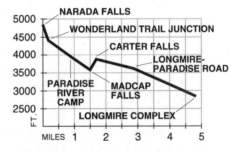

Finding the trailhead: Hiking this trail one way requires a short two-car shuttle. From the Nisqually Entrance Station, drive 6.7 miles east on Longmire-Paradise Road to the Longmire complex on the right (south). Park one car here and continue 8.4 miles east on Longmire-Paradise Road and turn right (east) into the parking lot signed for Narada Falls. The Narada Falls Trail is on the far east side of the parking lot before the bathrooms. Park and walk over the bridge until you see the trailhead on the right (south).

Parking & trailhead facilities: There are restrooms and generous parking at both the Narada Falls parking lot and the Longmire complex. On sunny weekends, however, parking is a potential problem and you might have to find an alternate hike. The Longmire complex has toilets, a grocery store, a museum, a restaurant, and the National Park Inn.

Key points:

0.2	(0.3)	Wonderland Trail junction.
0.9	(1.4)	Paradise River Camp.
1.5	(2.4)	Madcap Falls.
1.7	(2.7)	Carter Falls.
2.8	(4.5)	Longmire-Paradise Road.
4.5	(7.2)	Longmire complex.

The hike: If you like to hike downhill and love waterfalls, this is the hike for you! You begin at the astonishing Narada Falls, then hike by two other waterfalls, Madcap Falls and Carter Falls. The only disadvantage of this hike is that it requires two vehicles.

Narada Falls

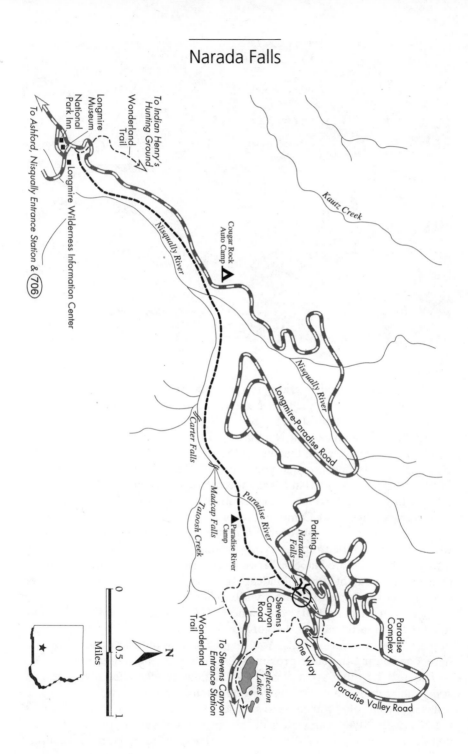

Bridge over the Nisqually River.

From the Narada Falls parking lot, go down the stone steps of the Narada Falls Trail that run along the falls. Narada Falls is wondrous, and on a hot day the cool spray of the falls is very refreshing. Do be careful on the slippery rocks. The first 0.2 mile on the Narada Falls Trail is usually extremely crowded, considering how close the magnificent falls are to the road. Fortunately, the traffic nearly disappears when you join the Wonderland Trail. Go right and head west on the Wonderland Trail. You can hear the Paradise River flowing directly to your right, which you cross about 1 mile into your hike (about 0.1 mile past Paradise River Camp on the left).

Three bridges take you over the relatively calm forks of the Paradise River. About 0.5 mile from here you encounter Madcap Falls, 1.5 miles total into your hike, where Tatoosh Creek flows into the Paradise River. Instead of dropping straight down, Madcap Falls slope at a diagonal. The water gushes over the rocks to create a white wonder.

Soon after Madcap Falls, you come to Carter Falls, 1.7 miles into your hike. A sign reaffirms that the gorgeous waters you see dropping straight down are in fact Carter Falls. You might come upon a number of people here, considering the close proximity to Cougar Rock Campground.

The next 1.1 miles are a pleasant walk along the Paradise River, despite some metal drain pipes and power lines along the trail. When you are 2.8 miles into your hike, you come to another set of bridges that take you across the Nisqually River. The waters of the Nisqually River are thick with "glacial flour," fine sediments deposited by active glaciers at the river's source.

After you cross the bridges, climb up to Longmire-Paradise Road. The Wonderland Trail continues left (west), with a sign indicating that it is 1.6 miles to Longmire. In 0.2 mile, you come to another junction. The trail to your right (north) goes to Cougar Rock Campground, and the trail left (south) goes to the horse ford for the Nisqually River. Continue heading southwest on the Wonderland Trail through old-growth forest all the way to the Longmire complex.

Options: If you do not have two cars, you can hide a bike at the end of the hike and ride back to the car. Consider doing the hike in reverse so that the person biking the shuttle doesn't have to ride uphill after the hike. Keep in mind that Longmire-Paradise Road has a narrow shoulder, leaving little room for cyclists.

Another option is to start at the Paradise complex instead of Narada Falls, making your trip 1.2 miles longer. This allows you to travel all the way from the Paradise complex to the Longmire complex. Park one car at the Longmire complex, as indicated previously, and park the other car at the Paradise complex. To get to the Paradise complex from the Longmire complex, drive 11.4 miles east on Longmire-Paradise Road. Park in the parking lot in front of the Paradise Ranger Station and the Paradise Inn. Walk to the Lakes Trailhead, located in the southeast corner of the parking lot. Stay on the Lakes Trail for less than 0.6 mile until you intersect with the Narada Falls Trail. Then go west on the Narada Falls Trail for a little over 0.1 mile until you cross Longmire-Paradise Road. Travel along the Narada Falls trail for another 0.5 mile until you reach Narada Falls. At this point, refer to the above hike description.

Camping & services: If you choose to stay overnight, you can stay at Paradise River Camp. Fires are not permitted, as in all of the backcountry camps in Mount Rainier National Park. Paradise River Camp has three individual sites and one group site. All of the sites are small and flat. Site 2 is the most secluded, but it overlooks site 1. Site 3 is nearest to the bathrooms and directly off the spur trail. The Paradise River is the water source for this backcountry camp.

If you would like to car camp and day hike, both Cougar Rock Campground and Sunshine Point Campground are options, but Cougar Rock Campground is closer. Campfires are allowed at both campgrounds. Some groceries and supplies can be obtained at the Longmire General Store located in the National Park Inn, but supplies are limited. The nearest place to obtain gas and extensive supplies is Ashford on Washington Highway 706, about 5 miles west from the park boundary.

For more information: Contact the Longmire Wilderness Information Center or the Longmire Museum (see Appendix A).

9 Comet Falls

Type of hike:	Out-and-back; day hike.
Total distance:	3.8 miles (6.1 kilometers).
Difficulty:	Easy.
Elevation gain:	1,600 feet.
Best months:	Early July–September.
Maps:	USGS Mount Rainier West; Trails Illustrated Mount Rainier National Park; Astronaut's Vista: Mount Rainier National Park, Washington; Earthwalk Press Hiking Map & Guide.
Starting point:	Van Trump Park Trailhead (commonly referred to as Comet Falls Trailhead).

General description: A short ascent through an enchanting forest to a waterfall that drops over a 300-foot cliff.

Finding the trailhead: From the Nisqually Entrance Station, drive 10.7 miles east on Longmire-Paradise Road. The trailhead and parking lot are on your left.

Parking & trailhead facilities: The parking lot at the Van Trump Park Trailhead is often overcrowded on sunny weekends. If you cannot find a space in the parking lot or in the few spaces across the street, you might have to find an alternate hike.

Key points:
0.3	(0.5)	Christine Falls
1.9	(3.0)	Comet Falls

The hike: This hike takes you past two other waterfalls before you reach the highest waterfall accessible by trail in Mount Rainier National Park. In August, salmonberries line the trail. It is uphill all the way to Comet Falls, but well worth every step.

From the Van Trump Park parking lot, travel up the Van Trump Park Trail. Only 0.3 mile into your hike, you come to a bridge over a beautiful falls, the top of Christine Falls. This is also Van Trump Creek. The trail stays mainly in the forest all the way, but it opens up before Comet Falls. At that point, you can relish Van Trump Creek on your left and salmonberries to your right.

You come to a bridge before you reach Comet Falls. The trail seems to fork before the bridge, but stay to the left. The trail to the right (east) is a small spur trail that wraps around the bend to below an unnamed falls. You also have a nice view of the falls from the bridge.

When you reach your first view of Comet Falls, 1.7 miles from the beginning of your hike, several viewing areas await you. The white waters of Comet Falls resemble the tail of a comet and this is the inspiration for its name. The spectacular falls are visible from the bottom of the switchbacks,

Comet Falls

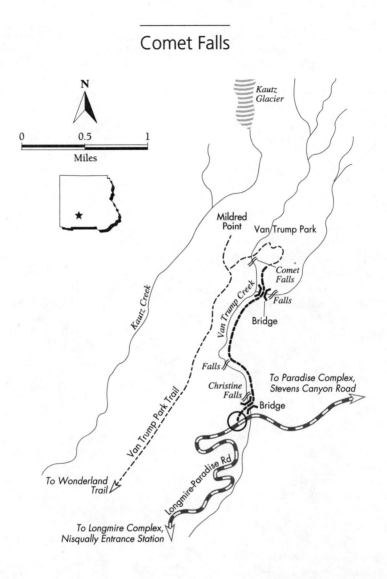

but you have to travel 0.2 mile up the steep switchbacks adjacent to the falls to get a close-up view of the falls. You might even get a little wet!

Options: You can hike up to Van Trump Park. It is 1 mile away, making your trip 2 miles longer. (See Hike 6: Van Trump Park.)

Camping & services: If you would like to car camp and day hike, both Cougar Rock Campground and Sunshine Point Campground are options. Cougar Rock Campground is closer to the trailhead. Campfires are allowed at both campgrounds.

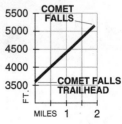

Comet Falls.

Some groceries and supplies can be obtained at the Longmire General Store located in the National Park Inn, but supplies are limited. The nearest place to obtain gas and extensive supplies is Ashford on Washington Highway 706, about 5 miles west from the park boundary.

For more information: Contact the Longmire Wilderness Information Center or the Longmire Museum (see Appendix A).

10 Trail of the Shadows

Type of hike: Loop; day hike.
Total distance: 0.7 mile (1.2 kilometers).
Difficulty: Easy, and wheelchair-accessible for the first 0.25 mile.
Elevation gain: Minimal.
Best months: May–October.
Maps: USGS Mount Rainier East; Trails Illustrated: Mount Rainier National Park; Astronaut's Vista: Mount Rainier National Park, Washington; Earthwalk Press Hiking Map & Guide.
Starting point: Longmire complex.

General description: A 20-minute stroll around the Longmire Meadow that informs the hiker about the Longmire family and its stake in the park.

Finding the trailhead: From the Nisqually Entrance Station, drive 6.7 miles east on Longmire-Paradise Road. Look for the Longmire complex on the right (east). Park in one of the many spaces available, then cross the road along one of teh two crosswalks to find the trailhead.

Parking & trailhead facilities: Park in one of the parking lots around the Longmire Wilderness Information Center, the Longmire Museum, and the National Park Inn. Parking is a potential problem on sunny weekends and you might have to choose an alternate hike. There are pay phones and bathrooms next to the Longmire Museum.

Key points:
0.1	(0.2)	Masonry spring.
0.2	(0.3)	Longmire's cabin.
0.2	(0.3)	Iron Mike.
0.5	(0.8)	Travertine Mound.

The hike: If you are a history buff who likes casual strolls, you will enjoy this hike. The trail winds around an enchanting meadow, while taking you to many informative stations. The theme of the stations is James Longmire, his crusade for a natural health spa, and his love of the mountain.

Starting to the right (north), the first stop is a work of stone masonry with bubbling water, said in the nineteenth century to cure any illness. As the sign ironically reads, do NOT drink this water; it can make you very ill.

Trail of the Shadows

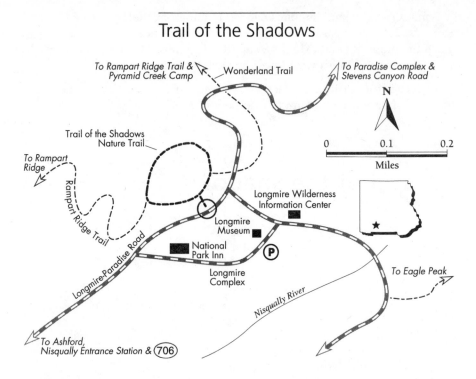

The next stop, 0.2 mile into the hike, is the cabin that Longmire built. It still has the original furniture, also constructed by Longmire. Next door is Iron Mike, a spring which is tinted orange by iron minerals.

A very small side trip at 0.5 mile from the trailhead leads to the Travertine Mound, another orange mass bursting with mineral water. A bench here provides a nice place to sit and view the meadow.

The home stretch of the loop includes a variety of interesting wild vegetation. After completing the loop, cross the same street to your car and the large present-day Longmire complex. Notice the great disparity between the present-day edifices and the shadows of the past.

Camping & services: A hotel room, groceries, and limited supplies can be obtained in the Longmire area. The nearest place to fill up on gas and extensive supplies is Ashford, located on Washington Highway 706, about 5 miles west from the park boundary.

For more information: Contact the Longmire Wilderness Information Center or the Longmire Museum (see Appendix A).

View of Rampart Ridge from the Trail of the Shadows.

11 West Wonderland

Type of hike: One-way with a lengthy vehicle shuttle; three- to five-night backpack.
Total distance: 34.1 miles (54.6 kilometers).
Difficulty: Strenuous.
Elevation gain: 8,420 feet total, with a total elevation loss of 9,300 feet.
Best months: Late July–September.
Maps: USGS Golden Lakes, Mount Wow; Trails Illustrated Mount Rainier National Park; Astronaut's Vista: Mount Rainier National Park, Washington; Earthwalk Press Hiking Map & Guide
Starting point: Paul Peak Trailhead on Mowich Lake Road.

General description: An outstanding backpack trip that covers the entire west side of the Wonderland Trail, which has been coined the "pie crust" by previous hikers.

Finding the trailhead: This hike requires a two-car shuttle between the start and finish. First, leave a car at the finish at the Longmire complex. From the Nisqually Entrance Station, drive 6.7 miles east on Longmire-Paradise Road to the Longmire complex and park one car here.

From here, the drive to the hike's start in the northwestern section of the park can take up to two hours—make sure you account for this time when planning your trip. Drive back to the Nisqually Entrance Station and continue 13 miles west on Washington Highway 706. In the town of Elbe, stay to the right when the road forks and drive north, now on WA 7. Continue about 10 miles north on WA 7 and take the exit for Eatonville and WA 161. Drive north on WA 161 and take the exit for Kapowsin on your right. Continue north through Electron to the town of Orting and WA 162. Turn right and drive about 10 miles east on WA 162 to the junction with WA 165. Go right (south) on WA 165, through Wilkeson, another 9 miles until the road forks. Stay to the left (south) at this fork, signed for Mowich Lake. After 3.2 miles, the road turns into a well-maintained dirt road, although it can be very slippery when muddy. Follow this road another 8.8 miles to the Paul Peak Trailhead on the right (south) side of the road. If you come to Mowich Lake, you have gone too far and need to turn around. Be sure to pay the park entrance fee before heading off on your hike.

Parking & trailhead facilities: The Paul Peak Trailhead has one restroom and a sizable parking lot that is rarely full.

Key points:

0.6	(1.0)	Meadow Creek.
3.1	(5.0)	Wonderland Trail junction.
4.0	(6.4)	South Mowich River.

West Wonderland

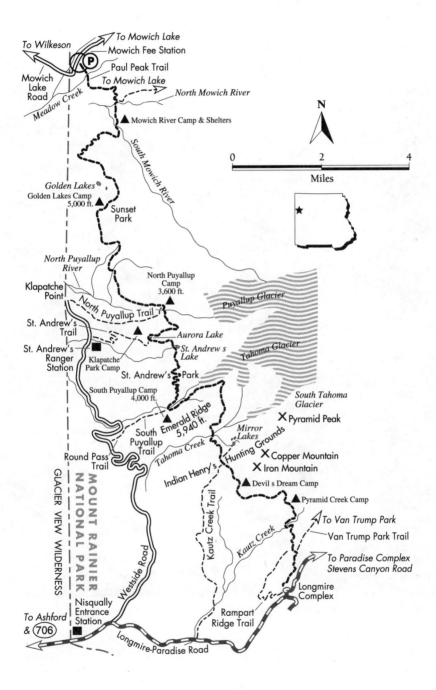

To Wilkeson

To Mowich Lake
Mowich Fee Station
Paul Peak Trail

Mowich
Lake
Road

To Mowich Lake
North Mowich River

Meadow Creek

Mowich River Camp & Shelters

N

0   2   4
Miles

South Mowich River

Golden Lakes
Golden Lakes Camp
5,000 ft.
Sunset
Park

Puyallup Glacier

North Puyallup
River

North Puyallup
Camp
3,600 ft.

Klapatche
Point

North Puyallup Trail

Tahoma Glacier

St. Andrew's
Trail

Aurora Lake

St. Andrew's
Ranger
Station

Klapatche
Park Camp

St. Andrew's
Lake

St. Andrew's Park

South Puyallup Camp
4,000 ft.

South Tahoma
Glacier

X Pyramid Peak

South Emerald Ridge
5,940 ft.

Mirror
Lakes

South
Puyallup
Trail

Tahoma Creek

Hunting Grounds

X Copper Mountain
X Iron Mountain

Round Pass
Trail

Indian Henry's

Devil's Dream Camp

Pyramid Creek Camp

To Van Trump Park
Van Trump Park Trail

GLACIER VIEW WILDERNESS

MOUNT RAINIER NATIONAL PARK

Westside Road

Kautz Creek Trail

Kautz Creek

To Paradise Complex
Stevens Canyon Road

Longmire
Complex

Nisqually
Entrance
Station

To Ashford
& (706)

Rampart
Ridge Trail

Longmire-Paradise Road

North Puyallup River. PHOTO BY BILL SCHNEIDER

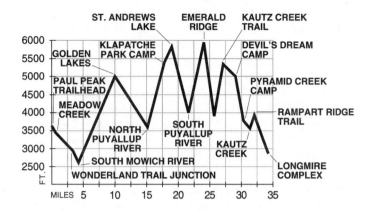

10.1 (16.0)   Golden Lakes.
15.1 (24.2)   North Puyallup River.
17.8 (28.5)   Klapatche Park Camp.
18.6 (29.8)   St. Andrews Lake.
21.8 (34.9)   South Puyallup River.
23.4 (37.4)   Emerald Ridge.
25.5 (40.8)   Suspension bridge over Tahoma Creek.
27.2 (43.5)   Kautz Creek Trail.
29.5 (47.8)   Devil's Dream Camp.
30.6 (49.0)   Pyramid Creek Camp.
31.3 (50.1)   Kautz Creek.
32.3 (51.7)   Rampart Ridge Trail junction.
34.1 (54.6)   Longmire complex.

The hike: This is a fantastic hike if you want to experience the Wonderland Trail (but do not have the time or facilities to hike the entire trail, decribed in Hike 60: The Wonderland Trail). This 34.1-mile hike takes you along the entire west side of the Wonderland Trail, commonly called the "pie crust" due to its severe elevation changes. The trail gives you spectacular views of Mount Rainier, Klapatche Park, St. Andrews Park, and other astonishing backcountry in Mount Rainier National Park.

From the Paul Peak Trailhead, head down a few switchbacks to Meadow Creek. The trail then turns slightly uphill through magnificent old-growth forest for the next 1.5 miles until you hit steep switchbacks downhill. The switchbacks continue almost all the way to the Wonderland Trail, 3.1 miles into your hike. At the junction with the Wonderland Trail, go right (south) toward the South Mowich Shelter. The trail continues downhill all the way to the North Mowich River.

Two bridges take you over the North Mowich River and put you on the North Mowich River Bar. You might still be able to see the remains of the North Mowich Shelter, which was torn down in 1993, atop this river bar. About 0.25 mile after you cross the North Mowich River, you come to South Mowich Camp and its shelter. Depending on how long you have decided to make your trip, you will or will not set up camp here. This is also the last place to filter water until Golden Lakes.

Beyond South Mowich Camp, you cross the South Mowich River, 4 miles into your hike. The area around the South Mowich River is scattered with debris and crushed trees from previous glacial outburst floods from the ever-changing south fork of the Mowich River. When we hiked this trail, one of the three bridges over the South Mowich River was washed out, and it apparently washes out several times a year. Be aware that it is a tricky ford and glacial boulders in the river are a possible hazard. It is a good idea to call ahead to the Wilkeson Wilderness Information Center to find out if the bridge is down so you can prepare accordingly, but understand that washouts are unpredictable and the bridge may be gone on the day you arrive.

After you leave the South Mowich River, the trail climbs uphill all the way to Golden Lakes, 6.1 miles away. At first the grade is slight, but after a mile or so, the switchbacked trail becomes steep and maintains this steep grade to the top of the ridge. At the top, the trail descends briefly and then sustains a slight pitch for almost a mile to Golden Lakes, 10.1 miles into your hike. The scattered pools you see around you are Golden Lakes. Wildflowers, such as shooting stars and avalanche lilies, line their banks in mid-July.

The next day, head south for Klapatche Park. A 0.5-mile ascent will bring you to Sunset Park in all its glory. Magenta paintbrushes and avalanche lilies fill the meadows of the park. At the edge of Sunset Park, the hillside is filled with ghost trees, the eerie remains of a fire from years ago. The trail is all downhill for the next 5 miles to the North Puyallup River, 15.1 miles into your hike.

Just before you cross the North Puyallup River, a spur trail leads to North Puyallup Camp to the left (north), and the Wonderland Trail continues to the right (south). As you cross the river, make sure to look down at the raging white waters of the North Puyallup River and up at the Puyallup Glacier. If the bridge makes you uneasy, you can enjoy the sights from a more grounded viewpoint on the other side of the river.

The junction with the North Puyallup Trail is also on the other side of the bridge. The trail forks right (west) and runs directly left of the horse camp and its toilet. Stay to the left, unless you are taking the side trip to Klapatche Point, and head up Klapatche Ridge. (See Options.)

Watch your step as you hike up this ridge; the trail is very steep and has an unstable ledge that drops straight off. At the top of the ridge, Klapatche Park unfolds in front of your eyes. Beautiful wildflowers fill the meadows and surround Aurora Lake in mid-July. Aurora Lake is only a shallow pool of snowmelt, but it looks astonishing with Mount Rainier towering above it. If you are staying at Klapatche Park Camp, it is located at the west end of the lake.

The next day, take off for St. Andrews Lake and St. Andrews Park. At the south end of Aurora Lake, the St. Andrews Trail forks off to the right (west). Stay to the left (south), unless you plan to take a side trip to Denman Falls. (See Options.) It is only 0.8 mile to St. Andrews Lake from this junction.

Previous hikers have greatly impacted St. Andrews Lake by creating numerous social trails along the fragile banks of this subalpine lake. Minimize your impact by admiring the lake from the designated trail. You can also see a west-side climbing route that many have used to attempt the summit. Fortunately, the trails do not entirely take away from the deep blue waters of St. Andrews Lake. As much as you will hate leaving the lake, do not worry because St. Andrews Park will soon stun you with its subalpine beauty. In mid-July, avalanche lilies, lupine, and magenta paintbrush fill the meadows with their splendor.

From the end of St. Andrews Park, it is another 2.5 miles down to the South Puyallup River, 21.8 miles into your hike. The descent is steep, and the trail is surrounded by scratchy brush. At the end of your descent, you cross the silty waters of the South Puyallup River and come to the junction with the South Puyallup Trail. South Puyallup Camp is to your right, west on the South Puyallup Trail. Go left (east) toward Emerald Ridge on the Wonderland Trail, unless you had previously decided to stay at South Puyallup Camp.

It is 1.7 miles to the top of Emerald Ridge from the junction with the South Puyallup Trail. The Tahoma Glacier and its moraine are to your left (north) as you head east on the Wonderland Trail. If you look up at Mount Rainier, you will see the top of the Tahoma Glacier, accompanied by the South Tahoma Glacier to the right. Between the two glaciers is Glacier Island. Mountain goats often can be seen grazing on Glacier Island, a green haven in a sea of glaciers: if you look closely, you can see fields of lupine.

The top of Emerald Ridge is an emerald green meadow filled with wildflowers in mid-July. The scent of lupine fills hikers' nostrils with its sweet perfume. A plethora of hoary marmots lives in the meadows. Do not feed these wild animals; they need to emain self-sufficient to survive in their natural habitat. Also, it is illegal to feed the wildlife in Mount Rainier National Park.

The trail along the north side of Emerald Ridge has washed out many times and lines a steep, unstable ledge. Be very careful. Take the new trail that diagonally crosses the ridge.

After Emerald Ridge, you head down toward Indian Henry's Hunting Ground. The trail takes you on the other side of Emerald Ridge to the South Tahoma Moraine. Hike over the moraine and head back into the forest. From there, it is more downhill switchbacks until you reach the suspension bridge over Tahoma Creek, 2.1 miles from the top of Emerald Ridge. Just before you reach the bridge, you will see a sign for the Tahoma Creek Trail on your right that connects with Westside Road. As the sign indicates, the trail is not recommended for use.

From the suspension bridge, there is an amazing view of Tahoma Creek. If it is not too windy, take the time to look up the creek. Tahoma Creek continually experiences glacial outburst floods, and if you hear a loud, roaring sound, immediately proceed to higher ground.

Uphill switchbacks await you on the other side of the bridge. It is about a 1,000-foot climb to Indian Henry's Hunting Ground. When you arrive there, the trail winds through the pretty meadows of Indian Henry's Hunting Ground from which you have an excellent view of Mount Rainier. You might want to take a break here before heading off to Devil's Dream Camp.

After you pass the Kautz Creek Trail Junction, the trail begins to drop to Devil's Dream Camp, which is 29.5 miles into your hike. You will pass Squaw Lake on your left before you reach the camp. This is the water source for Devil's Dream Camp when the stream below the camp dries up in late summer. As you will see, it is a little hike from the camp.

From Devil's Dream Camp, the Longmire complex is only 5.5 miles away. This should be your last day and it's all downhill. It is 2.1 miles to Pyramid Creek Camp and then under 0.7 mile to Kautz Creek. During a hot spell, the waters of Kautz Creek can rise, washing out the footbridges.

After Kautz Creek, the trail is relatively flat to the intersection with the Rampart Ridge Trail, 1.8 miles from the end. You travel downhill through the forest for the rest of your trip. It is not very scenic, but shady heaven on a hot day.

Options: If you cannot complete the whole hike as outlined, you can take the option of heading out to Westside Road after spending the night at Klapatche Park. It is 2.5 miles down the St. Andrews Trail from Klapatche Park to reach Westside Road. If the road is still closed, it is another 7.8 miles to the closure, making your total trip 28.1 miles long.

Two possible side trips for this hike are Klapatche Point and Denman Falls. From the junction with the North Puyallup Trail, go right (west) by the group/horse site of North Puyallup Camp. The trail is flat all the way to Westside Road. Due to the closure of the road, this trail receives minimum use and has become overgrown with bushes, particularly salmonberries. This could explain the bear scat we saw everywhere. At the end of the North Puyallup Trail is Klapatche Point, from which you can see out of the park.

The other option is Denman Falls. At the west end of Aurora Lake, you come to the junction with the St. Andrews Trail. You hike 2.5 miles down steep switchbacks to Westside Road. The Denman Falls Trail begins on the other side of the road a couple of steps north. Denman Falls is a little over 0.1 mile from road. The first spur trail that forks off from the Denman Falls Trail takes you to St. Andrews Creek above the falls. The Denman Falls Trail continues on and takes you below the falls.

Camping & services: Campfires are not permitted at any of the seven camps available. Most hikers need anywhere from three to five nights to complete this trip. If you choose to go for three nights, you must average more than 10 miles per day. We recommend staying at Golden Lakes Camp, Klapatche Park Camp, and Devil's Dream Camp. If you choose to take five nights, you will hike 4 to 7 miles per day and stay at Mowich Camp, Golden Lakes Camp, Klapatche Park Camp, South Puyallup Camp, and Devil's Dream Camp. Of course, these itineraries are not final and you might have to adjust them according to what camps are available to you.

Mowich Camp, the first camp, has four individual sites and a group site. (The South Mowich Shelter is considered one of the individual sites.) Sites 3 and 4 are closer to the South Mowich River, while sites 1 and 2, along with the group site, are crunched together and near the trail. There is an outhouse here.

There are five individual campsites and one group site at Golden Lakes Camp. The camp also has a food storage pole to hang your food. Numbers 1, 2, and 3 are near the outhouse. The group site (number 4) and number 5 are near the lake. You have a fantastic view at site 5, as well as a close water source. The group site is closest to the lake.

North Puyallup Camp is along the North Puyallup River, although you do not see the river from any of the sites. The camp, tucked away in the forest, has three individual sites and one group/horse site. Each individual site is flat, small, and directly next to the trail. The group/horse site is rather spacious and open, separate from the three individual sites, and located across the foot bridge over North Puyallup River.

The campsites at Klapatche Park spoil you. There are four individual sites. The toilet is near all the sites, although the food storage pole is too close. Number 1 is closest to the lake and has an incomparable view. Watching the sun rise and reflect Mount Rainier in Aurora Lake will take your breath away. You cannot see Mount Rainier clearly from any of the other sites, but the view down the north side of Klapatche Ridge from sites 2, 3, and 4 is very pleasant.

There are four individual sites at South Puyallup Camp and one group site. Number 1 is probably the best campsite. It is private, with a close water source. Be forewarned that the toilet is 0.1 mile from all the campsites. Site 2 also has its own water source with good tent sites. Sites 3 and 4 have just been improved, and if seclusion is your primary concern, site 4 is your best bet.

The seven campsites at Devil's Dream Camp are nothing to dream about, but all are very nice and flat. Sites 5 and 6 offer the most privacy. There are two pit toilets, and the camp is often filled with Wonderland Trail hikers. Be careful when you use the toilet near site 4 because it is likely that the residents there can see you! All of the other sites are next to the trail, spacious, and flat. Usually the water source for Devil's Dream Camp is near site 1, but it often dries up in late summer. If this is the case, you will have to hike about 0.25 mile to Squaw Lake or to the creek directly after Squaw Lake, depending on where you prefer to obtain your water.

Pyramid Creek Camp has only two sites, but the National Park Service is currently adding another. It has a pit toilet and its water source is Pyramid Creek, less than 0.1 mile north on the Wonderland Trail. Both are flat and nice, site 2 being more private and more spacious.

For more information: Contact the Wilkeson Wilderness Information Center, the Longmire Wilderness Information Center, or the Longmire Museum (see Appendix A).

Paradise

For many reasons, more people tour the Paradise region than the other areas of Mount Rainier. Situated high on the south slope of Mount Rainier, the Paradise area offers close-up views of massive glacial formations. Most noted is the Nisqually Glacier, a debris-and crevice-ridden glacier that inches farther down the mountain yearly. A plethora of trails encircles Paradise, all with spectacular views of Mount Rainier, the Tatoosh Range, Mount St. Helens, alpine rock fields, and subalpine meadows filled with rather bold animals.

Recent tourists were not the first to appreciate the wonders of Paradise. The name itself, taken from the native *Saghalie Illahe*, literally means "Land of Peace." For the surrounding Native American tribes, this area signified not only a wonderland of beauty, but also a haven from an often tumultuous life. Fighting was prohibited in Paradise.

Today, with so many visitors yearly, Paradise faces a new challenge. Incessant tromping on the fragile meadows has led to extreme erosion. Recent efforts at meadow restoration prove promising, but without the cooperation of those enjoying Paradise no improvements will last. Please, in this and all areas around Mount Rainier National Park, stay on the designated trails, do not feed the animals, and enjoy the splendors of conservation.

12 Nisqually Vista

Type of hike: Out-and-back; day hike.
Total distance: 1.2 miles (1.9 kilometers).
Difficulty: Easy.
Elevation gain: Minimal.
Best months: Early July–September.
Maps: USGS Mount Rainier East; Trails Illustrated Mount Rainier National Park; Astronaut's Vista: Mount Rainier National Park, Washington; Earthwalk Press Hiking Map & Guide.
Starting point: Dead Horse Creek Trailhead.

General description: A short hike through beautiful forest overlooking the Nisqually Glacier.

Finding the trailhead: From the Nisqually Entrance Station, drive 15.9 miles east on Longmire-Paradise Road to the turnoff for the Ohanapecosh area. Stay to the left and continue on Longmire-Paradise Road for 2.1 miles. Park in the parking lot in front of the Jackson Visitor Center.

Nisqually Vista

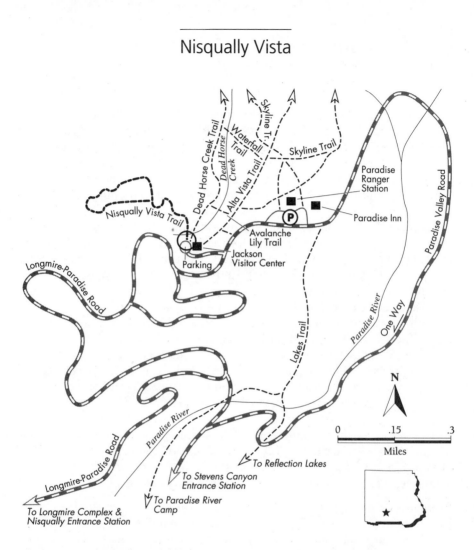

Parking & trailhead facilities: Parking at the Paradise complex can get really hectic. Watch for a flashing sign when you enter the park that indicates whether or not the parking lots at Paradise are full. Even if all of the lots are not full, the lot in front of the visitor center is likely to be full. In this case, you can drive another 0.1 mile up the road to the parking lot in front of the Paradise Ranger Station and the Paradise Inn. Bathrooms are located inside the Jackson Visitor Center and in the upper lot next to the Paradise Ranger Station. The Paradise complex offers food, phones, restrooms, an inn, a visitor center, and limited supplies.

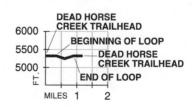

Key points:

0.3	(0.5)	Beginning of loop.
0.6	(1.0)	First viewpoint of the Nisqually Glacier.
0.9	(1.4)	End of loop.
1.2	(1.9)	Dead Horse Creek Trailhead.

The hike: This is a great hike for kids and adults alike. The trail takes you through beautiful forested areas and wonderful meadows to an overlook of the Nisqually Glacier. The Nisqually Vista Trail is a self-guiding trail, but the National Park Service offers a guided tour of this hike. Inquire inside the Jackson Visitor Center for more information. It is downhill all the way to the lookout and then uphill back to the parking lot, but both gradients are gradual.

To begin the hike, head to the northwest end of the Jackson Visitor Center parking lot. Look for a trail sign for the Dead Horse Creek Trail. Go left (northwest) onto the Nisqually Vista Trail. The trail forks less than 0.3 mile down the trail. Go right (southwest). Halfway through the loop and halfway through your hike, you come to a viewpoint. There are three viewpoints total, and the last one has a display on the Nisqually Glacier.

From all the viewpoints, you can see where the Nisqually River comes out of the Nisqually Glacier and the massive moraine the glacier has dug out. The Nisqually Glacier is currently advancing at approximately 6 inches per day. At one point, the glacier extended all the way to Ricksecker Point. You might have seen Ricksecker Point on the way from the Longmire complex to the Paradise complex. It is visible from the only bridge between the two areas.

The rest of the loop is a little over 0.3 mile long, and it takes you through quaint forest with meadows of lupine and bistort (commonly called bottlebrush). When you come to the end of the loop, stay to the left, toward the visitor center. Enjoy a leisurely hike back to the parking lot.

Camping & services: You can stay at the Paradise Inn located near the Paradise Ranger Station. The nearest place to obtain gas and other supplies is Ashford on Washington Highway 706, about 5 miles west from the park boundary. Any other supplies should be obtained in Ashford.

For more information: Contact the Jackson Visitor Center on the Paradise Ranger Station, (see Appendix A).

13 Alta Vista Summit

Type of hike: Out-and-back; day hike.
Total distance: 1.6 miles (2.6 kilometers).
Difficulty: Easy.
Elevation gain: Minimal.
Best months: Early July–September.
Maps: USGS Mount Rainier East; Trails Illustrated Mount Rainier National Park; Astronaut's Vista: Mount Rainier National Park, Washington; Earthwalk Press Hiking Map & Guide.
Starting point: Jackson Visitor Center.

General description: A short hike up to the Alta Vista summit, where you have an excellent view of Paradise Park and the Tatoosh Range.

Finding the trailhead: From the Nisqually Entrance Station, drive 15.9 miles east on Longmire-Paradise Road to the turnoff for the Ohanapecosh area. Stay to the left and continue on Longmire-Paradise Road for 2.1 miles. Park in the parking lot in front of the Jackson Visitor Center.

Parking & trailhead facilities: Parking at the Paradise complex can get really hectic. If you do find a parking spot, the Paradise complex offers food, phones, restrooms, an inn, a visitor center, and limited supplies. Watch for a flashing sign when you enter the park that indicates whether or not the parking lots at Paradise are full. Even if all of the lots are not full, the lot in front of the visitor center is likely to be full. In this case, you can drive another 0.1 mile up the road to the parking lot in front of the Paradise Ranger Station and the Paradise Inn. Bathrooms are located inside the Jackson Visitor Center and in the upper lot next to the Paradise Ranger Station.

Key Points:
0.1	(0.2)	Junction with Avalanche Lily Trail.
0.2	(0.3)	Junction with Waterfall Trail.
0.5	(0.8)	Beginning of loop.
1.1	(1.8)	End of loop.
1.6	(2.6)	Jackson Visitor Center.

The hike: This hike is excellent for children. It is short, scenic, and gives you a little taste of Mount Rainier National Park. If you take this hike in July or August, an abundance of wildflowers will line the trails. Please preserve

Alta Vista Summit

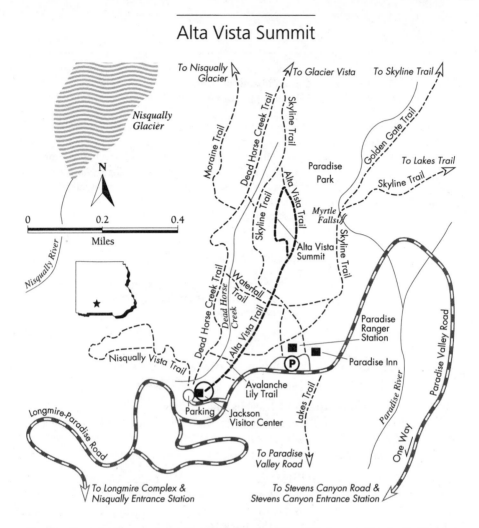

the fragile meadows where the flowers grow by staying on the trail. Expect to see a lot of people on this popular trail.

The trail, paved and well maintained, begins directly west of the Jackson Visitor Center. No trailhead sign marks the beginning of the Alta Vista Trail, but follow the paved steps that head north for just a few steps and you will come to a display of trails in the Paradise area. Do not take the spur trail heading to the right (east); it leads to the Paradise Ranger Station.

Continue 0.1 mile north on the Alta Vista Trail to the Avalanche Lily Trail, which runs west to the Dead Horse Creek Trail and east to the Paradise Ranger Station. Go straight and immediately pass another small spur trail that connects with the Avalanche Lily Trail on your left heading southwest. Stay on the Alta Vista Trail traveling north. There are detailed signs to help you stay on the Alta Vista Trail.

After another 0.1 mile, the Waterfall Trail goes left (west) to connect with the Dead Horse Creek Trail or right (east) to the Skyline Trail. Again, stay on the Alta Vista Trail heading north. Very soon after this junction, you come to the Skyline Trail. Again, stay on the Alta Vista Trail. At this point, the trail grade turns markedly steep. Pace yourself.

About 0.5 mile into your hike, you come to the beginning of the loop to the Alta Vista summit. Go left (northwest) and uphill toward the summit with the help of a sign that points you in the correct direction. Below, Paradise Park is to the right (east). You can see tons of people milling about below you on other Paradise trails. Turn around and look to the south for a fabulous view of the jutting peaks of the Tatoosh Range.

If you need a rest, enjoy the view from one of many rock benches along the trail. Please preserve the meadows by staying on the trail or in a designated rest area.

When you have enjoyed yourself to the fullest, complete the loop by continuing north on the Alta Vista Trail, or simply turn around and go back the way you came. If you decide to complete the loop, you reach the east side of the loop 0.1 mile from the summit, about 0.8 mile from the Jackson Visitor Center. Turn right and head south on the east side of the Alta Vista Trail until the loop rejoins itself, 1.1 miles into your hike. From this point, head back down the trail to the parking lot.

Camping & services: You can stay at the Paradise Inn near the Paradise Ranger Station. The nearest place to obtain gas and supplies is Ashford on Washington Highway 706, about 5 miles west from the park boundary.

For more information: Contact the Jackson Visitor Center (Paradise), or the Paradise Ranger Station (see Appendix A).

14 Camp Muir

Type of hike:	Out-and-back; day hike or overnighter.
Total distance:	8.6 miles (13.8 kilometers).
Difficulty:	Strenuous.
Elevation gain:	4,680 feet.
Best months:	Mid July–August.
Maps:	USGS Mount Rainier East; Trails Illustrated Mount Rainier National Park; Astronaut's Vista: Mount Rainier National Park, Washington; Earthwalk Press Hiking Map & Guide.
Starting Point:	Skyline Trailhead.

General description: A very steep hike up to Camp Muir, the most popular base camp used by climbers, from which you can see Mount Adams, the Goat Rocks, Mount St. Helens, and the Tatoosh Range.

Camp Muir

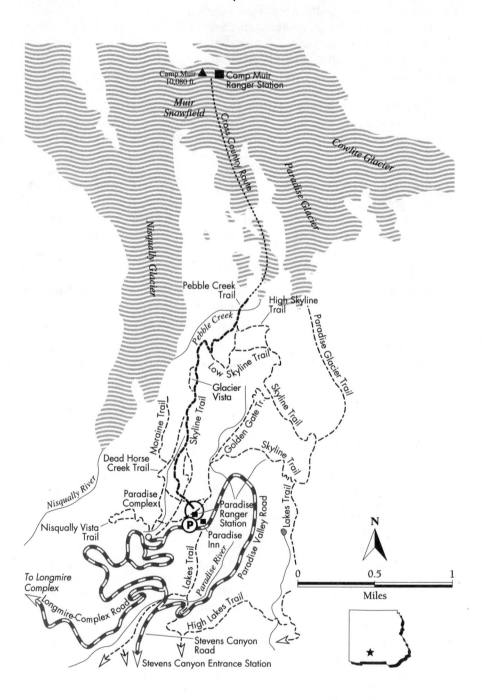

Camp Muir ▲ ■ Camp Muir
10,080 ft.   Ranger Station

Muir
Snowfield

Cowlite Glacier

Nisqually Glacier

Cross County Route

Paradise Glacier

Pebble Creek
Trail

High Skyline
Trail

Pebble Creek

Low Skyline Trail

Paradise Glacier Trail

Glacier
Vista

Skyline Trail

Golden Gate Tr.

Skyline Trail

Moraine Trail

Skyline Trail

Dead Horse
Creek Trail

Skyline Trail

Nisqually River

Paradise
Complex

Lakes Trail

Paradise
Ranger
Station

Nisqually Vista
Trail

Paradise
Inn

Paradise Valley Road

Lakes Trail

Paradise River

To Longmire
Complex

Longmire-Complex Road

High Lakes Trail

Lakes Trail

Stevens Canyon
Road

Stevens Canyon Entrance Station

N

0   0.5   1

Miles

Camp Muir. PHOTO BY JOHN CALDWELL.

Finding the trailhead: From the Nisqually Entrance Station, drive 15.9 miles east on Longmire-Paradise Road to the turnoff for the Ohanapecosh area. Stay to the left and drive another 2.2 miles on Longmire-Paradise Road. Pass the Jackson Visitor Center on the left after 2.1 miles, keep going, and park in the lot in front of the Paradise Ranger Station.

Parking & trailhead facilities: Parking at the Paradise complex can get really hectic. Watch for a flashing sign when you enter the park that indicates whether or not the parking lots at Paradise are full. If you do find a parking spot, the Paradise complex offers food, phones, restrooms, an inn, a visitor center, and limited supplies. If it is full, you might have to find an alternate hike. Bathrooms are next to the Paradise Ranger Station.

Key Points:
    1.6   (2.6)   Junction with Pebble Creek Trail.
    1.9   (3.0)   Junction with High Lakes Trail.
    2.2   (3.5)   End of Pebble Creek Trail.
    4.3   (6.9)   Camp Muir.

The hike: From Camp Muir, you can see all the way to Mount Adams and Mount St. Helens. The Goat Rocks and the Tatoosh Range are also visible. This hike reaches an elevation of 10,080 feet, which feels like the top of the world. Expect an intense workout because this hike has an elevation gain of 4,680 feet in 4.3 miles. Bring plenty of sunscreen and apply it on all exposed skin. Make sure you apply some under your chin and nose to protect against the sun's rays reflected off the snow.

From the parking lot, go up one of the two paved trails to the north. Both trails soon intersect with the Skyline Trail. Go left (northwest) on the Skyline Trail and continue northwest/north on the west side of the Skyline Trail for 1.6 miles to the High Skyline Trail. A maze of trails intersects with the Skyline Trail, but there are signs at every intersection. Remember to con-

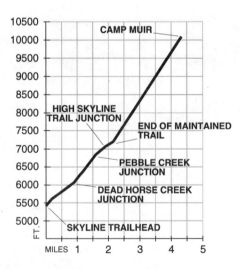

tinue traveling north. The Skyline Trail is relatively steep, gaining about 1,200 feet in the first 1.6 miles.

Go left (north) up the High Skyline Trail. Turn left into the Pebble Creek Trail on the right, staying left and heading north. Soon you will reach the end of the Pebble Creek Trail at a steep snowfield, 2.2 miles into your hike. From this point on, the route is unmaintained. The National Park Service reminds you to travel safely and cause a minimal amount of impact beyond this point. Head up the snowfield, keeping to the snow. Do not walk on fragile rock.

The rest of your ascent will be on snow, gaining 2,888 feet in the next 2.1 miles. By August, footprints cover the snowfield. You can choose to follow someone else's tracks or make your own. This decision may depend on the traction of your hiking boots. The route passes over several ridges before reaching Camp Muir. The camp itself rests next to Cowlitz Cleaver, and if you strain your eyes you might be able to see it on the approach.

The view from the snowfield is amazing. As you rise higher and higher, the Tatoosh Range, Mount St. Helens, and the Goat Rocks become more prominent. You also have a close-up view of the Nisqually Glacier.

At the top, the amount of development might be surprising. The buildings on the left are for those partaking in an RMI-guided climb. RMI (Rainier Mountaineering, Inc.) has a contract with the National Park Service to allow its operation within the park. The buildings to your right are National Park Service buildings. The first one is a bunkhouse open to climbers on a first-come, first-served basis. From the campsites to the left of the bunkhouse you can see a slice of the eastern portion of the park, and all other vantages provide a panorama of the southern end of the park. Find a place to rest and enjoy the view.

Camping & services: You can camp at one of the sites at Camp Muir, whether or not you intend to rock climb. There are special regulations for base camps, especially pertaining to the disposal of human waste. The snowfield itself is your water source.

Day hikers can stay at the Paradise Inn near the Paradise Ranger Station. Groceries and limited supplies can be obtained at a store in the Longmire area. The nearest place to obtain gas is Ashford on Washington Highway 706, about 5 miles west from the park boundary.

For more information: Contact the Jackson Visitor Center (Paradise), or the Paradise Ranger Station (see Appendix A).

15 Lakes Trail

Type of hike: Loop; day hike.
Total distance: 4.5 miles (7.5 kilometers).
Difficulty: Moderate.
Elevation gain: Minimal, with a short climb at the end.
Best months: Mid July–September.
Maps: USGS Mount Rainier East; Trails Illustrated: Mount Rainier National Park; Astronaut's Vista: Mount Rainier National Park, Washington; Earthwalk Press Hiking Map & Guide.
Starting point: Paradise complex.

General description: A popular three-hour loop that descends from subalpine forest, through a meadow, along Mazama Ridge to a scenic lake, then up a steep pitch to the trailhead parking lot.

Finding the trailhead: From the Nisqually Entrance Station, travel 15.9 miles east on Longmire-Paradise Road. Stay to the left (north) where the road forks, following the road to Paradise. Bypass the visitor center, at 2.1 miles, and park in the Paradise Inn parking lot in front of the Paradise Ranger Station and Paradise Inn.

Parking & trailhead facilities: Parking at the Paradise complex can get really hectic. Watch for a flashing sign when you enter the park that indicates whether or not the parking lots at Paradise are full, a common scenario on weekends from 11 A.M. until early evening. You can hope for a vacant spot, but if one does not open up promptly, we suggest finding an alternate hike. If you do find a parking spot, the Paradise complex offers food, phones, restrooms, an inn, a visitor center, and limited supplies.

Key points:
0.4	(0.7)	Myrtle Falls and Golden Gate Trail junction.
0.7	(1.2)	4th Crossing Trail junction.
1.1	(2.8)	Lakes Trail junction.
2.7	(4.5)	High Lakes Trail junction.
3.2	(5.3)	Wonderland Trail junction.
3.4	(5.7)	Stevens Canyon Road.
3.5	(5.8)	Reflection Lakes.
3.9	(6.5)	Second High Lakes Trail junction.
4.4	(7.3)	Paradise Valley Road.
4.5	(7.5)	Narada Falls Trail junction.
5.1	(8.5)	Paradise.

The hike: The Lakes Trail begins in the most popular tourist area of the park. After parking in the Paradise Inn lot, follow the well-marked trail in the northernmost part of the parking lot. Start hiking to the right (east), following the signs that read "Skyline Trail." Wide and paved, the first 0.5 mile of the trail is barrier free and wheelchair accessible.

Lakes Trail

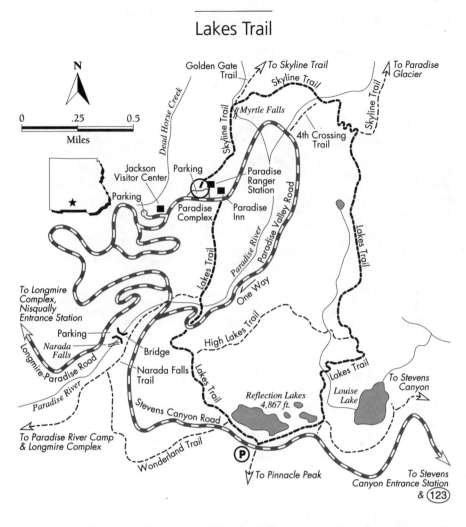

In 0.4 mile the trail comes to Myrtle Falls. A very short but steep walk down to the bottom of the falls gives you a view of a small, pretty waterfall. Back on the main trail, cross Edith Creek and come to a junction with the Golden Gate Trail. Once again, stay to the right along the Skyline Trail.

In 0.3 mile, the 4th Crossing Trail intersects with the Skyline Trail to the right (south). Stay on the Skyline Trail heading east. For 0.4 mile the trail climbs, sometimes with switchbacks, until it intersects with the Lakes Trail. Take a right (south) onto the Lakes Trail. The trail now descends gradually for 2 miles. This area is renowned for its subalpine forest and alpine views, so catch a good look before descending into denser forest. About 1.6 mile from the junction with the Lakes Trail, a fork in the trail marks the High Lakes Trail junction. Stay to the left (south) for the best view of Reflection Lakes.

When you come to the Wonderland Trail junction, in 0.5 mile, stay to the right (south). Continue descending for another 0.3 mile, until you reach Stevens Canyon Road. You can see Reflection Lakes to the right (east). Walk

Reflection Lakes.

along the road toward the lakes for only 0.1 mile. On a clear day, Mount Rainier's image reflects on the surface of the lake.

Proceed along the road and by the lakes until you see the Lakes Trail heading north. Turn right (north) onto that trail. It skirts the lake for 0.25 mile, then moves away, climbing abruptly. Less than 0.5 mile after leaving Stevens Canyon Road, the Lakes Trail meets the High Lakes Trail once again. Stay to the left (west). The trail immediately begins to descend and continues the descent for 0.4 mile, at which point it crosses Paradise Valley Road. On the opposite side of the road, look for a small parking area. The trail continues from the northernmost corner of this lot.

The trail quickly descends to the bank of the crystal clear waters of the Paradise River. The trail follows the banks, then crosses the river. About 0.1 mile beyond Paradise Valley Road, the trail meets the Narada Falls Trail. Turn right (north). You have now come 4.5 miles and have only 0.6 mile to go. Unfortunately, this is the steepest section of the hike. Climb steadily and steeply until the trail leads into the southeastern corner of the Paradise complex parking lot. Remember where you parked your car?

Camping & services: The Paradise Inn is located near the Paradise Ranger Station. Groceries and limited supplies can be obtained at a store in the Longmire area. The nearest place to obtain gas is Ashford on Washington Highway 706, about 5 miles west from the park boundary.

For more information: Contact the Jackson Visitor Center (Paradise) or the Paradise Ranger Station (see Appendix A).

16 Dead Horse Creek

Type of hike: Loop; day hike.
Total distance: 2.3 miles (3.7 kilometers).
Difficulty: Easy.
Elevation gain: 600 feet.
Best months: Early July–September.
Maps: USGS Mount Rainier East; Trails Illustrated Mount Rainier National Park; Astronaut's Vista: Mount Rainier National Park, Washington; Earthwalk Press Hiking Map & Guide.
Starting point: Jackson Visitor Center parking lot.

General description: A short spur trail that connects with the Skyline Trail and has great views of the Tatoosh Range, Mount Rainier, and the Nisqually Glacier.

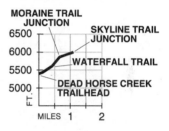

Finding the trailhead: From the Nisqually Entrance Station, drive 15.9 miles east on Longmire-Paradise Road to the turnoff for the Ohanapecosh area. Stay to the left and continue on Longmire-Paradise Road for 2.1 miles. Park in the parking lot in front of the Jackson Visitor Center.

Parking & trailhead facilities: Parking at the Paradise complex can get really hectic. Watch for a flashing sign when you enter the park that indicates whether or not the parking lots at Paradise are full. Even if all of the lots are not full, the lot in front of the visitor center is likely to be full. In this case, you can drive another 0.1 mile up the road to the parking lot in front of the Paradise Ranger Station and the Paradise Inn. Restrooms are located inside the Jackson Visitor Center and in the upper lot next to the Paradise Ranger Station. If you do find a parking spot, the Paradise complex offers food, phones, restrooms, an inn, a visitor center, and limited supplies.

Key points:
0.1   (0.2)   Junction with Avalanche Lily Trail.
0.4   (0.6)   Junction with Waterfall Trail.
0.7   (1.1)   Junction with Moraine Trail.
1.1   (1.8)   Junction with Skyline Trail.

The hike: If you desire to hike the Skyline Trail, but want a more gradual ascent, you should consider taking this trail. This is also a shorter alternative to the Skyline Trail. In August, the trail is lined with wildflowers, from lupine to Lewis monkeyflower. Please preserve these flowers by staying on designated trails.

To begin the hike, head to the west end of the parking lot. Look for a trail sign for the Dead Horse Creek Trail. Stay to the right, heading north on the

Dead Horse Creek

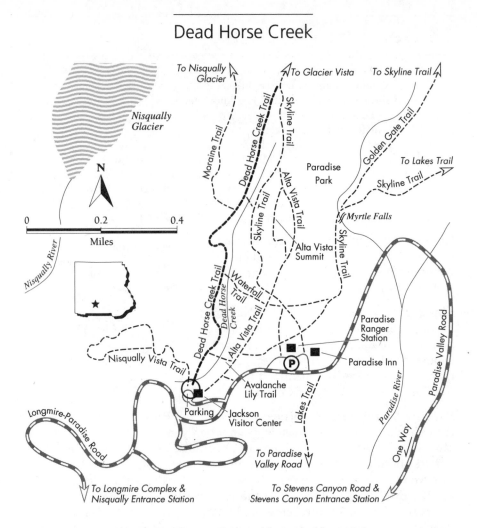

Dead Horse Creek Trail. The trail goes through beautiful, serene forest. Although the Paradise area is extremely busy, this trail receives less use than other local trails.

Wildlife is commonly seen along the trail. Deer, grouse, and marmots often venture into this area. Remember not to feed these wild animals because they need to remain self-sufficient to survive in their natural habitat. Also, it is illegal to feed the wildlife in Mount Rainier National Park.

Continue going north on the trail and ignore the two trails that come in from the right at 0.1 mile (the Avalanche Lily Trail) and 0.4 mile (the Waterfall Trail). Both of the trails travel to the Paradise Ranger Station and the Paradise Inn. There are signs at every intersection to help you stay on the Dead Horse Creek Trail. The Nisqually Glacier is visible to the west. The National Park Service has set up several rock benches to help you enjoy this view. Please use the provided benches to minimize your impact on the fragile subalpine meadows.

The Moraine Trail comes in from the left at 0.7 mile. Stay to the right (northeast), unless you plan to take the Moraine Trail option. Not far from the junction with the Moraine Trail, a small spur trail goes right, connecting with the Skyline Trail. Stay on the main trail.

The trail is considerably steeper at this point, but you have only 0.4 mile to the end of the trail, over 1.1 miles into your hike. The end of Dead Horse Creek Trail is the Skyline Trail. You have the option of hiking down the way you just came or making a loop by following the Skyline Trail. If you choose to take the Skyline Trail, follow the signs for it until you see a sign for the visitor center. Then follow the signs that point to the visitor center.

Options: More than halfway up the Dead Horse Creek Trail is the Moraine Trail. This trail, maintained for less than 0.1 mile, is a total of 0.5 mile long. Taking this option will make your trip 1 mile longer. The trail takes you down to the Nisqually Glacier Moraine where the Nisqually River flows out of the Nisqually Glacier. People often hear and see chunks of ice falling from the end of the glacier. Beware, the Moraine Trail is extremely steep.

Camping & services: You can stay at the Paradise Inn near the Paradise Ranger Station. The nearest place to obtain gas and supplies is Ashford on Washington Highway 706, about 5 miles west from the park boundary.

For more information: Contact the Jackson Visitor Center or the Paradise Ranger Station (see Appendix A).

17 High Lakes Trail

Type of hike: Loop; day hike.
Total distance: 2.7 miles (4.3 kilometers).
Difficulty: Easy.
Elevation gain: Minimal.
Best months: Mid July–September.
Maps: USGS Mount Rainier East; Trails Illustrated Mount Rainier National Park; Astronaut's Vista: Mount Rainier National Park, Washington; Earthwalk Press Hiking Map & Guide.
Starting point: Reflection Lakes.

General description: A short loop with a great view of the Tatoosh Range and Reflection Lakes.

Finding the trailhead: From Stevens Canyon Entrance Station, drive 17 miles west on Stevens Canyon Road to Reflection Lakes.

High Lakes Trail

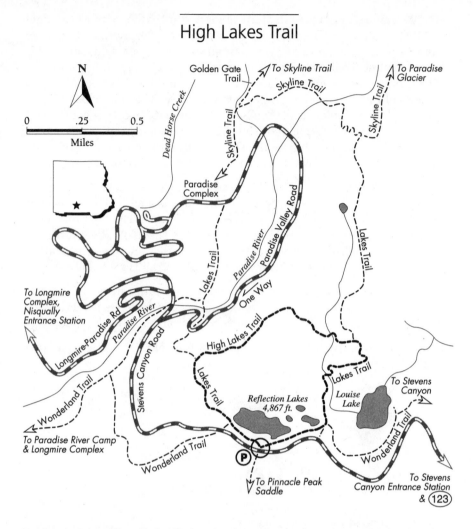

Parking & trailhead facilities: Park in the parking lot in front of Reflection Lakes. If you need additional services or supplies, the Paradise complex offers food, phones, restrooms, an inn, a visitor center, and limited supplies.

Key points:

0.7	(1.1)	High Lakes Trail junction.
1.9	(3.0)	Junction with Lakes Trail.
2.4	(3.7)	Wonderland Trail junction.
2.7	(4.3)	Reflection Lakes.

The hike: This is an easy day hike that explores the area around Reflection Lakes. The trail goes partway up Mazama Ridge, gaining just enough elevation to afford an excellent view of the Tatoosh Range.

From the Reflection Lakes parking lot, walk east along Stevens Canyon Road until you hit the Lakes Trail. Go left (northeast) onto the Lakes Trail.

Mt. Rainier as seen from the Lakes Trail.

Continue on the Lakes Trail up the south side of Mazama Ridge—a relatively steep but short section—to the High Lakes Trail, 0.7 mile into your hike.

Turn left (west) onto the High Lakes Trail. This trail is mostly downhill or flat, with many opportunities to view the Tatoosh Range. You can see Pinnacle Peak, Plummer Peak, and Unicorn Peak jutting toward the sky.

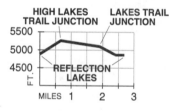

After 1.2 miles, the High Lakes Trail rejoins the Lakes Trail. Go left (south) and downhill on the lower Lakes Trail for 0.5 mile to a junction with the Wonderland Trail. Stay to the left and head toward Reflection Lakes for the next 0.2 mile to Stevens Canyon Road. Walk 0.1 mile east along the road to where you parked.

Camping & services: You can stay at the Paradise Inn located near the Paradise Ranger Station. The nearest place to obtain gas is Ashford on Washington Highway 706, about 5 miles west from the west park boundary.

For more information: Contact the the Jackson Visitor Center or the Paradise Ranger Station (see Appendix A).

18 Pinnacle Peak Saddle

Type of hike:	Out-and-back; day hike.
Total distance:	2.6 miles (4.2 kilometers).
Difficulty:	Easy.
Elevation gain:	970 feet.
Best months:	Late July–September.
Maps:	USGS Mount Rainier East; Trails Illustrated Mount Rainier National Park; Astronaut's Vista: Mount Rainier National Park, Washington; Earthwalk Press Hiking Map & Guide.
Starting point:	Pinnacle Peak Trailhead located across from Reflections Lake.

General description: A short climb up to the saddle between Pinnacle Peak and Plummer Peak, with great views of Mount Rainier along the trail and at the saddle.

Finding the trailhead: From the Stevens Canyon Entrance Station, drive about 18 miles west on Stevens Canyon Road until you see Reflections Lake on your right. You can park anywhere along Reflection Lakes to get to the Pinnacle Peak Trailhead, but it would be a good idea to go as far west as possible. Look for the trailhead on the left (south) side of the road and near the end of the lake.

Parking & trailhead facilities: There is usually parking at Reflection Lakes, but no restrooms or other facilities. If you need additional services or supplies, the Paradise complex offers food, phones, restrooms, an inn, a visitor center, and limited supplies.

Key points:

0.0	(0.0)	Pinnacle Peak Trailhead.
1.3	(2.1)	Pinnacle Peak saddle.

The hike: This hike is uphill all the way to the turnaround point. Wildflowers, such as lupine and magenta paintbrush, often grow along the trail in July and August. Many pikas inhabit the rockfields along the trail, 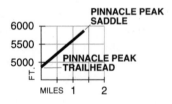 squeaking at passersby. The saddle offers an excellent view of Mount Rainier. Hope for a clear day.

There are no tricky turns or trail junctions on this trail. Simply start from the trailhead, directly across from the west end of Reflection Lakes, and hike all the way to the saddle. The first half of the trail is in the forest and climbs gradually. Keep in mind that once you hit the first rockfield, the trail becomes steep and rocky. Snow lingers on these rockfields late into the summer—sturdy hiking boots are the footwear of choice here.

Pinnacle Peak Saddle

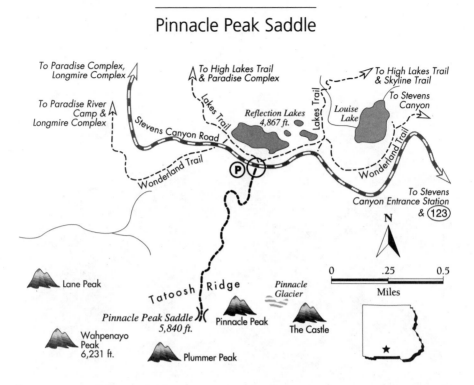

Once you reach the saddle, you can see to the south boundary of the park and all the way to Packwood. Plummer Peak resides to the right (west) and Pinnacle Peak to the left (east). Looking southeast, you can see both Unicorn Peak and the Castle, and to the southwest Wahpenayo Peak is visible. Enjoy the amazing view before heading back the way you came.

Options: The maintained trail ends 1.3 miles into the hike. There are unmaintained trails heading along the ridges of both Pinnacle and Plummer Peaks. The climb up to Pinnacle Peak does not actually require technical climbing equipment, but it is hazardous and should be approached with caution.

Camping & services: You can stay at the Paradise Inn near the Paradise Ranger Station. The nearest place to obtain gas and supplies is Ashford on Washington Highway 706, about 5 miles west from the park boundary.

For more information: Contact the Jackson Visitor Center (Paradise), the Paradise Inn, or the Paradise Ranger Station (see Appendix A).

Pinnacle Peak.

19 Skyline Trail

Type of hike:	Loop; day hike.
Total distance:	5.2 miles (8.7 kilometers).
Difficulty:	Strenuous.
Elevation gain:	1,400 feet.
Best months:	Mid-July–September.
Maps:	USGS Mount Rainier East; Trails Illustrated: Mount Rainier National Park; Astronaut's Vista: Mount Rainier National Park, Washington; Earthwalk Press Hiking Map & Guide.
Starting point:	Skyline Trailhead.

General description: Quite possibly the most popular hike in Mount Rainier National Park, the Skyline Trail is very well maintained, and partly paved, with a close-up view of the Nisqually Glacier.

Finding the trailhead: From the Nisqually Entrance Station, travel 15.9 miles east on Longmire-Paradise Road to where the road forks. Stay to the left (north) on the road to the Paradise complex. Bypass the visitor center, at 2.1 miles, and park in the large parking lot in front of the Paradise Ranger Station, at 2.2 miles.

Parking & trailhead facilities: Parking at the Paradise complex can get really hectic. Watch for a flashing sign when you enter the park that indicates whether or not the lots at Paradise are full, a common scenario on weekends from 11 A.M. until early evening. You can hope for a vacant spot, but if one does not open up promptly, consider an alternate hike. If you do find a parking spot, the Paradise complex offers food, phones, restrooms, an inn, a visitor center, and limited supplies.

Key points:

1.1	(1.8)	Glacier Vista Trail junction.
1.6	(2.7)	Low Skyline Trail junction to Panorama Point.
2.0	(3.3)	Pebble Creek Trail junction.
2.8	(4.7)	Golden Gate Trail junction.
3.4	(5.7)	Paradise Glacier Trail junction and Van Trump Monument.
4.8	(8.0)	Myrtle Falls/Golden Gate Trail Junction.
5.2	(8.7)	Paradise.

The hike: For good reason, more people tour Paradise than any other location on Mount Rainier. The views are absolutely spectacular, the services plentiful, and the trails many. Of all the trails in Paradise, Skyline is the most well known and frequently hiked. As you might guess by the name, the Skyline Trail goes above timberline onto alpine terrain with an awe-inspiring look at the Nisqually Glacier.

For the longest and best view of Mount Rainier, hike this trail clockwise. Start from the Skyline Trailhead in the northwestern corner of the Paradise

Skyline Trail

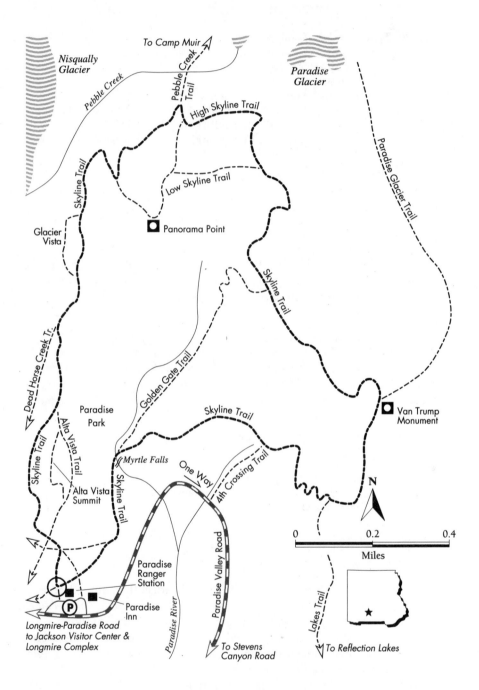

Nisqually Glacier

To Camp Muir

Pebble Creek

Pebble Creek Trail

Paradise Glacier

High Skyline Trail

Skyline Trail

Low Skyline Trail

Glacier Vista

Panorama Point

Paradise Glacier Trail

Skyline Trail

Dead Horse Creek Tr.

Golden Gate Trail

Paradise Park

Van Trump Monument

Skyline Trail

Skyline Trail

Alta Vista Trail

Myrtle Falls

One Way

4th Crossing Trail

Alta Vista Summit

Skyline Trail

N

Paradise Valley Road

Paradise River

0   0.2   0.4

Miles

Paradise Ranger Station

P

Paradise Inn

Longmire-Paradise Road to Jackson Visitor Center & Longmire Complex

Lakes Trail

★

To Stevens Canyon Road

To Reflection Lakes

Van Trump Monument on Skyline Trail.

area parking lot. Rather than turning right (east), stay to the left (northwest), heading directly up the mountain. With so many trails, this area could be a bit confusing. Signs, however, explicitly point the way. Stay on the Skyline Trail through all of the intersections. Do not be surprised to see deer. Please, do not feed the wildlife. They have already become very bold from the constant handouts.

The trail ascends rather steeply for the next two miles, so prepare for a workout. At 1.1 miles, the Glacier Vista Trail intersects with the main trail. For a slightly closer view of the Nisqually Glacier and a few words on the wonders of glaciation, take the Glacier Vista Trail to your left (west). It parallels the Skyline Trail briefly and then rejoins it. Back on the main trail, continue north for 0.5 mile of switchbacks, at which point the Low Skyline Trail splits to the right toward Panorama Point. Turn left (northeast) to stay on the Skyline Trail.

Rocky alpine terrain provides the foreground for a powerful view of the mountain for 0.4 mile. At the junction with the Pebble Creek Trail, 2 miles into the hike, you reach the top of your ascent. This is the path many mountaineers take on their trek to the summit. To see the Camp Muir snowfield, turn left (north) onto the Pebble Creek Trail. A good glimpse of the path to the top can be had less than 0.5 mile from the turnoff, where Pebble Creek makes a good lunch spot.

Otherwise, stay to the right (east), following the Skyline Trail. You descend steeply along switchbacks in alpine terrain almost all the way to the Golden Gate Trail junction, about 0.8 mile. The Golden Gate Trail provides a shortcut back to Paradise, cutting about 2 miles off the hike length. To stay on the Skyline Trail, bear left.

In 0.7 mile a bizarre bench made of stone serves as a monument to P. B. Van Trump and Hazard Stevens, and their first ascent of Mount Rainier. It also serves as a marker for the trailhead to the Paradise Glacier. Sit and relax on the stone slabs before continuing south on the Skyline Trail. Behind the monument, facing south, you have an excellent view of the Tatoosh Range on a sunny day.

Another 1.3 miles of constant descent with sporadic switchbacks leads to Myrtle Falls, an unimpressive but pretty waterfall. You must walk to the bottom, a short side trip, to see it well. Return to the now-paved main trail. You should be able to see Paradise from the trail. Walk 0.4 mile back to the trailhead.

Options: If the day is clear, follow the Low Skyline Trail detour to Panorama Point. Less than 0.25 mile of good trail leads to an excellent viewpoint. Here a panoramic picture of the Tatoosh Range and other neighboring mountains is well labeled for your viewing pleasure and insight. A trail from Panorama Point joins the Skyline Trail to the north, so you can easily jump back on the loop.

Camping & services: You can stay at the Paradise Inn located near the Paradise Ranger Station. Limited supplies can be obtained at the Longmire General Store, but for a more extensive selection you should go to Ashford or Packwood. The nearest gas station is in Ashford on Washington Highway 706, about 5 miles west from the park boundary.

For more information: Contact Jackson Visitor Center (Paradise) or the Paradise Ranger Station (see Appendix A).

20 Paradise Glacier

Type of hike:	Out-and-back; day hike.
Total distance:	6.4 miles (10.6 kilometers).
Difficulty:	Moderate.
Elevation gain:	1,000 feet.
Best months:	Mid July–September.
Maps:	USGS Mount Rainier East; Trails Illustrated: Mount Rainier National Park; Astronaut's Vista: Mount Rainier National Park, Washington; Earthwalk Press Hiking Map & Guide.
Starting point:	Skyline Trailhead.

General description: A short day hike over a snowfield and to the foot of a small glacier.

Finding the trailhead: From the Nisqually Entrance Station, travel 15.9 miles east on the Longmire-Paradise Road to where the road forks. Stay to the left (north) on the road to the Paradise complex. Bypass the visitor center, at 2.1 miles, and park in the large parking lot in front of the Paradise Ranger Station, at 2.2 miles.

Parking & trailhead facilities: Parking at the Paradise complex can get really hectic. Watch for a flashing sign when you enter the park that indicates whether the lots at Paradise are full, a common scenario on weekends from 11 A.M. until early evening. You can hope for a vacant spot, but if one does not open up promptly, consider an alternate hike. If you do find a parking spot, the Paradise complex offers food, phones, restrooms, an inn, visitor center, and limited supplies.

Key points:

0.4	(0.7)	Myrtle Falls and Golden Gate Trail junction.
0.7	(1.2)	4th Crossing Trail junction.
1.4	(2.3)	Lakes Trail junction.
1.8	(3.0)	Paradise Glacier Trail junction and Van Trump Monument.
3.2	(5.3)	Paradise Glacier.

The hike: The ice caves of yesteryear that once drew many to this trail have melted with the general increase in global temperature. This means a less sensational hike, but it also means fewer passersby and the same spectacular view as before.

Start hiking along the Skyline Trail in the northwestern corner of the parking lot; the trailhead is well marked. Proceed to the right (east), counterclockwise along the loop. Many trails congest this area, but just follow the Skyline Trail signs eastbound and you will reach your destination.

Hike gradually uphill along a wide, paved trail for 0.4 mile to arrive at Myrtle Falls. The path to the bottom of the falls is short but steep and offers a closer look. Back on the main trail, cross Edith Creek, the source of Myrtle Falls, and stay to the right beyond the Golden Gate Trail junction.

Climb steadily, through occasional switchbacks, for 0.3 mile to the 4th Crossing Trail. Stay to the left, continuing east. Much like previous parts of the trail, this is a medium ascent through subalpine forest. You soon reach the Lakes Trail junction, 1.4 miles into the hike. Again, stay to the left, heading northeast.

The trail turns to head north; 0.4 mile after the Lakes Trail junction look for a stone bench at a fork in the trail. This firm resting spot was erected by the Mountaineers and the Mazamas as a tribute to Hazard Stevens and Philamon Beecher Van Trump. The monument marks the campsite from which the two made the first recorded ascent of Mount Rainier. It also marks the Paradise Glacier Trail junction.

Turn right (east) onto the Paradise Glacier Trail. From here, the ascent is gradual, but it leads into alpine terrain. Even in late summer expect to encounter quite a bit of snow, so wear boots if you have them. The trail ends in a snowfield—hike only as far as you feel comfortable. No sign marks the end of the maintained trail. Cairns guide you to the snowfield where the ice caves once were.

A good view of the Paradise Glacier is not the reason to hike this trail. The snowfield, however, is a good place to play "name that glacier." Facing

Paradise Glacier

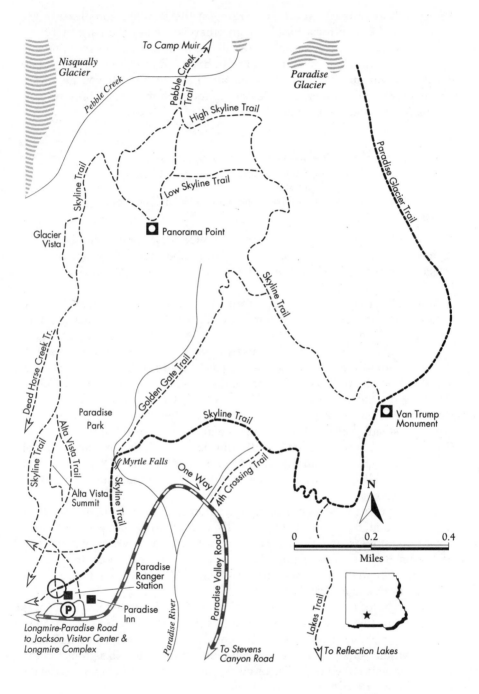

To Camp Muir

Nisqually Glacier

Paradise Glacier

Pebble Creek

Pebble Creek Trail

High Skyline Trail

Low Skyline Trail

Skyline Trail

Panorama Point

Glacier Vista

Paradise Glacier Trail

Skyline Trail

Dead Horse Creek Tr.

Golden Gate Trail

Paradise Park

Skyline Trail

Van Trump Monument

Alta Vista Trail

Skyline Trail

Myrtle Falls

One Way

4th Crossing Trail

Alta Vista Summit

Skyline Trail

N

Paradise Ranger Station

Paradise River

Paradise Valley Road

Paradise Inn

0   0.2   0.4

Miles

Longmire-Paradise Road to Jackson Visitor Center & Longmire Complex

Lakes Trail

To Stevens Canyon Road

To Reflection Lakes

View of Little Tahoma Peak along the Paradise Glacier Trail.

north up the trail, you have a close view of the glaciated mountain. To the east are the headwaters of Stevens Creek, and directly behind you (south) is an amazing view of the Tatoosh Range, the Goat Rocks, and Mount Adams. When you are ready, return to Paradise along the same trail.

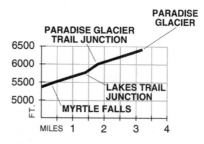

Camping & services: You can stay at the Paradise Inn located near the Paradise Ranger Station. Limited supplies can be obtained at the Longmire General Store, but for a more extensive selection you should go to Ashford or Packwood. The nearest gas station is in Ashford on Washington Highway 706, about 5 miles west from the park boundary.

For more information: Contact the Jackson Visitor Center (Paradise), the Paradise Inn, or the Paradise Ranger Station (see Appendix A).

21 Snow Lake

Type of hike: Out-and-back; day hike.
Total distance: 2.5 miles (4.2 kilometers).
Difficulty: Easy.
Elevation gain: Minimal.
Best months: Mid-July–September.
Maps: USGS Mount Rainier East; Trails Illustrated: Mount Rainier National Park; Astronaut's Vista: Mount Rainier National Park, Washington; Earthwalk Press Hiking Map & Guide.
Starting point: Snow Lake Trailhead.

General description: Perfect for children, this two-hour day hike passes one lake, then ends at a lake in a glacial cirque.

Finding the trailhead: From the Stevens Canyon Entrance Station, drive 15.5 miles west along the winding Stevens Canyon Road. A small parking lot on the left (south) marks the trailhead to Snow Lake.

Parking & trailhead facilities: The Snow Lake Trailhead has a small parking lot, not always adequate for the number of hikers. If you need other services, such as restrooms, food, equipment, and lodging, the Paradise complex has all of these.

Key points:
    0.7   (1.2)   Bench Lake.
    1.3   (2.0)   Snow Lake Camp.
    1.2   (2.2)   Snow Lake.

The hike: Trees obscure the Snow Lake Trailhead. After parking, walk to the eastern corner of the parking lot to see the trail, heading south. The trail immediately begins to ascend rather steeply, but do not worry, it eventually levels off and descends as it crosses several ridges throughout the hike.

The trail leads 0.7 mile through silver subalpine forest to the junction to Bench Lake on the left (east). The path down to the lake is steep, but the bank is worth the struggle, particularly if you fish. We saw many fish rising in Bench Lake, and, as is true throughout the park, fishing is free and the limits are few.

Returning to the main trail, you only have 0.5 mile of hiking before you reach Snow Lake. When you arrive at the mountain meadow, turn around. This area offers a beautiful view of Mount Rainier. The last 0.2 mile of trail slopes upward until you see the lovely lake. In a glacial cirque, the peaks of the Tatoosh Range frame the lake, and glacial waters cascade down their flanks into the ice-cold, turquoise waters.

If you would like to camp here or see the marvelous view from the campsites, turn left (east) at the fork in the trail—a sign points the way. Descend for less than 0.2 mile until the trail crosses a stream out of Snow Lake. To

Snow Lake

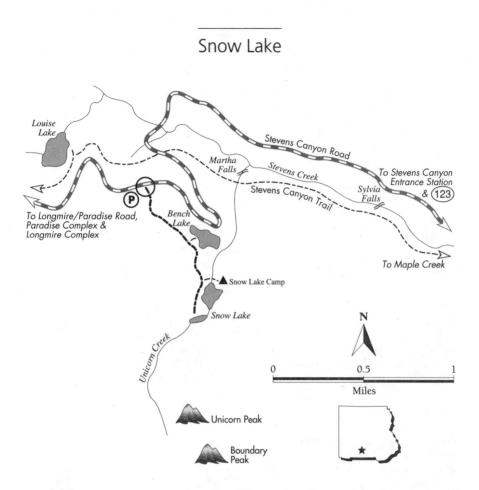

cross this stream, you must hop from log to log. Be careful, since some of these logs are not quite as stable as they appear. As soon as you cross the stream, you reach Snow Lake Camp. The toilet is almost immediately to your left, and the campsites are farther down (southeast) and along the lakeside. Campsite 1 sits on a small peninsula with a view of Unicorn Peak across the aqua waters. A jutting rock makes for a great place to jump in the freezing waters for a refreshing dunk or a painful swim.

You can also follow the path to the right (southwest) at the fork before the lake. This path is 0.3 mile, and ends in a small lake access point. If you hike this trail, you should plan to spend some time at one of these places; they are lovely. When you're ready to return, just retrace your steps.

Camping & services: As mentioned above, you can camp at one of two campsites on Snow Lake. Both offer spectacular views. Campsite 1 is nearer the toilet with better water access. Campsite 2, though, offers quite a bit of privacy. You can also stay at the Paradise Inn. For services, you can buy limited supplies in the Longmire area, but gas is available only outside of the park. The nearest towns are Packwood, 12 miles south of the park on U.S. Highway 12, or Ashford, 5 miles west of the park on Washington Highway 706.

The Tatoosh Peaks over Snow Lake.

For more information: Contact the Jackson Visitor Center or the Paradise Ranger Station (see Appendix A).

22 Stevens Canyon

        Type of hike: One-way, with a vehicle shuttle; day hike.
      Total distance: 6.6 miles (11.0 kilometers).
         Difficulty: Moderate.
    Elevation gain: 2,267 feet.
      Best months: June–September.
            Maps: USGS Mount Rainier East; Trails Illustrated: Mount Rainier National Park; Astronaut's Vista: Mount Rainier National Park, Washington; Earthwalk Press Hiking Map & Guide.
   Starting point: Stevens Creek Trailhead/Box Canyon Picnic Area.

General description: A half-day hike through a canyon strewn with wildflowers, wildlife, and waterfalls.

Finding the trailhead: From the Stevens Canyon Entrance Station, drive 10.8 miles west on Stevens Canyon Road to the Box Canyon Picnic Area on the left, about 0.3 mile beyond the Box Canyon exhibit. The hike begins from the picnic area.

As this hike is a shuttle, however, you must leave a bike or car at the trail's end at Reflection Lakes, or face twice the hiking. To reach the Reflection Lakes Trailhead from the Box Canyon Picnic Area, drive 7.5 miles west on Stevens Canyon Road. Look for a parking lot in front of a scenic lake on the right (north) side of Stevens Canyon Road. After leaving a bike or vehicle here, return to the Box Canyon Picnic Area to start hiking.

Parking & trailhead facilities: Stevens Creek Trailhead, in the Box Canyon Picnic Area, has several tables for eating, restrooms, garbage cans, and recycling bins. If you want to fill water bottles ahead of time, stop at the Box Canyon exhibit 0.3 mile east on Stevens Canyon Road, where potable water is available. The Box Canyon Picnic Area has a large parking lot that may fill on sunny weekends.

Key points:

0.5	(0.8)	River viewpoint.
0.6	(1.0)	Wonderland Trail junction.
0.7	(1.2)	Stevens Creek crossing.
2.1	(3.5)	Maple Creek Camp and Maple Falls.
3.3	(5.5)	Sylvia Falls.
4.3	(7.2)	Martha Falls.
5.0	(8.3)	Stevens Canyon Road.
6.0	(10.0)	Louise Lake.

Stevens Canyon

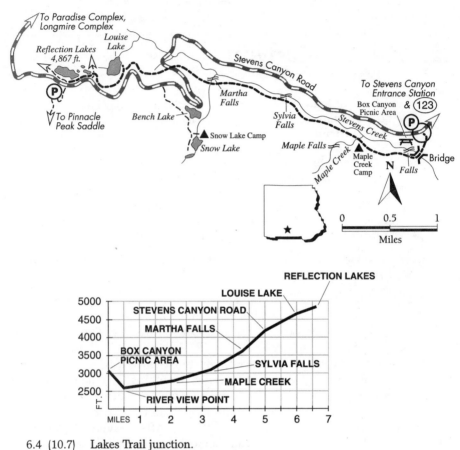

6.4 (10.7)   Lakes Trail junction.
6.5 (10.8)   Stevens Canyon Road.
6.6 (11.0)   Reflection Lakes/Trail's end.

The hike: If you love crashing water, you will adore this hike. You pass five falls while hiking through a canyon replete with wildflowers and wildlife. Do not let deer or snakes startle you; they are a common sight in this area. Wildflowers such as phlox and glacier lilies line the trail in late spring, but Stevens Canyon is best known for its many falls.

To begin hiking, follow the sign that points south at the Box Canyon Picnic Area. Two unnamed falls are visible in the first 0.6 mile of the hike alone. Just 0.5 mile from the trailhead, a sign points west to a river view-point, which offers a nice view of the first falls. Return to the trail, and continue west 0.1 mile to the junction of the Stevens Creek Trail and the Wonderland Trail. Turn right (west) onto the Wonderland Trail. Cross the bridge where Stevens Creek falls in churning rapids over gray, black, and turquoise boulders.

Martha Falls.

After hiking on relatively flat terrain, you come upon Maple Creek Camp, 2.1 miles into your hike. Unless you want to explore campsites or use the pit toilet, stay to the right (northwest) toward a deceptively narrow part of the trail. The trail, however, widens and crosses a stream along a small log. While crossing, look up and to your left to see Maple Falls in the distance.

Continue west to Sylvia Falls, 1.2 miles beyond Maple Falls. Sylvia Falls is obscured by large trees, but what is visible is engaging. It appears as though the water shoots directly out of the land from no source. A small clearing that looks out upon Sylvia Falls makes a nice, cool lunch spot for summer hikers.

A gradual ascent begins here and continues for 1 mile to Martha Falls, the most impressive of the five falls, if just for its size. The gradual ascent soon becomes a steep ascent for 0.7 mile of switchbacks. The sound of cars tells you that you have neared Stevens Canyon Road. The trail crosses Stevens Canyon Road and continues west.

The ascent continues for 1 mile before you reach Louise Lake. The trail, however, becomes dangerously narrow and obscured by brush, so tread carefully until you reach the lake. If you would like a closer look, choose the marked and maintained trail to the lake. After the lake, the main trail widens, a sign of more frequent use. A more gradual ascent heads to the junction with the Lakes Trail. Turn left (south) to once more encounter Stevens Canyon Road in 0.1 mile. The trail's end, Reflection Lakes, can be seen 0.1 mile up the road to your right (west). Bike or drive back to the Box Canyon Picnic Area to complete the hike.

Option: If you have two cars and would prefer to hike downhill rather than uphill, you may consider leaving your car at the Box Canyon Picnic Area and starting from Reflection Lakes.

Camping & services: With a backcountry permit, you can camp along the trail at Maple Creek Camp. You can also stay at the Paradise Inn located near the Paradise Ranger Station. Limited supplies can be obtained at the Longmire General Store. For most services, your best bet is the town of Packwood, 12 miles south of the Stevens Canyon entrance station on Washington Highway 123.

For more information: Contact the Jackson Visitor Center or the Paradise Ranger Station (see Appendix A).

23 Stevens Creek

Type of hike:	Out-and-back; day hike.
Total distance:	1.4 miles (2.5 kilometers).
Difficulty:	Easy.
Elevation gain:	Minimal.
Best months:	Late May–October.
Maps:	USGS Mount Rainier East; Trails Illustrated: Mount Rainier National Park; Astronaut's Vista: Mount Rainier National Park, Washington; Earthwalk Press Hiking Map & Guide.
Starting point:	Box Canyon Picnic Area.

General description: A one-hour hike in the southern section of the park, which leads to two different unnamed falls along the same river.

Finding the trailhead: From the Stevens Canyon Entrance Station, drive 10.8 miles west on Stevens Canyon Road to the Box Canyon Picnic Area on the left, about 0.3 mile beyond the Box Canyon wayside exhibit. The hike begins at the picnic area.

Parking & trailhead facilities: The Box Canyon Picnic Area has a large parking lot, restrooms, and picnic tables. Water is available at the Box Canyon wayside exhibit 0.3 mile east on Stevens Canyon Road.

Key points:
```
0.5  (0.8)   River viewpoint.
0.6  (1.0)   Wonderland Trail junction.
0.7  (1.2)   Stevens Creek crossing.
```

The hike: This trail descends rather steeply through woods full of wildlife to reach two unnamed falls. Well marked and well maintained, the trail is easy to follow. The first point of interest comes after only 0.5 mile. A sign marks the river viewpoint to your right (west). Only a few paces more, and you stand in a fenced clearing, admiring the first falls.

Return to the main trail, and head right (south) to see the other nameless falls. Walk 0.1 mile beyond the river viewpoint, a total of 0.6 mile from the trailhead, to a junction with the famed Wonderland Trail. Stay to the right (southwest) for 0.1 mile more to reach the bridge over Stevens Creek.

This bridge marks an incredible meeting of stream and stone. Iceberg white water rushing from the glaciers above has rounded these boulders and shaped them into something out of a fairy tale.

When you have appreciated the falls to your content, turn around and follow the same path back to the picnic area. The returning trail is not long, but it is a rather steep ascent, so do not be surprised if you are winded by the end.

Stevens Creek

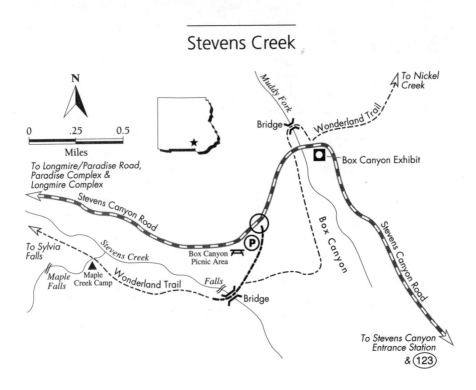

Camping & services: You can stay at the Paradise Inn located near the Paradise Ranger Station. Limited supplies can be obtained at a store located in the Longmire area. For most services, your best bet is the town of Packwood, 12 miles south of the Stevens Canyon Entrance Station on Washington Highway 123.

For more information: Contact the Jackson Visitor Center (Paradise), the Paradise Inn, or the Paradise Ranger Station (see Appendix A).

24 Box Canyon

Type of hike:	Loop; day hike.
Total distance:	0.3 mile (0.5 kilometer).
Difficulty:	Easy.
Elevation gain:	Minimal.
Best months:	May–September
Maps:	USGS Mount Rainier East; Trails Illustrated Mount Rainier National Park; Astronaut's Vista: Mount Rainier National Park, Washington; Earthwalk Press Hiking Map & Guide.
Starting point:	Box Canyon wayside exhibit.

Stevens Creek.

General description: A very short loop with a bridge over a canyon carved by a powerful glacier.

Finding the trailhead: From the Stevens Canyon Entrance Station, drive 10.5 miles west on Stevens Canyon Road to the Box Canyon wayside exhibit. Parking is on the left (south). If you pass the Box Canyon Picnic Area, you have gone 0.3 mile too far west. The paved trail begins across the street from the parking lot to the right (east) of the bridge.

Parking & trailhead facilities: The Box Canyon Picnic Area has a large parking lot, restrooms, and picnic tables. Water is available at the Box Canyon wayside exhibit 0.3 mile east on Stevens Canyon Road.

The hike: This hike is great for those interested in glaciers. Many years ago, a glacier gouged dirt and boulders out of the mountainside to create Box Canyon. The paved trail takes you past wildflowers and the thundering canyon itself. For the first half of this hike, the paved trail is wide, smooth, and wheelchair accessible. The whole hike is in fact paved, eliminating most mud and muck, although the second half of the loop is considerably rougher.

At the trailhead, there is an informational sign about the hike. After reading it, head straight up the trail. The trail merging from the right (northeast) is the Wonderland Trail. Notice the bare rocks on the right side of the canyon where a powerful glacier once wiped out the vegetation.

Less than 0.2 mile into your hike is a bridge over Muddy Fork. Take the time to look down and enjoy the unique canyon. After you cross the bridge, the trail is paved, but less maintained all the way to where it rejoins Stevens Canyon Road. Either retrace your steps or walk along the road to loop back to your car.

Box Canyon

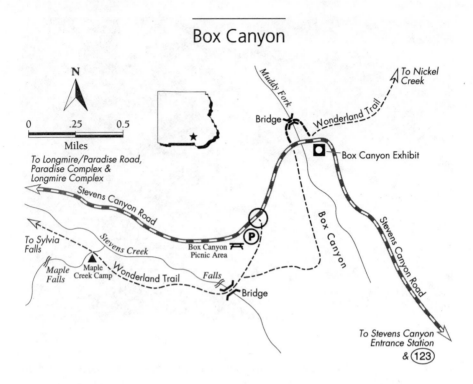

Camping & services: You can stay at the Paradise Inn located near the Paradise Ranger Station. Limited supplies can be obtained at a store located in the Longmire area. For-most services, your best bet is the town of Packwood, 12 miles south of the Stevens Canyon Entrance Station on Washington Highway 123.

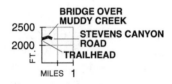

For more information: Contact Jackson Visitor Center or the Paradise Ranger Station (see Appendix A).

Ohanapecosh

The Ohanapecosh region is situated in the southeast corner of Mount Rainier National Park. Because it is farther from Seattle and Portland than other parts of the park, Ohanapecosh sees fewer visitors. Nestled in dense forest, the hikes in the Ohanapecosh region offer few views of Mount Rainier—and, frankly, few views whatsoever. What this area does offer, however, is freedom from the crowds that plague other regions, many waterfalls, massive trees, and a crystal clear glacial river, the Ohanapecosh.

25 Silver Falls

Type of hike: Loop; day hike.
Total distance: 2.7 miles (4.3 kilometers).
Difficulty: Easy.
Elevation gain: Minimal.
Best months: May–September.
Maps: USGS Ohanapecosh Hot Springs; Trails Illustrated Mount Rainier National Park; Astronaut's Vista: Mount Rainier National Park, Washington; Earthwalk Press Hiking Map & Guide.
Starting point: Silver Falls Loop Trailhead.

General description: A short, beautiful day hike to spectacular Silver Falls.

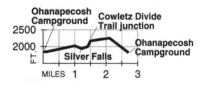

Finding the trailhead: From the Stevens Canyon Entrance Station, drive 1.8 miles south on Washington Highway 123 to the turnoff for Ohanapecosh Campground. Turn right (west), and immediately right again at the fork in the road toward the campground. Continue on this road as it winds past the visitor center until you come to another junction. Again, go right (north) toward the day parking, which is immediately to your right. You cannot enter the parking lot here—you have to loop around to enter the parking lot from the other (east) side. As you loop around, you will see the Silver Falls Trailhead to your left (north). Park and walk to the trailhead.

Parking & trailhead facilities: Restrooms are located at the Ohanapecosh Visitor Center. Remember to park in day parking to avoid all fines. Unfortunately, the day parking lot is rather small and if it is full you might have to find an alternate hike.

Silver Falls

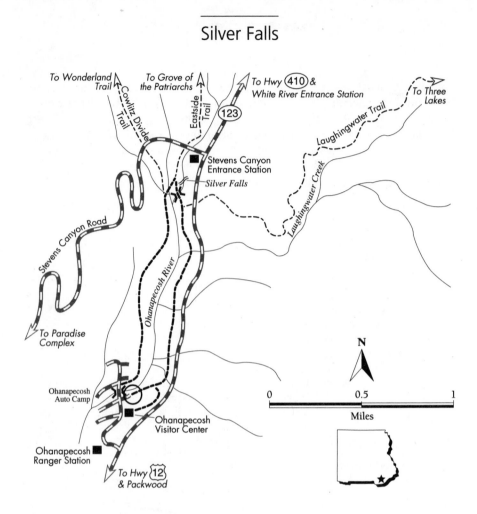

Key points:

0.1	(0.2)	Junction with Hot Springs Trail.
1.0	(1.6)	Junction with Laughingwater Trail.
1.2	(1.9)	Silver Falls.
1.4	(2.2)	Eastside Trail junction.
1.5	(2.4)	Cowlitz Divide Trail junction.
2.7	(4.3)	Ohanapecosh Campground.

The hike: Silver Falls opens early in the year due to its low elevation, and visitors can enjoy the falls as early as May. Plus, the trail wanders through a beautiful forest. Keep in mind that the traffic can be very heavy on this trail, due to the fact that the trailhead is located at Ohanapecosh Campground.

The first 0.1 mile of this hike is also part of an educational self-guided loop trail that explains the Mount Rainier ecosystem. The numbered posts along the trail correspond to text in an interpretive pamphlet available in

Silver Falls.

the Ohanapecosh Visitor Center. Stay left (north) when the Hot Springs Trail forks off to the right.

The beginning of the trail runs through a thermal area. You will see hot springs and interpretive signs telling you more about the thermal features. Keep in mind that the ground is fragile and easily damaged here, making it especially important that you stay on the trail. Walking off the trail in this area is illegal and violators may be cited. Keep in mind that water originating from hot springs is unsafe for human consumption.

The trail gains a bit of elevation in the beginning. You will pass over two bridges before you reach the bridge over Laughingwater Creek. The first bridge is over 0.2 mile into your hike and the second bridge is a little less than 0.8 mile into your hike. Both of these bridges cross streams that empty into the Ohanapecosh River, which is to your left (west). At 0.9 mile, you reach Laughingwater Creek. It is easy to see where the creek gets its name, as the water bounces and frolics over the rocks. Cross Laughingwater Creek and walk 0.1 mile to the Laughingwater Trail junction. Stay to the left and on the Silver Falls Loop.

Silver Falls is 0.2 mile from the Laughingwater Trail junction, 1.2 miles into your hike. An overlook, 0.1 mile from where you first see the falls, looks over the shining waters of Silver Falls. Take your time and enjoy the marvelous view until you are ready move on. The rocks at Silver Falls are moss-covered and slippery. People have died as a result of slipping on the rocks and falling. Please stay behind the guardrails.

The second half of the loop is not as eventful as the first half, but the trail winds through a pleasant mixture of western hemlock, Douglas-fir, and western red cedar. The trail exits at a different location than where it began, but simply walk over the bridge and head back to the day parking lot.

Camping & services: If you wish to car camp and day hike, you can stay at the Ohanapecosh Campground. Unlike backcountry camps, campfires are allowed here. The nearest place to obtain gas and supplies is the town of Packwood, 12 miles south of the park on Washington Highway 123.

For more information: Contact the Ohanapecosh Visitor Center (see Appendix A).

26 Grove of the Patriarchs

Type of hike: Loop; day hike.
Total distance: 1.1 miles (1.8 kilometers).
Difficulty: Easy.
Elevation gain: Minimal.
Best months: May–September.
Maps: USGS Ohanapecosh Hot Springs; Trails Illustrated Mount Rainier National Park; Astronaut's Vista: Mount Rainier National Park, Washington; Earthwalk Press Hiking Map & Guide.
Starting point: Eastside Trailhead.

General description: A short interpretive hike through magnificent old-growth forest.

Grove of the Patriarchs

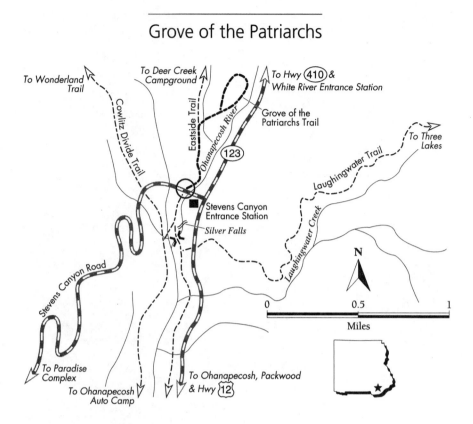

Finding the trailhead: From Stevens Canyon Entrance Station, go west 0.2 mile on Stevens Canyon Road to a parking lot on your right (north). The trailhead is to the left (west) of the restrooms.

Parking & trailhead facilities: Grove of the Patriarchs has a fairly big parking lot but is almost always packed. You might have to find an alternate hike on a sunny weekend. There are wheelchair-accessible restrooms at the trailhead.

The hike: The trail is very well maintained but often muddy. Wear your hiking boots and remember to step through the mud instead of around to avoid widening the trails. Interpretive signs line the trail, helping you identify the difference between western hemlock, Douglas-fir, and western red cedar. This is a great trail to take if you are interested in learning more about the complexities of old-growth forests.

The Eastside Trail begins to the right of the restrooms and heads north. The Ohanapecosh River is to the right for the first 0.3 mile as the trail meanders through old-growth forest. The waters are abnormally clear for a glacial river because the Ohanapecosh Glaciers are relatively inactive, reducing the amount of suspended glacial flour. If it is a sunny day, you can see the sun sparkling off the river's clear surface.

The Grove of the Patriachs Trail.

The trail forks 0.3 mile into the hike. The Eastside Trail continues heading north and the Grove of the Patriarchs Trail veers off to the right (southeast) toward a steel suspension bridge over the Ohanapecosh River. The bridge links to an island rich with old-growth forest. Some of the trees are more than 1,000 years old, towering over the forest floor.

Around 0.1 mile past the Grove of the Patriarchs junction, the trail splits to form a loop. Go left (northeast) around the loop. Make sure to check out the big cedar tree about halfway through the loop. The enormity of the cedar tree is very humbling. Then continue along the loop until you are back to the beginning. The return trip will give you a chance to apply the knowledge of trees you have just gained.

Camping & services: If you wish to car camp and day hike, you can stay at the Ohanapecosh Campground. The nearest place to obtain gas and supplies is the town of Packwood, 12 miles south of the park on Washington Highway 123.

For more information: Contact the Ohanapecosh Visitor Center (see Appendix A).

27 Three Lakes

Type of hike: Out-and-back; day hike or overnighter.
Total distance: 12 miles (20 kilometers).
Difficulty: Strenuous day hike or moderate overnighter.
Elevation gain: 2,800 feet.
Best months: Mid-July–September.
Maps: USGS Ohanapecosh Hot Springs; Trails Illustrated Mount Rainier National Park; Astronaut's Vista: Mount Rainier National Park, Washington; Earthwalk Press Hiking Map & Guide.
Starting point: Laughingwater Trailhead.

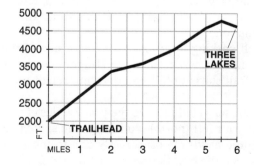

General description: A long day hike or moderate overnighter that ends at three marshy lakes on the eastern border of the park.

Three Lakes

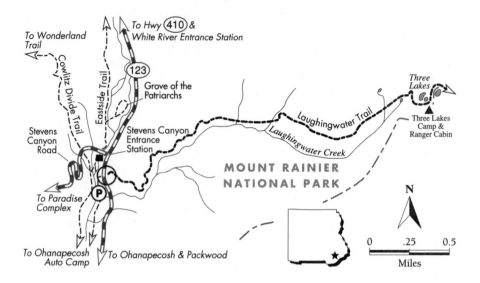

Finding the trailhead: From the Stevens Canyon Entrance Station, drive 0.5 mile south on Washington Highway 123. A hiking sign points to the left (east) and a pulloff marks the parking lot just beyond the sign and on the right (west).

Parking & trailhead facilities: Only a small parking lot, the trailhead has no facilities and few parking spaces. If you need water or toilets, the Ohanapecosh Visitor Center has both. Just drive 1 mile south on WA 123 and follow signs right (west) to the turnoff to Ohanapecosh. Turn right, then immediately right (north) again. This road leads directly to the visitor center.

The hike: As you may have noticed, we have listed no key points for the hike to Three Lakes. The truth is, the hike itself has no distinguishing characteristics. The path constantly ascends through little-changing forest up until it reaches the lakes. You will see little wildlife, few people, no waterfalls, and no views of Mount Rainier on this trail. That is, not until you reach your destination.

From the small parking lot, cross to the east side of the road and walk north along WA 123 a few paces to the Laughingwater Trailhead to your right (east). The trail starts uphill and does not relent until 0.25 mile from the lakes.

Winding switchbacks characterize the first 2 miles of trail. When you see a marshy pool to your left (north), you know the switchbacks have ended. The rest of the route heads almost directly east for nearly 4 miles.

Beyond the marsh, the trail flattens out a bit for 1.5 miles. The end of this more gradual incline is marked by the crossing of three streams. By late August, these streams have dried up, so carry adequate water for the entire

Pensive by the last of the Three Lakes.

6 miles. From this point, the trail begins to ascend steeply and continues for nearly 2 miles. It contours along a ridge, nearing the top, but never quite reaches it. About 0.5 mile from Three Lakes, the trail passes through a small meadow and begins to descend. When you see a small patrol cabin to your left (north) and two lakes beyond it, you have reached your destination.

A small peninsula that separates the two lakes has a campsite that would make a nice place to lunch and relax, as long as ferocious bugs do not bother you. If you have chosen to hike this in one day, follow the same trail back to the parking lot. Otherwise, see the information below for campsite advice.

Options: The last of the three lakes is located 0.1 mile east of the two lakes and just outside of the park's boundary. To visit this lake, continue along the same trail. This side trip increases your hike length to 12.2 miles total, but the sight of the many newts frolicking in the water is worthwhile.

Camping & services: Three Lakes Camp has three available campsites. If you are the first to arrive, claim campsite 1. The site is flat and the location lovely. The other two campsites do not have views of the lakes, and the group site is very close to the toilet. Day hikers can stay at the Ohanapecosh Campground, where campfires are allowed. The nearest place to obtain gas and supplies is Packwood, 12 miles south of the park on WA 123.

For more information: Contact the Ohanapecosh Visitor Center (see Appendix A).

28 Pacific Crest Trail

Type of hike: Loop; three-night backpack.
Total distance: 29.3 miles (48.8 kilometers).
Difficulty: Moderate.
Elevation gain: 3,600 feet.
Best months: Late July–September.
Maps: USGS Ohanapecosh Chinook Pass; Trails Illustrated
Mount Rainier National Park; Astronaut's Vista:
Mount Rainier National Park, Washington; Earthwalk
Press Hiking Map & Guide.
Starting point: Laughingwater Trailhead.

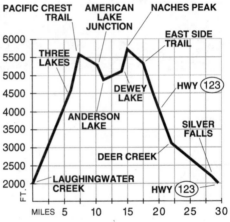

General description: A three-night backpacking trip mostly through forest, with the exception of a portion of the Pacific Crest Trail that follows a ridge and passes many lakes.

Finding the trailhead: From the Stevens Canyon Entrance Station, drive 0.5 mile south on Washington Highway 123. A hiking sign points to the left (east) and a pulloff marks the parking lot just beyond the sign and on the right (west).

Parking & trailhead facilities: Only a small parking lot, the trailhead has no facilities and few parking spaces. If the pullout is full, you can begin this backpacking loop at two other places: Tipso Lake and the Grove of the Patriarchs Trailhead. If you need water or toilets, the Ohanapecosh Visitor Center has both. Just drive 1 mile south on WA 123 and follow signs right (west) to the turnoff to Ohanapecosh. Turn right, then immediately right (north) again. This road leads directly to the visitor center.

Key points:
6.0 (10.0)   Three Lakes.
7.3 (12.2)   Pacific Crest Trail junction.

Pacific Crest Trail

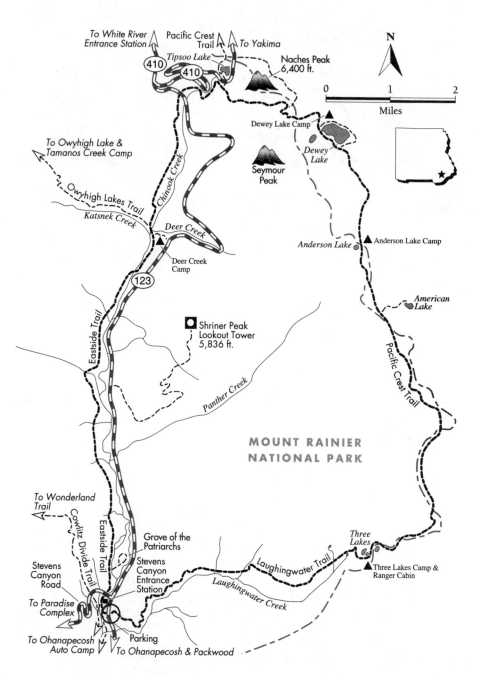

To White River Entrance Station
Pacific Crest Trail
To Yakima
410
410
Tipsoo Lake
Naches Peak 6,400 ft.

N

0   1   2
Miles

Dewey Lake Camp
Dewey Lake

To Owyhigh Lake & Tamanos Creek Camp

Owyhigh Lakes Trail
Katsnek Creek
Chinook Creek

Seymour Peak

Deer Creek
Deer Creek Camp

123

Anderson Lake
Anderson Lake Camp

Eastside Trail

■ Shriner Peak Lookout Tower 5,836 ft.

American Lake

Panther Creek

Pacific Crest Trail

MOUNT RAINIER NATIONAL PARK

To Wonderland Trail

Cowlitz Divide Trail

Eastside Trail

Grove of the Patriarchs

Stevens Canyon Road

Stevens Canyon Entrance Station

Three Lakes

Laughingwater Trail

▲ Three Lakes Camp & Ranger Cabin

Laughingwater Creek

To Paradise Complex

To Ohanapecosh Auto Camp

Parking

To Ohanapecosh & Packwood

Small falls on Chinook Creek. PHOTO BY JOHN CALDWELL.

10.3 (17.2)	American Lake Trail junction.
11.3 (18.8)	Anderson Lake.
14.0 (23.3)	Dewey Lake.
15.0 (25.0)	Naches Peak Loop junction.
17.5 (29.2)	East Side Trail junction/WA 410.
19.0 (31.7)	WA 123.
21.8 (36.3)	Owyhigh Lakes Trail junction.
21.9 (36.7)	Deer Creek Camp.
28.3 (47.0)	Grove of the Patriarchs junction.
28.6 (47.5)	Stevens Canyon Road.
29.1 (48.3)	Silver Falls Loop junction.
29.2 (48.7)	Laughingwater Trail junction.
29.3 (48.8)	WA 123.

The hike: From the small parking lot, cross to the east side of the road and walk north along WA 123 a few paces to the Laughingwater Trailhead to the right (east). The trail starts uphill and does not relent until 0.25 mile from the lakes. A marshy pool about 2 miles into the hike marks the end of the switchbacks. From this point, the trail heads due east until you reach Three Lakes. The last 2 miles before the lakes are at a steep pitch, and the sources for water on this section of the hike are nil in late summer, so if you hike this trail in those months bring plenty of water.

Three Lakes Camp makes a nice place to stay, and after the 2,800 feet of ascent you might need the rest. If not, there are many places to camp along the Pacific Crest Trail. To reach the Pacific Crest Trail, continue east along the Laughingwater Trail. A few spur trails might lead you astray here, but stay on the better-maintained trail, and you should be fine.

You pass one well-marked county trail, but stay to the left and head north. The Laughingwater Trail intersects with the Pacific Crest Trail less than a mile beyond the county trail. Because the Pacific Crest Trail is not a part of Mount Rainier National Park and falls under different management, it is not as well maintained as trails within the park boundaries. This means a few more jutting rocks and downed trees in the way.

After three miles, the Pacific Crest Trail intersects with the American Lake Trail to your right (east). Look at the option below for more details on this day hike, but otherwise proceed north on the Pacific Crest Trail. The trail ascends steeply until you reach the top of a ridge with a few sites for camping. A very short descent on the other side of the ridge leads you to the banks of Anderson Lake. Because it is in the park, no camping is permitted around Anderson Lake, but you can stay in the sites on the ridge just above the lake.

Dewey Lake provides many good campsites also. About 14 miles into the hike, 2.7 miles beyond the Anderson Lake trail junction, the trail forks. Both of the trails encircle Dewey Lake. For the best luck in campsite grabbing, stay to the left, north along the Pacific Crest Trail. Most of the good sites are on the northern part of the lake. If you stay here, set camp at least 100 feet from the lake, keep stock animals at least 200 feet from water, and do not set campfires. Otherwise, enjoy one of the few lakes on this loop that is clear, warm, and large enough to swim in.

When you leave Dewey Lake, you leave behind the privacy and nature of the first part of the hike. Only 1 mile from Dewey Lake, the trail comes to the Naches Peak Loop. Many visitors come to this area, particularly on weekends. At this intersection, you have a choice to round the loop to the left (northwest) or the right (northeast). We suggest going left. On a clear day, you have a good view of the surrounding peaks. This direction also intersects sooner with the Eastside Trail.

If you would like to picnic on the Naches Peak Picnic Area tables, cross WA 410 and follow the path to the left (west) of Tipsoo Lake. If you would rather avoid the masses of people and cars, when you reach the intersection, just before WA 410, turn left (west) onto the Eastside Trail. In 1.5 miles, after a gradual downhill, you come to WA 123. Cross the road and look for the continuation of the trail a bit to the right (north).

From this point on the trail proceeds downhill very near WA 123. The first mile of the 3 miles to Deer Creek are sometimes dangerously steep. Grab onto trees for support. The pitch then levels out. Stay to the left (south) past the Owyhigh Lakes Trail junction. Only 0.1 mile beyond the junction, 22 miles into the trip, you come to Deer Creek Camp. If you do not want to stay here (the mice are terrible), you have to hike 7.4 more miles before reaching your car.

The rest of the trip is much the same. You are surrounded by forest, but you occasionally cross very pretty streams. The forest grows denser and wetter on your way to the Grove of the Patriarchs Trail junction, 6.3 miles beyond Deer Creek (see Options for details on this possible side trip). If you choose not to enter the Grove of the Patriarchs, stay to the right (south) and hike for 0.3 mile, where you come to Stevens Canyon Road. The trail continues on the south side of the road.

You now have only 0.8 mile of trail left to hike. The Eastside Trail intersects with the Silver Falls Loop in 0.5 mile. Get onto the Silver Falls Loop, and cross the Ohanapecosh River to the left (east). Enjoy Silver Falls for a while, then continue east about 0.1 mile. A sign points the way to the Laughingwater Trail and your car, both on your left (east).

Options: You should keep in mind two possible day hikes along this backpacking trip. The trail to the first side trip, American Lake, intersects with the Pacific Crest Trail 3 miles north of the junction with the Laughingwater Trail. The hike to American Lake is only 0.5 mile, adding only 1 mile to the total hiking distance. Innumerable trails, a result of careless use, circle this pretty lake. It has good swimming potential but small fish for anglers.

The second recommended side trip, the Grove of the Patriarchs, is listed as a separate day hike (see Hike 26). The trip adds less than 0.3 mile, and the massive trees make quite an impression.

Camping & services: Three Lakes Camp has three available campsites. If you are the first to arrive, claim campsite 1. The site is flat and the location lovely. The other two campsites do not have views of the lakes, and the group site is very close to the toilet. In any place along the Pacific Crest Trail that is outside of the park, you may camp for free. We suggest Dewey or American Lake. Deer Creek is a below-average campground with two individual sites. Hang your packs and your food very carefully—when we were here, an onslaught of mice ate through one pack and the food bag.

You can also stay at Ohanapecosh Campground if you plan to car camp. The nearest place to obtain gas and supplies is the town of Packwood, 12 miles south of the park on WA 123.

For more information: Contact the Ohanapecosh Visitor Center (see Appendix A).

29 Shriner Peak

Type of hike: Out-and-back; day hike or overnighter.
Total distance: 8.4 miles (13.5 kilometers).
Difficulty: Strenuous.
Elevation gain: 3,436 feet.
Best months: Early July–September.
Maps: USGS Chinook Pass; Trails Illustrated Mount Rainier National Park; Astronaut's Vista: Mount Rainier National Park, Washington; Earthwalk Press Hiking Map & Guide.
Starting Point: Shriner Peak Trailhead.

Shriner Peak

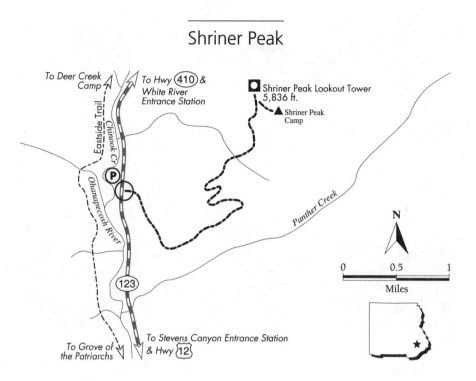

General description: A steep climb to a lookout with spectacular views of the "Four Sisters": Mount Rainier, Mount Adams, Mount Hood, and Mount St. Helens.

Finding the trailhead: From Stevens Canyon Entrance Station, turn left onto Washington Highway 123 and drive 3.6 miles north. At this point, you will pass the trailhead on your right. Continue driving to the pullout just past the trailhead on your left.

Parking & trailhead facilities: No restrooms are available at the trailhead.

The hike: This is a very steep hike. The steepness, combined with little shade and limited water sources, makes this hike seem undesirable, but we can not emphasize enough how incredible the view is from the top of Shriner Peak. You can see the whole east side of Mount Rainier National Park. Just remember to bring plenty of water and start early in the morning.

The first 1.4 miles of the trail wander through a forest, but then the trail enters an area that was burned by a fire several years ago and is presently in the beginning stages of the forest cycle. A switchbacked trail leads through open meadows, created by the fire, all the way to the top. Wildflowers and wild strawberries line these switchbacks.

At the top, you have an amazing view. On a clear day, you can see the "Four Sisters": Mount Rainier, Mount Adams, Mount Hood, and Mount St. Helens: Shriner Peak Camp is located southeast of the lookout. When we were there, there were panoramic photos propped up in the lookout. If the photos are still there, they really help you identify the surrounding landmarks.

Shriner Peak Lookout.

Camping & services: Campfires are not allowed at Shriner Peak Camp, as is the case for every backcountry camp. Shriner Peak Camp has two campsites, but there is no reliable water source. Snowmelt can be used as a water source early in the season, but after the snow melts the only water source is a small stream 1 mile from camp. Keep in mind that this small stream often dries up in midsummer. The nearest place to obtain gas and supplies is the town of Packwood, 12 miles south on WA 123.

For more information: Contact the Ohanapecosh Visitor Center (see Appendix A).

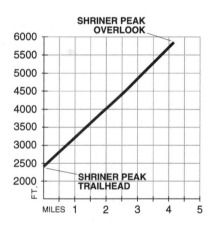

30 Ohanapecosh Park

Type of hike: Loop; three- to four-night backpack.
Total distance: 34.1 miles (56.9 kilometers).
Difficulty: Strenuous.
Elevation gain: 2,800 feet.
Best months: Late July–September.
Maps: USGS Ohanapecosh Hot Springs; Trails Illustrated Mount Rainier National Park; Astronaut's Vista: Mount Rainier National Park, Washington; Earthwalk Press Hiking Map & Guide.
Starting point: Fryingpan Creek Trailhead.

General description: Touted as one of the most spectacular hikes in Mount Rainier National Park, Ohanapecosh Park does not disappoint as an amazing four-day backpacking trip.

Finding the trailhead: From the White River Ranger Station, drive 7.8 miles west on White River Road. Adequate parking becomes visible just after you cross Fryingpan Creek. The trailhead is well marked on the left (south) side of the road.

Parking & trailhead facilities: The Fryingpan Trailhead usually has enough parking for the many hikers, but it has no facilities. The White River Entrance Station has a line of toilets in the process of repair in the summer of 1998. For running water, more toilets, and a picnic area, continue 1.1 miles west on White River Road to the White River Picnic Area and Campground.

Key points:

4.2	(7.0)	Summerland.
6.6	(11.0)	Panhandle Gap.
8.7	(14.5)	Indian Bar.
14.6	(24.3)	Olallie Creek Camp.
17.2	(28.7)	Stevens Canyon Road.
17.5	(29.2)	Eastside Trail junction.
18.7	(31.2)	Grove of the Patriarchs.
25.0	(41.7)	Deer Creek Camp.
25.1	(41.9)	Owyhigh Lakes Trail junction.
29.8	(49.7)	Owyhigh Lakes.
30.6	(50.1)	Tamanos Creek Camp.
33.6	(56.0)	Sunrise Road.
34.1	(56.9)	Fryingpan Trailhead.

The hike: Before we hiked this trail for the first time, different rangers on separate occasions informed us that it was the best hike in the park. It very well might be. The trail begins in dense forest and ascends into subalpine forest, then alpine terrain, even crossing snowfields. The hike offers awesome views of Mount Rainier, fields of wildflowers, alpine lakes, and small ice caves.

Ohanapecosh Park

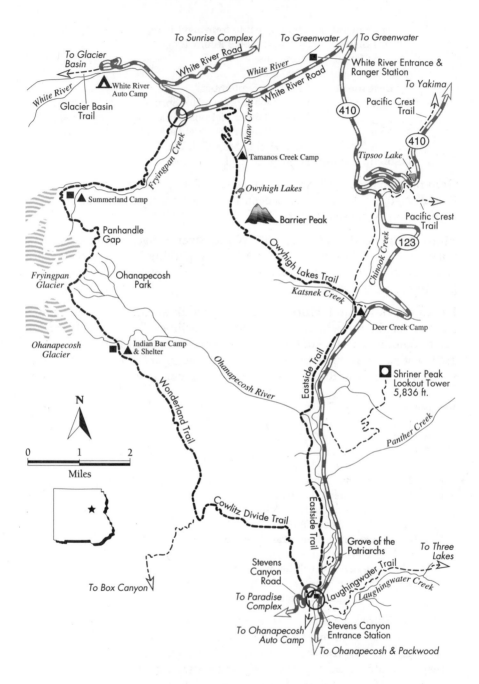

Approaching Panhandle Gap.

Heading south from the Fryingpan Creek Trailhead, the trail climbs moderately through woods. A few switchbacks indicate that you are nearing the Fryingpan Creek crossing, about 2 miles into the hike. Just beyond the creek, you enter a gap in the forest that allows for a good glimpse of Mount Rainier. The trail gets steeper. When the trail turns south, you have only 1 mile of switchbacks to go until you reach Summerland, 4.2 miles into the hike.

After crossing the creek that provides water for Summerland campers, the fields of subalpine flowers turn into rock fields as you enter alpine terrain. The mountain looms over you as you pass an iceberg lake and Panhandle Gap, a saddle between two rocky rises. At this point you have reached the zenith of the hike.

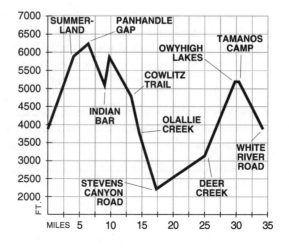

In this area snow is a constant. Prepare to cross several steep and slippery snowfields even in the heat of late summer. After leaving the last snowfield, you have only 1.5 miles of hiking left before reaching Indian Bar. Descend along a ridge flanked by cliffs and waterfalls on one side and a flowered valley on the other. A few switchbacks take you down to a mountain meadow covered with lupine and magenta paintbrush. The Indian Bar Shelter is just across the meadow. If you are camping here, follow the sign that points left (east) to an available site. Otherwise, continue south along the main trail.

From Indian Bar, the trail heads steadily uphill. Make sure you turn around for another great view of the mountain. The top of a nearby knoll makes for a great photo opportunity if the weather is nice. The descent from the top leads to a wooded ridge. The mountain disappears. For 3 miles, walk along this ridge until you reach a fork in the trail.

Head left (southeast) toward Olallie Camp and Ohanapecosh. After descending abruptly for 1.3 miles, cross Olallie Creek. Immediately after the crossing, a trail spurs to the left (north). The wooden sign for the camp is camouflaged in the forest, so keep an eye out for it if you plan to stay there.

The main trail keeps descending steeply until highway noises indicate that you are approaching Stevens Canyon Road, 17.2 miles from the trailhead. Cross the road and look for the other side of the trail a bit to the right (west). You reach the intersection with the Eastside Trail only 0.3 mile from the road. Take a sharp left (north) onto the Eastside Trail. Stevens Canyon Road bisects the 1.2-mile path to the junction with the Grove of the Patriarchs Trail. Walk along the small lollipop loop and admire massive trees if you have the time for the extra 0.3 mile, or else stay to the left (north).

Six miles of trail through woods and over a few pretty streams leads to Deer Creek Camp near the merging of three rivers. Only 0.1 mile beyond Deer Creek Camp, the path forks again. Stay to the left (west) toward Owyhigh Lakes. Nearly 2 miles from the intersection, the trail takes you just west enough to glimpse a sliding falls along a tributary to Needle Creek. Now the ascent begins. Gradual but numerous switchbacks lead you to a meadow below Barrier Peak.

When you enter the woods again, you know that the lakes are only 1 mile away. Unfortunately, this area may still have quite a bit of snow through July. You might need some orienteering skills to reach Owyhigh Lakes. From the lakes, you do not have a view of Mount Rainier, because it is obscured by the Cowlitz Chimneys, but the view of Governors Ridge and the Cowlitz Chimneys is quite lovely.

About 0.5 mile beyond the lakes, you reach Tamanos Camp, then Tamanos Creek. Cross the prepared log and descend through the forest for 3 miles to reach White River Road. Head left (west) for 0.5 mile to find your car.

Options: If you have two cars and less time, see Hike 48 to Indian Bar for a shuttle in the same area.

Camping & services: You have five options for backcountry camps along this loop: Summerland, Indian Bar, Olallie Creek, Deer Creek, and Tamanos Creek. We highly recommend both Summerland and Indian Bar. Deer Creek has mice problems, but you may not be able to avoid staying there. If the campsites are full, which is very possible on this popular section of the Wonderland Trail, choose another hike.

If you plan to car camp, you can stay at Ohanapecosh Campground or White River Campground. The nearest places to obtain gas and supplies are south on Washington Highway 123 in the town of Packwood or northwest on WA 410 in the town of Greenwater.

For more information: Contact the Ohanapecosh Visitor Center or the White River Ranger Station (see Appendix A).

Sunrise

Sunrise, the northeastern section of the park, is home to many natural wonders and scenic treasures of Mount Rainier National Park. As the name implies, the morning light here rises dramatically on Mount Rainier, accentuating the massive glaciers, sliced crevasses, and jagged ridges. The radiant Mount Rainier is visible from almost all of the hikes in this section, as is the jutting peak of Little Tahoma rising from the east flank of Mount Rainier. In Native American legends, Little Tahoma is said to be Mount Rainier's son sitting on her shoulder. Rising into the alpine zones, most of the hikes around Sunrise enter terrain similar to that found in arctic tundra, though the difficulties of the trails vary drastically.

The Sunrise complex, the highest point in the park accessible by car, consists of the Sunrise Ranger Station, the Sunrise Visitor Center, and a snack bar and gift shop. Besides Mount Rainier, several other dormant Cascade volcanoes are visible from the Sunrise complex, including Mount Hood, Mount Adams, and Mount Baker, as well as two massive glaciers, Emmons and Winthrop.

31 Owyhigh Lakes

Type of hike: Out-and-back to the lakes, or a one-way to Eastside Road with a vehicle shuttle; either is a day hike.

Total distance: 7 miles (11.6 kilometers) to lakes (round trip); 8.8 miles (14.7 kilometers) to Eastside Road.

Difficulty: Moderate.

Elevation gain: 1,300 feet.

Best months: Mid-July–September.

Maps: USGS Mount Rainier East; Trails Illustrated: Mount Rainier National Park; Astronaut's Vista: Mount Rainier National Park, Washington; Earthwalk Press Hiking Map & Guide.

Starting point: Owyhigh Lakes Trailhead.

General description: A steep, then gradual ascent to mountain lakes surrounded by a meadow of wildflowers and a jutting ridge. Round trip, the hike takes about four hours.

Finding the trailhead: From the White River Entrance Station, drive 2.1 miles west on White River Road. A small parking area to the right (north) and a hiking sign to the left (south) mark the Owyhigh Lakes Trailhead.

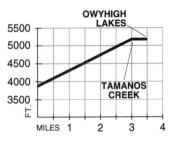

Owyhigh Lakes

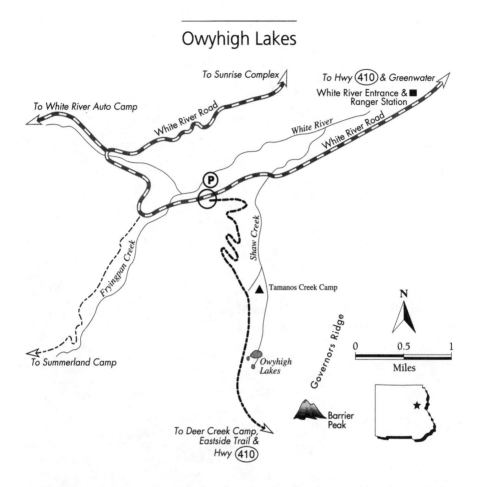

To hike one way to Eastside Road, you must first leave a shuttle car at the Deer Creek Trailhead. From the northern entrance to the park, drive south on Washington Highway 410 to the junction with WA 123. Stay to the right (southbound), turning onto WA 123. Follow this road for 5.1 miles. Watch for a sign for Deer Creek just before a widening of the road and a hiking sign. Leave your car in the pulloff on the left (east), and drive to the Owyhigh Lakes Trailhead to begin hiking.

Parking & trailhead facilities: The Owyhigh Lakes Trailhead has no facilities. The White River Entrance Station should have plumbing, although they were in the process of repair when we were there.

Key points:

3.0	(5.0)	Tamanos Creek Campground.
3.5	(5.8)	Owyhigh Lakes.

Eastside Road Option:

6.9	(11.5)	Falls.
8.3	(13.8)	Boundary Creek and Deer Creek crossing.
8.4	(14.0)	Eastside Trail junction.
8.8	(14.7)	WA 123.

View of Governors Ridge from Owyhigh Lakes.

The hike: The trail to Owyhigh Lakes sees fewer hikers than many other hikes in the park, perhaps because it offers an uneventful first 3 miles of uphill and no view of Mount Rainier. However, those who forego the Owyhigh Lakes trails are missing out. An extensive field of assorted wild-flowers separates the well-maintained trail from the picturesque lakes, and the jutting bluffs of Governors Ridge frame the lakes beautifully.

The hike begins with a 3-mile moderate ascent through forest to the top of the hill. The eastern edge of a few long switchbacks gives you a glimpse of Shaw Creek, but beyond that obscured view the only scenery to be found lies in the surrounding forest. A prepared log stretching across Tamanos Creek marks the end of the ascent. Immediately after Tamanos Creek crossing, a trail splits left to Tamanos Creek Campground. Unless you need to visit the pit toilet, stay on the main trail, walking south for 0.5 mile. Just before reaching the lakes, the trees become more sparse and are replaced by wildflowers. No maintained trail leads to the lake, only casual use trails. Please stay on the main Owyhigh Lakes Trail—these mountain meadows are very fragile and susceptible to damage from tromping humans.

From the lakes, you do not have a view of Mount Rainier because it is obscured by the Cowlitz Chimneys, but the view of Governors Ridge and the Cowlitz Chimneys is quite lovely. After you have rested, snacked, or admired long enough on a nearby boulder, return along the same path to your vehicle.

Options: Rather than turning around at Owyhigh Lakes you can continue along the trail heading southeast. For nearly 3 miles, the trail drops gently through flowered meadows, then dense forest. Then 0.5 mile of switchbacks takes you down to a falls made unique by volcanic rock and sliding water. Only 1.4 more miles of a mild descent, and you reach a place where three creeks merge. Cross Boundary Creek, then Deer Creek. A sign points east toward WA 123. The last 0.4 mile to WA 123 is very steep, but the sound of traffic tells you that you are near the end.

Camping & services: If you would like to backcountry camp, Tamanos Camp is only 0.5 mile north of Owyhigh Lakes. Car campers can stay at Ohanapecosh Campground or White River Campground.

The nearest places to obtain gas and supplies are south on WA 123 in the town of Packwood or northwest on WA 410 in the town of Greenwater.

For more information: Contact the Ohanapecosh Visitor Center or the White River Wilderness Information Center (see Appendix A).

Naches Peak

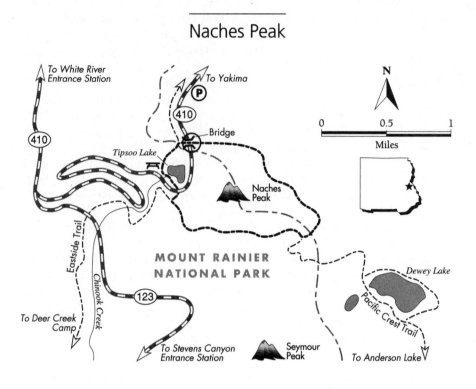

32 Naches Peak

Type of hike:	Loop; day hike.
Total distance:	5 miles (8.3 kilometers).
Difficulty:	Easy.
Elevation gain:	Minimal.
Best months:	Late July–September.
Maps:	USGS Chinook Pass; Trails Illustrated Mount Rainier National Park; Astronaut's Vista: Mount Rainier National Park, Washington; Earthwalk Press Hiking Map & Guide.
Starting point:	Naches Peak Trailhead.

General description: A popular loop in late summer, Naches Peak Trail offers small mountain lakes, subalpine forest, good views of Mount Rainier, and a worthwhile side trip to Dewey Lake.

Finding the trailhead: From the junction of Washington Highway 410 and WA 123 on the eastern edge of the park, drive east on WA 410 to Chinook Pass. Continue east, out of the park, and park in the Tipsoo Lake parking lot on the right (south) side of the road just west of Chinook Pass. Walk west along the highway for less than 0.5 mile to the large park entrance sign

View from the Naches Peak Loop. JOHN CALDWELL PHOTO.

above the road. The top of the sign doubles as a bridge, and the trailhead sign is on the north side of the bridge.

Parking & trailhead facilities: The parking lot has a few toilets. The Tipsoo Picnic Area at the end of the loop has tables for food.

Key points:
    2.2   (3.7)   Pacific Crest Trail junction.
    4.6   (7.7)   WA 410.
    4.7   (7.8)   Tipsoo Lake.
    5.0   (8.3)   WA 410.

The hike: For good reason, the loop around Naches Peak is a very popular hike. The first 2 miles of trail are outside of the park and along the Pacific Crest Trail. Because this trail is pet-friendly, you may see many hikers with leashed dogs and the occasional horseback rider. If you have a pet you would like to walk, however, you cannot complete the loop. Pets are not allowed on the section of trail inside park boundaries, so you must turn around at the park entrance signs where teh Naches Peak Trail intersects with the Pacific Crest Trail.

From the Naches Peak Trailhead, cross the bridge to the southeast side of WA 410. The trail ascends steadily, passing a few small subalpine lakes. Trails lead to the lakes, but they are not maintained and trekking through such fragile meadow is discouraged. Stay on the trail.

The trail reaches its highest point just before entering the park and curves eastward. Soon, 2.2 miles into the hike, the Pacific Crest Trail intersects with the trail returning to the Tipsoo Lake area. To go to Tipsoo Lake or return to your car, turn right (east) here. To continue the Naches Peak Loop, stay on the Pacific Crest Trail going left. Just as you round the bend, you catch a great view of Mount Rainier.

The trail wraps to the right around Naches Peak. Wildflowers blanket the meadows in midsummer, and huckleberries do the same in late summer. The trail also passes a small mountain lake on this side of the peak, and as the trail turns north, you can see Tipsoo Lake with its parking lot and picnic tables.

To reach the picnic area, 4.7 miles into the hike, you must cross WA 410. The continuing trail is visible across the road. A maintained trail loops around Tipsoo Lake, if you are up for a casual stroll.

The steepest incline on the hike is left for the end. The trail passes just north of the picnic area, switches back a few times, then sets you back at the trailhead. Walk east along WA 410 to return to your car.

Options: If you have the time and the desire, a side trip to Dewey Lake is worthwhile. Halfway through the hike described above, follow the signs for Dewey Lake leading southeast. The path down to the lake is a bit steep, but in warm weather the lake is perfect for swimming, fishing, and admiring. This side trip adds almost 2 miles to the total trip distance.

Camping & services: If you do not want to camp at Dewey Lake for no charge, you can stay at Ohanapecosh Campground or White River Campground. The nearest places to obtain gas and supplies are south on WA 123 in the town of Packwood or northwest on WA 410 in the town of Greenwater.

For more information: Contact the Ohanapecosh Visitor Center or the White River Wilderness Information Center (see Appendix A).

33 Crystal Lakes

Type of hike: Out-and-back; day hike or overnighter.
Total distance: 6 miles (9.6 kilometers).
Difficulty: Moderate.
Elevation gain: 2,328 feet.
Best months: Mid-July–September.
Maps: USGS White River; Trails Illustrated Mount Rainier National Park; Astronaut's Vista: Mount Rainier National Park, Washington; Earthwalk Press Hiking Map & Guide.
Starting point: Crystal Lakes Trailhead.

General description: A steep climb to two beautiful mountain lakes.

Finding the trailhead: Since there are no entrance stations on Washington Highway 410, you can access this trailhead without actually passing through an entrance station (Remember, you still need a backcountry permit to camp at Lower or Upper Crystal Lake.)

Crystal Lakes

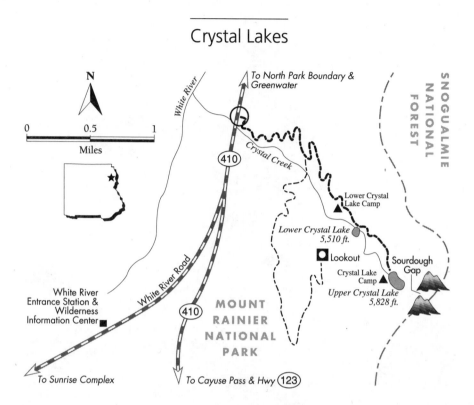

From the junction with White River Road, drive north 0.5 mile on WA 410. Look for a hiking sign on the left pointing east. The parking lot is on the right.

Parking & trailhead facilities: Parking is located just south of the trailhead. Front-in parking is encouraged to make the most of this small parking area. If the lot is full, you can park on the other side the road, but be extra careful not to block the maintenance building. There are no restrooms at this trailhead. Flush toilets can be found at the White River Wilderness Information Center, and additional limited facilities are available at the Sunrise complex.

Key points:
    1.3   (2.1)   Junction with Crystal Lakes Lookout Trail.
    2.3   (3.7)   Lower Crystal Lake.
    3.0   (4.8)   Upper Crystal Lake.

The hike: This steep hike climbs through serene forest into flower-filled meadows, ending at two lovely mountain lakes. Elk are often seen grazing around the lakes and mountain goats gambol along the ridges lining Upper Crystal Lake. This is a very popular hike, so plan on seeing a lot of fellow hikers.

Upper Crystal Lake.

The first 2.3 miles of switchbacks climb up to Lower Crystal Lake. This part of the trail is heavily forested, except where it crosses an avalanche slope. The avalanche slope ends just before you reach the Crystal Lakes Lookout Trail, 1.3 miles into your hike. This unmaintained trail takes you to Crystal Lakes Lookout, more than 2.7 miles away. From the avalanche slope, you have a great view of Mount Rainier and White River.

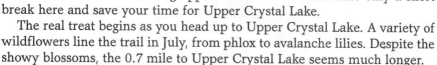

At Lower Crystal Lake, a trail goes down to the lake and to the campsites. No designated trail leads around the lake, and there are limited viewing opportunities of the lake. Take only a short break here and save your time for Upper Crystal Lake.

The real treat begins as you head up to Upper Crystal Lake. A variety of wildflowers line the trail in July, from phlox to avalanche lilies. Despite the showy blossoms, the 0.7 mile to Upper Crystal Lake seems much longer.

When you reach Upper Crystal Lake, take the time to walk around the lake. Don't be surprised if a snowbank or two lies in the way. Glacier lilies are often seen in midsummer along the shores of Upper Crystal Lake, and Sourdough Gap towers above the lake. When you have enjoyed yourself to the fullest, head back the way you came. The steep downhill really does a job on your knees, so take several breaks.

Camping & services: If you want to stay overnight, there are camps at both Crystal Lakes. Fires are not permitted, as in all of the backcountry campgrounds. The lakes are the water source for both campgrounds. Lower Crystal Lake has two flat tent sites, but limited scenery. The two campsites at Upper Crystal Lake are on the south side of the lake and are considerably more scenic. The nearest place to obtain gas and supplies is Greenwater, north on WA 410.

For more information: Contact White River Wilderness Information Center or Sunrise Visitor Center (see Appendix A).

34 Palisades Lakes

Type of hike: Out-and-back; day hike or overnighter.
Total distance: 7 miles (11.6 kilometers).
Difficulty: Moderate.
Elevation gain: Minimal.
Best months: Mid July–September.

Palisades Lake

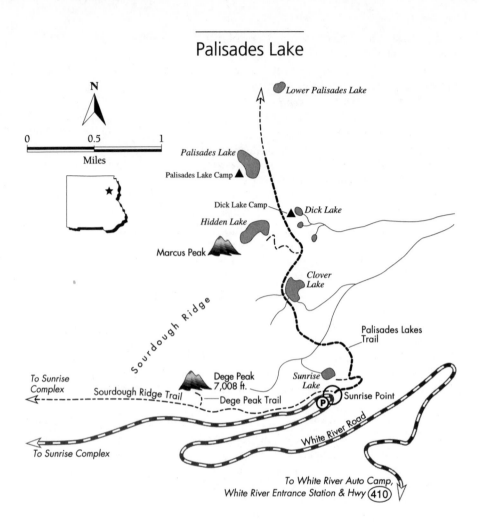

Maps: USGS White River Basin; Trails Illustrated Mount
Rainier National Park; Astronaut's Vista: Mount
Rainier National Park, Washington; Earthwalk Press
Hiking Map & Guide.
Starting point: Palisades Trailhead.

General description: A sharp descent into a valley with many lakes.

Finding the trailhead: From the White River Ranger Station, drive west
11.2 miles on White River Road to well-marked Sunrise Point.

Parking & trailhead facilities: This popular viewpoint has adequate parking most of the time. For all facilities (water, food, toilet, information, gifts, etc.),
continue west on Sunrise Road another 2.6 miles to the Sunrise complex.

Key points:
0.5	(0.8)	Sunrise Lake.
1.5	(2.5)	Clover Lake.

A troop descending to Sunrise Lake.

2.6 (4.3) Hidden Lake Trail junction.
2.9 (4.8) Dick Lake.
3.5 (5.8) Upper Palisades.

The hike: After parking at Sunrise Point, cross White River Road to the east. The trail begins at the easternmost corner of the point beyond a few informational displays. At first the trail descends gradually, but the slight grade soon gives way to a steep, rocky trail. Wear shoes with good traction. We saw more than one person in inadequate shoes slip on the dusty trail. The steep switchbacks end in 0.5 mile at a junction. The westbound trail heads to Sunrise Lake, a pretty lake that is unfortunately close to a busy road.

To continue toward Palisades Lakes, stay to the right (north). The next 1 mile to Clover Lake is almost completely flat. You walk alternately through forest and meadow. When the forest opens to reveal a lake, you have reached Clover Lake. You cannot camp here, but it makes a lovely spot for a break. Stay on the maintained trails—the terrain encircling Clover Lake is very fragile.

Immediately north of Clover Lake the trail climbs a low ridge. The ascent is not long, but it is steep. From the top of the ridge, it's all downhill or flat to the junction with the Hidden Lake Trail, 2.6 miles into the hike (see Options).

If you do not plan to take the Hidden Lake option, stay to the right (north) on the main trail. Another 0.3 mile of trail takes you to Tom, Dick, and Harry Lakes, and Dick Camp. If you plan to stay at Dick Camp, follow signs for Dick Lake, a short trek through the woods. Situated in forest, these green lakes are filled with grass. In midsummer, beware of the bugs. Mosquitoes thrive here.

Mosquitoes are also abundant at Upper Palisades Lake. When we were here, one of the backpacking groups abandoned camp for fear of the infestation of bugs. It really was not that bad, but be forewarned. To get to Palisades Lake, stay to the north on the main trail. A very slight ascent leads you first through forest then field. When you reach a large emerald meadow that "resembles a golf course" as a ranger told us, turn around. From this spot, you have a nice view of the Cowlitz Chimneys over rolling mounds of green.

Beyond this meadow, it is less than 0.5 mile to Upper Palisades Lake. The trail stays relatively flat until you reach the fork to Upper Palisades Camp. To head toward the camp, take the trail to the left (southwest). To filter water from the lake, take the path straight down to the lake (west). To see Lower Palisades Lake from a distance, stay on the main trail (north).

Upper Palisades Lake is beautiful. From the direction you approach, a field of flowers leads all the way to the water's edge. Striated rock formations, the Palisades, provide the backdrop for the deep blue and aqua waters of the lake. If you planned only a day hike, retrace your steps along the main trail.

Options: The side trip to Hidden Lake should not be missed. At the junction, 2.6 miles into the hike, turn left (west). A steep, dusty ascent with a few switchbacks leads to a lovely lake. In a glacial cirque, the cool waters of the lake are surrounded on three sides by jutting rocks. A maintained trail runs around a large peninsula, then stops abruptly. Although some social trails have been created around Hidden Lake, stay on the main trail. The Park Service very recently restored the soil and vegetation in this area.

Camping & services: You have two options for backcountry camping: Dick Camp and Upper Palisades Camp. Dick Camp is the less desirable of the two. It is also situated in a place that requires a hike to reach both the toilet and the lake. Upper Palisades Lake has two very nice sites. Campsite 1 has the view, and campsite 2 is nearer the water and toilet.

You can also stay at White River Campground, 5 miles past the White River Entrance Station. Fires are allowed. The nearest place to obtain gas and supplies is Greenwater, north on Washington Highway 410.

For more information: Contact the White River Wilderness Information Center or the Sunrise Visitor Center (see Appendix A).

35 Dege Peak

Type of hike: Out-and-back; day hike.
Total distance: 2.8 miles (4.5 kilometers).
Difficulty: Easy.
Elevation gain: 928 feet.
Best months: Mid-July–September

Dege Peak

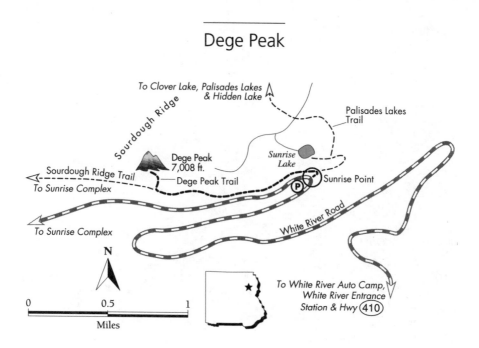

Maps: USGS White River; Trails Illustrated Mount Rainier National Park; Astronaut's Vista: Mount Rainier National Park, Washington; Earthwalk Press Hiking Map & Guide.
Starting point: Sunrise Point.

General description: A short climb to the top of Dege Peak with views of Mount Rainier, the North Cascades, Mount Adams, Mount Baker, and Sunrise Lake.

Finding the trailhead: From the White River Entrance Station, drive 11 miles west on White River Road to the Sunrise point turnout.

Parking & trailhead facilities: There is a sizable parking lot at Sunrise Point, but it is always busy. If the parking lot is full, parking along the road is not an option. Instead, consider climbing Dege Peak from the west side (see Options.)

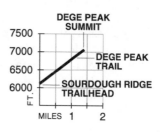

Key points:
   1.1   (1.8)   Junction with the trail to Dege Peak.
   1.4   (2.2)   Dege Peak summit.

The hike: Although this hike is only 2.8 miles long, it is all uphill for the first 1.4 mile to Dege Peak. Make sure to bring plenty of water and pace yourself throughout the climb. From the top of Dege Peak, jaw-dropping scenery surrounds you in every direction.

Sunrise and Clover Lakes from the Sourdough Ridge Trail.

The Sourdough Ridge Trail begins from the west end of the parking lot. Head west on the Sourdough Ridge Trail. Wildflowers, such as lupine and magenta paintbrush, often line the trail in midsummer, and trees provide much-needed shade on a hot day. Marcus Peak rises on the right (north), and when you have gained enough elevation, Mount Rainier comes into view to the west.

After hiking 1.1 miles, you come to the junction with the Dege Peak Trail. Turn right (northeast) on this trail. It is only 0.3 mile to the summit from this point, but the trail follows steep switchbacks all the way to the top. At the top of Dege Peak, you have entered the alpine zone. The peak consists of rock; little vegetation grows on the rocky surface. You can see two dormant volcanoes, Mount Baker and Mount Adams, and enjoy an impressive view of majestic Mount Rainier.

When you decide to head back, it is all downhill! Relish the view of Clover and Sunrise Lakes as you descend the peak. Sunrise Lake is closest to Sunrise Point, where you began your hike, and Clover Lake is farther north, near Marcus Peak.

Options: If the parking lot is full or if you want to start from the Sunrise complex, park in the Sunrise parking lot, 2.6 miles west from Sunrise Point on White River Road. There is a huge parking lot there, but on a sunny weekend it, too, might be full. In this case, you might have to choose an alternate hike.

Head up the paved path to the right of the restrooms leading to the Sourdough Ridge Nature Trail. Turn right (northeast) up the nature trail and stay on it for a little over 0.3 mile to the junction with the Sourdough Ridge

Trail. Turn right (east) onto the Sourdough Ridge Trail and head east toward Dege Peak, which is 1.5 miles away. This option has a total distance out-and-back of 3.8 miles (6.1 kilometers).

Camping & services: You can stay at the White River Campground, 5 miles past the White River Entrance Station. Unlike backcountry camps, campfires are allowed. The nearest place to obtain gas and supplies is Greenwater, north on Washington Highway 410.

For more information: Contact the White River Wilderness Information Center or Sunrise Visitor Center (see Appendix A).

36 Sourdough Ridge Nature Trail

Type of hike: Lollipop loop; day hike.
Total distance: 1.5 miles (2.5 kilometers).
Difficulty: Easy.
Elevation gain: Minimal.
Best months: Mid-July–September.
Maps: USGS Sunrise; Trails Illustrated Mount Rainier National Park; Astronaut's Vista: Mount Rainier National Park, Washington; Earthwalk Press Hiking Map & Guide.
Starting point: Sunrise complex.

General description: A one-hour self-guiding informative stroll along Sourdough Ridge.

Finding the trailhead: From the White River Entrance Station, drive 13.8 miles west on the White River Road to the Sunrise complex parking lot. Park and walk to the trailhead on the northwestern end of the lot, to the right of the restrooms.

Parking & trailhead facilities: Even though the Sunrise complex offers a large parking lot, it fills beyond capacity on some sunny weekends. Visitors are turned away. Some circle the lot hoping for a vacancy. The Sunrise complex also has a variety of facilities, including running water, a cafeteria, restrooms, a gift shop, and a museum.

The hike: To begin this hike, go to the northwestern part of the parking lot. Follow the wide trail running north beyond the restrooms. About 0.1 mile into the hike, a map and display on the right (east) delineates some of the trails in the Sunrise area, including elevation charts and short descriptions. Left (north) of the map a small box holds the accompanying pamphlet to Sourdough Ridge Nature Trail, entitled "Sourdough Ridge: Subalpine Meadow Ecology." If you plan to keep this pamphlet, put 50 cents in the fee box. Otherwise, return the pamphlet upon completion of the hike.

Sourdough Ridge Nature Trail

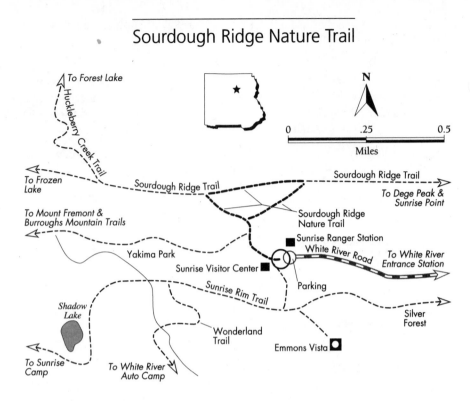

Continue north on this trail until it forks. Follow the sign pointing right (east). For stations 1 through 7, you walk along the south slope of Sourdough Ridge. You have a fantastic view of the grandeur of Mount Rainier, while the stations inform you about the small but crucial parts of the ecosystem.

After station 7, the path forks. Take the left (west) fork. From stations 8 to 13, you walk along the top of Sourdough Ridge with views off both sides of the ridge. On a clear day, you can see Mount Baker, Mount Adams, and Glacier Peak.

After station 13, turn left (south). The Sunrise complex comes into sight, as the lollipop reaches its end. As the pamphlet says, "We hope this walk has given you a look behind the scenery, into the ever changing environmental forces that influence this subalpine community."

Camping & services: If you want to car camp, you can stay at White River Campground, 5 miles past the White River Entrance Station. Campfires are allowed. The nearest place to obtain gas and supplies is Greenwater, which is north on Washington Highway 410.

For more information: Contact the White River Wilderness Information Center or the Sunrise Visitor Center (see Appendix A).

37 Silver Forest

Type of hike:	Out-and-back; day hike.
Total distance:	2 miles (5.7 kilometers).
Difficulty:	Easy.
Elevation gain:	Minimal.
Best months:	Mid-July–September.
Maps:	USGS Sunrise and White River Basin; Trails Illustrated Mount Rainier National Park; Astronaut's Vista: Mount Rainier National Park, Washington; Earthwalk Press Hiking Map & Guide.
Starting point:	Sunrise complex.

General description: An easy one-hour walk to informative viewpoints along a flowery subalpine meadow.

Finding the trailhead: From the White River Entrance Station, drive 13.8 miles west on White River Road to the Sunrise complex parking lot. Park in one of the many spaces provided. The trailhead is south of the parking lot.

Parking and trailhead facilities: Even though the Sunrise complex offers a large parking lot, it fills beyond capacity on some sunny weekends. Visitors are turned away. Some circle the lot hoping for a vacancy. The Sunrise complex also has a variety of facilities, including running water, a cafeteria, restrooms, a gift shop, and a museum.

Mt. Rainier from Emmons Vista.

Silver Forest

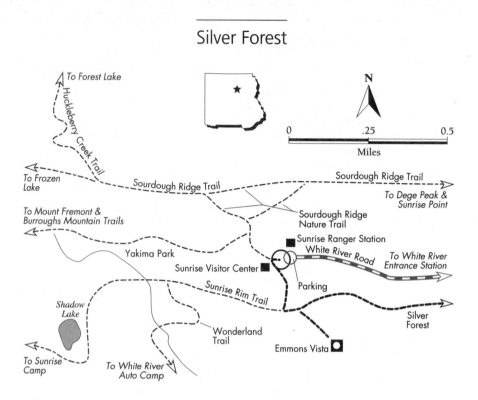

Key points:

0.1	(0.2)	Sunrise Rim Trail junction.
0.2	(0.3)	Emmons Vista exhibits.
1.0	(2.3)	End of maintained trail.

The hike: The Silver Forest Trail involves two parts. First, a short descent leads to two informative exhibits with great views of Mount Rainier. Then the trail continues east through subalpine forest and meadow.

To find the trailhead, park in the Sunrise parking lot. From the south side of the lot, directly across from the ranger station and cafeteria, a trail heads south and a dirt road heads west. As the sign directs, follow the southbound trail, the Emmons Vista Nature Trail.

In only 0.1 mile, you reach the junction with the Sunrise Rim Trail. Stay to the left (south). The path curves east and a sign points south to the first Emmons Vista exhibit. Walk down to the viewpoint and admire the tree-framed view of the Emmons and Winthrop Glaciers. The exhibit explains the various features of a glaciated mountain and how they were formed.

Return to the main trail and continue east. You soon come upon the second exhibit, again immediately south of the trail. This vista point has a nice, sheltered seating area and two more informative signs. The first, "Snow Shadow," includes climatic information about the winds and snow of Paradise. The other, "Rocks Riding on Air," gives a historical account of the Little Tahoma Peak rockslide of 1963.

Back on the main trail, head east once again. In less than 0.1 mile you come to a sign indicating that you have reached the Silver Forest portion of the trail. A fire of unknown origins incinerated this area long ago. Today, the only remnants of the old forest are "silver sentinels," long-dead but standing trees. In the fire's wake, subalpine trees and wildflowers have grown, making this forest particularly intriguing. Small, gnarled trees are dispersed in this meadow along with blankets of violet flowers in midsummer. Walk along this trail for 0.8 mile before reaching a sign that indicates the end of the maintained trail, 1 mile from the trailhead. The trail continues for quite some distance beyond this sign, so venture farther if you want an extended hike. Otherwise, turn around and walk back to the Sunrise complex.

Camping & services: If you want to car camp, you can stay at White River Campground, 5 miles past the White River Entrance Station. Campfires are allowed. The nearest place to obtain gas and supplies is Greenwater, which is north on Washington Highway 410.

For more information: Contact the White River Wilderness Information Center or the Sunrise Visitor Center (see Appendix A).

38 Emmons Moraine

> **Type of hike:** Out-and-back; day hike.
> **Total distance:** 2.8 miles (4.5 kilometers).
> **Difficulty:** Easy.
> **Elevation gain:** 960 feet.
> **Best months:** Early July–September.
> **Maps:** USGS Sunrise and White River; Trails Illustrated Mount Rainier National Park; Astronaut's Vista: Mount Rainier National Park, Washington; Earthwalk Press Hiking Map & Guide.
> **Starting point:** Glacier Basin Trailhead.

General description: A short hike up to the Emmons Moraine with an excellent view of the Emmons Glacier, the largest glacier in the contiguous United States.

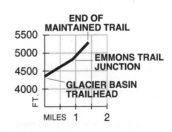

Finding the trailhead: From the White River Entrance Station, drive 3.9 miles west on White River Road to the White River Campground turnoff. Turn left (northwest) toward the campground and drive 1.2 miles to the parking area on the left. A sign indicates that the parking lot is for backpackers and climbers. Park here and walk to the Glacier Basin Trailhead in the middle of loop D, one of the many loops that make up White River Campground.

Emmons Moraine

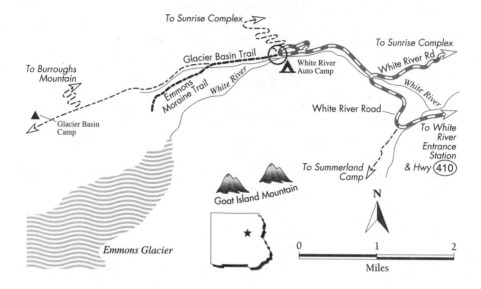

Parking & trailhead facilities: There are restrooms along loop C for you to use, and a pay phone at the entrance.

The hike: This short, gradual uphill hike is great for children. Hike along the Emmons Moraine for a close-up view of the Emmons Glacier. At one time, the Emmons Glacier filled the whole valley here. The glacier carved an amazingly flat and expansive section out of the earth.

Head west along the Glacier Basin Trail. Very near the beginning of the trail, you come to an informational billboard about this hike and other hikes in the immediate area. From here, hike 0.9 mile through tranquil forest to the junction with the Emmons Moraine Trail. At the junction, go left (southwest) up the Emmons Moraine Trail.

Travel slightly uphill for another 0.5 mile to the end of the maintained trail. Your feet sink into the sandy trail formed from silt deposits by the Emmons Glacier. On a hot day, the sand soaks up the sun, adding to the scorching heat. Also, the small trees along the Emmons Moraine provide little or no shade. Be sure to bring sunscreen. When you have marveled at the Emmons Glacier long enough, head back the same way you came.

Options: At the junction with Emmons Moraine Trail, you can head up to Glacier Basin. It will be another 2.2 miles from the junction to the end of the maintained trail, making your trip 4.4 miles longer. (See Hike 44: Glacier Basin.) From Glacier Basin, which is a lovely, mountain meadow, you can see the Inter Glacier and St. Elmo's Pass.

Camping & services: If you want to car camp, you can stay at White River Campground, 5 miles past the White River Entrance Station. Unlike

The Wedge between Emmons and Winthrop Glaciers. JOHN CALDWELL PHOTO.

backcountry camps, campfires are allowed. The nearest place to obtain gas and supplies is Greenwater, which is north on Washington Highway 410.

For more information: Contact the White River Wilderness Information Center or the Sunrise Visitor Center (see Appendix A).

39 Mount Fremont Lookout

Type of hike: Out-and-back; day hike.
Total distance: 5.4 miles (8.6 kilometers).
Difficulty: Easy.
Elevation gain: 781 feet.
Best months: Late July–September.
Maps: USGS Sunrise and White River; Trails Illustrated Mount Rainier National Park; Astronaut's Vista: Mount Rainier National Park, Washington; Earthwalk Press Hiking Map & Guide.
Starting point: Sunrise complex.

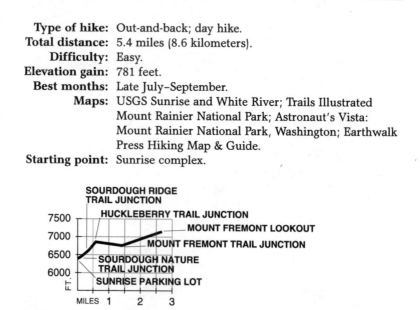

General description: A short ascent to a fire lookout on Mount Fremont that towers over the north side of the park and has great views of Mount Rainier, Skyscraper Mountain, Grand Park, and Sourdough Ridge.

Finding the trailhead: From the White River Entrance Station, drive 13.8 miles west on White River Road to the Sunrise parking lot. Park and walk to the trailhead on the north end of the lot, to the right of the restrooms.

Parking & trailhead facilities: You should have no trouble finding a parking spot unless it is a sunny weekend, in which case you might have to choose an alternate hike. A number of facilities are located at the Sunrise complex, including running water, a cafeteria, restrooms, a gift shop, and a museum.

Key points:
0.1 (0.2) Sourdough Ridge Nature Trail junction.
0.3 (0.5) Sourdough Ridge Trail junction.
0.6 (1.0) Huckleberry Creek Trail junction.
1.4 (2.2) Mount Fremont Trail junction.
2.7 (4.3) Mount Fremont Lookout.

The hike: Walk up the paved path to the right (east) of the restrooms until you see a dirt trail on your right (north). Get on that trail and travel north until you come to the junction with the Sourdough Ridge Nature Trail. Turn left (northwest) onto the Sourdough Ridge Nature Trail and walk 0.2 mile to the Sourdough Ridge Trail. Turn left (west) onto the Sourdough Ridge Trail.

Mount Fremont Lookout

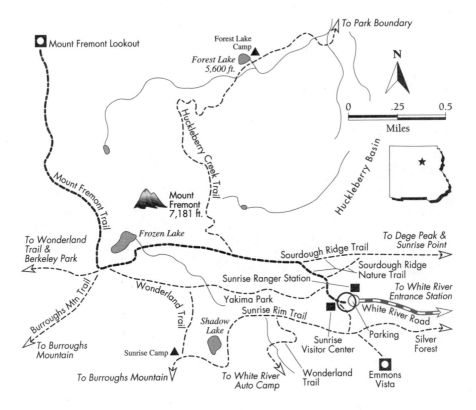

While you are walking along this trail, you can see the North Cascades to your right. Mount Rainier also looks magnificent from Sourdough Ridge. After 0.3 mile you pass the Huckleberry Creek Trail on your right, heading northwest. Keep going west another 0.8 mile to a five-way junction, immediately after Frozen Lake and 1.4 miles from the trailhead. The Mount Fremont Trail is the first trail on the right; head north on it. The trail runs above timberline for the remainder of the hike. Fat marmots inhabit the green meadows along the trail. Keep in mind that it is illegal to feed animals and detrimental to their survival skills.

Soon the trail threads along the rocky side of Mount Fremont. Watch your step—the ledge drops straight off the ridge! Low-growing subalpine wildflowers line the trail in late July. Walk along the ridge until you reach the lookout, 2.7 miles from the Sunrise complex. From the lookout, you can see all the way to the north end of the park, where the clearcuts start. Skyscrape Mountain is to your left, and Mount Rainier towers above it all. Take the time to get out your map and identify the landmarks around you.

Camping & services: If you want to car camp, you can stay at the White River Campground, 5 miles past the White River Entrance Station. Unlike

View from Mt. Fremont.

backcountry camps, campfires are allowed. The nearest place to obtain gas and supplies is Greenwater, which is north on Washington Highway 410.

For more information: Contact the White River Wilderness Information Center or the Sunrise Visitor Center (see Appendix A).

40 Forest Lake

Type of hike:	Out-and-back; day hike or overnighter.
Total distance:	5 miles (8 kilometers).
Difficulty:	Easy.
Elevation gain:	1,600 feet roundtrip.
Best months:	Late July–September.
Maps:	USGS Sunrise and White River; Trails Illustrated Mount Rainier National Park; Astronaut's Vista: Mount Rainier National Park, Washington; Earthwalk Press Hiking Map & Guide.
Starting point:	Sunrise parking lot.

General description: A short descent over rocky alpine terrain, through subalpine meadows, to a quaint mountain lake.

Forest Lake

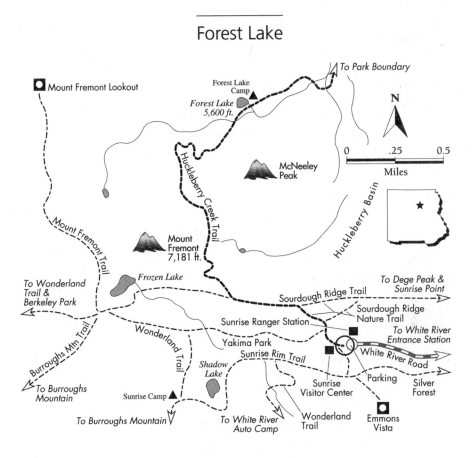

Finding the trailhead: From the White River Entrance Station, drive 13.8 miles west on White River Road to the Sunrise parking lot. Park and walk to the trailhead on the north end of the lot, to the right of the restrooms.

Parking & trailhead facilities: You should have no trouble finding a parking spot unless it is a sunny weekend, in which case you might have to choose an alternate hike. A number of facilities are located at the Sunrise complex, including running water, a cafeteria, restrooms, a gift shop, and a museum.

Key points:

0.1	(0.2)	Sourdough Ridge Nature Trail junction.
0.3	(0.5)	Sourdough Ridge Trail junction.
0.6	(1.0)	Huckleberry Creek Trail junction.
2.5	(4.0)	Forest Lake and Forest Lake Camp.

The hike: If you want to escape the crowd at Sunrise and experience a variety of different ecosystems, this is the hike for you. From the tundra on the north side of Sourdough Ridge to the deciduous forest that surrounds Forest Lake, you will have a taste of everything.

Walk up the paved path to the right (east) of the restrooms until the trail forks. Take the a dirt trail on your right (north). Get on that trail and walk up it until you come to the junction with the Sourdough Ridge Nature Trail. Turn left (northwest) onto the Sourdough Ridge Nature Trail and walk 0.2 mile to the Sourdough Ridge Trail. Turn left (west) onto the Sourdough Ridge Trail.

While you are walking along this trail, you can see the Cascades to the north, and Mount Rainier looks magnificent from here. Soon the Huckleberry Creek Trail splits right. Take the Huckleberry Creek Trail, 0.6 mile into your hike. The trail briefly ascends and then begins a long descent to Forest Lake. The first part of the trail is in the alpine zone and relatively rocky. There are low-growing wildflowers, such as red mountain heather, all around. Be aware that patches of snow might linger on the trail until August, but the trail is usually easy to follow.

We saw a lot of mountain goat tracks on this trail, so keep your eyes open for mountain goats on both Mount Fremont, to your left, and McNeeley Peak, to your right. The lush Huckleberry Basin is south of McNeeley Peak and is visible from Sourdough Ridge.

Soon the trail heads into the trees and wanders through forest and meadows, overflowing with wildflowers in late July, all the way to Forest Lake. Forest Lake is small, but charming. There is a great place right next to the campsite to take a break and enjoy the lake.

Camping & services: Forest Lake Camp has one individual campsite with slightly slanted tent sites and an incredible view. A pit toilet near the campsite is difficult to find—try heading almost directly north of the campsite. Fires are not permitted, as in all backcountry campgrounds.

If you want to car camp, you can stay at White River Campground, 5 miles past the White River Entrance Station. Unlike backcountry camps, campfires are allowed. The nearest place to obtain gas and supplies is Greenwater, which is north on Washington Highway 410.

For more information: Contact the White River Wilderness Information Center or the Sunrise Visitor Center (see Appendix A).

41 Berkeley Park

Type of hike: Out-and-back; day hike or overnighter.
Total distance: 7.6 miles (12.6 kilometers).
Difficulty: Moderate.
Elevation gain: 1,600 feet round trip.
Best months: Mid-July–September.
Maps: USGS Sunrise; Trails Illustrated Mount Rainier National Park; Astronaut's Vista: Mount Rainier National Park, Washington; Earthwalk Press Hiking Map & Guide.
Starting point: Sunrise complex.

General description: A mild descent to a lovely mountain meadow brimming with wildflowers and clear streams.

Finding the trailhead: From the White River Entrance Station, drive 13.8 miles west on White River Road to the Sunrise parking lot. Park and walk to the trailhead on the north end of the lot, to the right of the restrooms.

Parking & trailhead facilities: You should have no trouble finding a parking spot unless it is a sunny weekend, in which case you might have to choose an alternate hike. The Sunrise complex also has a variety of facilities, including running water, a cafeteria, restrooms, a gift shop, and a museum.

Key points:

0.1	(0.2)	Sourdough Ridge Trail junction.
1.4	(2.2)	Frozen Lake/Five Trail intersection.
2.4	(3.8)	Northern Loop Trail junction.
3.9	(6.2)	Berkeley Camp.

The hike: To begin this hike, go to the northwestern part of the parking lot. Follow the wide trail north beyond the restrooms. After about 0.1 mile, a map and display on the right (east) delineate some of the trails in the Sunrise area, including elevation charts and short descriptions. Continue 0.1 mile north of this sign to the junction with the Sourdough Ridge Trail. Turn left (west) onto this trail. This wide, dusty path runs along Sourdough Ridge, giving you various opportunities to admire the awesome views on both sides. In 1.1 miles you descend from the ridge, only to rise again to a junction of five trails.

Follow the Wonderland Trail heading directly west. The trail goes down a hill and toward a valley for 1.1 miles. At this point, the Northern Loop Trail goes right (north). Take this trail, entering the meadow below. This gap between Skyscrape Mountain to the west and Mount Fremont to the east is named Berkeley Park. Pink flowers line the creek that meanders beside you. If you look behind you (south), you can see Burroughs Mountain and Mount Rainier. Take your time appreciating the beauty of a subalpine meadow, because you soon leave it and enter the woods.

Berkeley Park

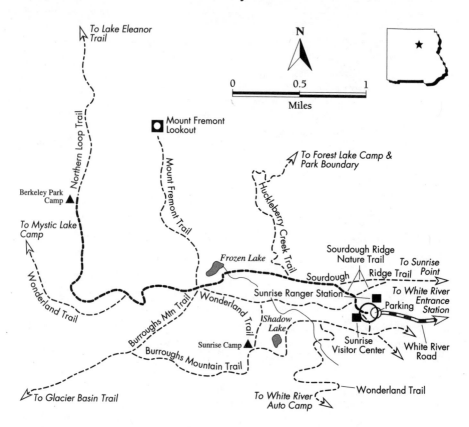

Continue to descend beyond the meadow and into a forested area. Berkeley Camp, 3.8 miles into the hike, is the destination. The camp rests right next to the trail (see Camping & services). Day hikers can filter water from Lodi Creek before beginning the 800-foot ascent back to the trailhead at the Sunrise complex.

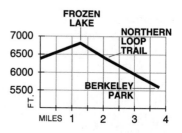

Camping & services: With a permit, you can camp at Berkeley Camp. It has four sites, three of them clustered at the southern end of camp. To find site 4, you must walk farther north along the trail and a sign will point you there. Sites 3 and 4 are the best for privacy, although site 4 is farther from water and the toilet.

If you want to car camp, you can stay at White River Campground, 5 miles past the White River Entrance Station. There is a fee of $10 per night and, unlike backcountry campsites, campfires are allowed. There are 117 sites available on a first-come, first-served basis. The nearest place to obtain gas and supplies is Greenwater, which is north on Washington Highway 410.

For more information: Contact the White River Wilderness Information Center or the Sunrise Visitor Center (see Appendix A).

42 Grand Park

Type of hike: Out-and-back; day hike or overnighter.
Total distance: 13.6 miles (22.3 kilometers).
Difficulty: Strenuous as a day hike; moderate as an overnighter.
Elevation gain: 1,600 feet round trip.
Best months: Mid-July–September.
Maps: USGS Sunrise; Trails Illustrated Mount Rainier National Park; Astronaut's Vista: Mount Rainier National Park, Washington; Earthwalk Press Hiking Map & Guide.
Starting point: Sunrise complex.

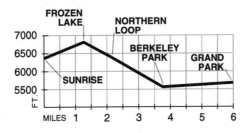

General description: A mild descent to a lovely mountain meadow brimming with wildflowers and clear streams, then a relatively flat hike to a massive expanse of meadow.

Finding the trailhead: From the White River Entrance Station, drive 13.8 miles west on White River Road to the Sunrise parking lot. Park and walk to the trailhead on the north end of the lot, to the right of the restrooms.

Parking & trailhead facilities: You should have no trouble finding a parking spot in the huge expanse of concrete unless it is a sunny weekend, in which case you might have to choose an alternate hike. The Sunrise complex also has a variety for facilities, including running water, a cafeteria, restrooms, a gift shop, and a museum.

Key points:
0.1	(0.2)	Sourdough Ridge Nature Trail junction.
1.4	(2.2)	Frozen Lake/Five Trail intersection.
2.4	(3.8)	Northern Loop Trail junction.
3.9	(6.2)	Berkeley Camp.
6.9	(11.0)	Lake Eleanor Trail junction/Grand Park.

Grand Park

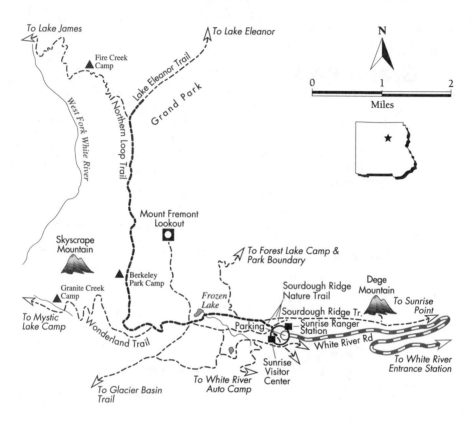

The hike: To begin this hike, go to the northwestern part of the parking lot. Follow the wide trail north beyond the restrooms. After about 0.1 mile, a map and display on the right (east) delineate some of the trails in the Sunrise area, including elevation charts and short descriptions. Go 0.1 mile north of this sign to the Sourdough Ridge Trail. Turn left (west) onto this trail. This wide, dusty path runs to and along Sourdough Ridge, giving you various opportunities to admire the awesome views on both sides. In 1.2 miles you descend from the ridge, only to rise again to a junction of five trails.

Follow the Wonderland Trail heading directly west. The trail goes down a hill and toward a valley for 1.1 miles. At this point, turn right onto the Northern Loop Trail and enter the meadow below. This gap between Skyscrape Mountain to the west and Mount Fremont to the east is named Berkeley Park. Pink flowers line the creek that meanders beside you. If you look behind you (south), you can see Burroughs Mountain and Mount Rainier. Take your time appreciating the beauty of a subalpine meadow, because you soon leave it and enter the woods.

Continue to descend beyond the meadow and into a forested area. Berkeley Camp, 3.9 miles into the hike, is a possible camp for an overnight stay.

Mt. Rainier from Grand Park.

The camp rests right next to the trail. (See Camping & Services.) If you plan to stay here, leave your packs before venturing to Grand Park.

Continue north on the main trail 3 miles to Grand Park. This 3 miles is divided into three sections. First, the trail climbs, then it descends, and finally it levels off for the final approach to Grand Park. The crest of the uphill affords a nice view of Mount Rainier to the rear, so be sure to turn around once in a while. The trail eventually leaves the sparse subalpine forest for an expansive meadow. At the junction with the Lake Eleanor Trail, 6.9 miles from the trailhead, turn right (northeast). You cannot miss Grand Park, the massive plateau with numerous wildflowers directly in front of you.

Aptly named, Grand Park is about 1.5 miles long and 0.5 mile wide, the flattest ground anywhere on or around Mount Rainier. It is absolutely spectacular. Walk along the Lake Eleanor Trail for a mile or so, and then turn around. Few places in Mount Rainier National Park offer such a majestic view of Mount Rainier.

Camping & services: There are several options for backcountry camps. Berkeley Camp, 3 miles south of Grand Park, has four sites, the first three clustered at the southern end of camp. To find site 4, you must walk farther north along the trail and a sign will point you there. Sites 3 and 4 are best for privacy, although site 4 is farther from water and the toilet. Lake Eleanor Camp, 3 miles northeast of Grand Park, has three individual campsites and one group site. The camp was built on a very pretty lake that has reasonably good fishing. The tent sites leave something to be desired and the path back to Grand Park is rather steep, but the location is nice. Fire Creek Camp, 1.6 miles beyond the Lake Eleanor Trail junction, has four mediocre sites with surprisingly good cooking areas. Once again, the pitch back to the Grand Park area would prove challenging.

If you want to car camp, you can stay at White River Campground, 5 miles past the White River Entrance Station. Campfires are allowed. The nearest place to obtain gas and supplies is Greenwater, which is north on Washington Highway 410.

For more information: Contact the White River Wilderness Information Center or the Sunrise Visitor Center (see Appendix A).

43 Burroughs Mountain

> **Type of hike:** Out-and-back; day hike.
> **Total distance:** 6 miles (10 kilometers).
> **Difficulty:** Moderate.
> **Elevation gain:** 1,000 feet.
> **Best months:** Late July–September.
> **Maps:** USGS Sunrise; Trails Illustrated Mount Rainier National Park; Astronaut's Vista: Mount Rainier National Park, Washington; Earthwalk Press Hiking Map & Guide.
> **Starting point:** Sunrise complex.

General description: A mild two-hour ascent to the top of a small mountain with tundra-like terrain.

Finding the trailhead: From the White River Entrance Station, drive 13.8 miles west on White River Road to the Sunrise parking lot. Park and walk to the trailhead on the north end of the lot, to the right of the restrooms.

Parking & trailhead facilities: You should have no trouble finding a parking spot in the huge expanse of concrete, unless it is a sunny weekend, in which case you might have to choose an alternate hike. The Sunrise complex also has a variety of facilities, including running water, a cafeteria, restrooms, a gift shop, and a museum.

Key points:
0.1	(0.2)	Sourdough Ridge Native Trail junction.
1.4	(2.1)	Frozen Lake/Five Trail intersection.
2.4	(3.8)	First Burroughs Mountain/South Loop junction.
3.1	(5.0)	Second Burroughs Mountain.

The hike: To begin this hike, go to the northwestern part of the parking lot. Follow the wide trail north beyond the restrooms. After about 0.1 mile, a map

Burroughs Mountain

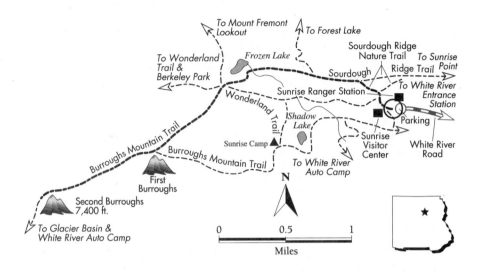

To Mount Fremont Lookout

To Forest Lake

To Wonderland Trail & Berkeley Park

Frozen Lake

Sourdough Ridge Nature Trail

To Sunrise Point

Sourdough

Ridge Trail

Wonderland Trail

Sunrise Ranger Station

To White River Entrance Station

Shadow Lake

Parking

Sunrise Visitor Center

White River Road

Sunrise Camp

Burroughs Mountain Trail

Burroughs Mountain Trail

To White River Auto Camp

First Burroughs

Second Burroughs 7,400 ft.

To Glacier Basin & White River Auto Camp

N

0   0.5   1

Miles

★

and display on the right (east) delineate some of the trails in the Sunrise area, including elevation charts and short descriptions. Continue 0.1 mile north of this sign to the Sourdough Ridge Native Trail. Turn left (west) onto this trail. This wide, dusty path runs to and along Sourdough Ridge, giving you various opportunities to admire the awesome views on both sides. In 1.1 miles you descend from the ridge, only to rise again to a junction of five trails.

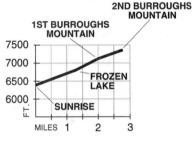

Follow the signs that point toward Burroughs Mountain (southwest). The trail follows Burroughs Mountain uphill with no switchbacks. The path is steep but fairly short. As you approach the top of the mountain, the turf on both sides of the trail has fewer and fewer plants. This region has terrain and fauna similar to that found in arctic regions. Stay on the trail; although this terrain looks rough and tumble, it is very susceptible to the damage caused by human tromping.

From the five-way intersection, you ascend 1.0 miles before reaching the top of First Burroughs Mountain. Walking southeast, you have a view of Mount Rainier throughout the first half of the hike. Take the time to identify the major glaciers and land forms in front of you: Emmons Glacier, Winthrop Glacier, Inter Glacier, and Little Tahoma Peak.

From the crest of First Burroughs Mountain, you have only 0.7 mile to the zenith of Second Burroughs Mountain. The trail drops at first, then climbs again. The top of Second Burroughs Mountain offers you much the same view as the first. When finished, retrace your steps to the trailhead.

Options: If you want to return along a different route, take the Southern Loop Trail to Shadow Lake and back to Sunrise. When returning east toward Sunrise, rather than heading back toward Frozen Lake at the junction atop First Burroughs Mountain, stay to the right (southeast). This trail descends steeply past Sunrise Camp to Shadow Lake. Stay to the right (east) at the junction with the Wonderland Trail, then to the left (east) toward the Emmons Vista Trail. This alternate route increases the total miles hiked by 0.5 mile. (See Hike 49: Sunrise Rim.)

Camping & services: If you want to car camp, you can stay at White River Campground, 5 miles past the White River Entrance Station. Campfires are allowed. The nearest place to obtain gas and supplies is Greenwater, which is north on Washington Highway 410.

For more information: Contact the White River Wilderness Information Center or the Sunrise Visitor Center (see Appendix A).

44 Glacier Basin

Type of hike:	Out-and-back; day hike or overnighter.
Total distance:	7 miles (10.2 kilometers).
Difficulty:	Moderate.
Elevation gain:	1,280 feet.
Best months:	Early July–September.
Maps:	USGS Sunrise and White River; Trails Illustrated Mount Rainier National Park; Astronaut's Vista: Mount Rainier National Park, Washington; Earthwalk Press Hiking Map & Guide.
Starting point:	Glacier Basin Trailhead.

General description: A moderate ascent near the Emmons Glacier Moraine to a camp at the foot of the Inter Glacier.

Finding the trailhead: From the White River Entrance Station, drive west 3.9 miles to the White River Campground turnoff. Turn left (west) toward the campground and drive 1.2 miles to the parking area on the left. A sign indicates that the parking lot is for backpackers and climbers. Park here and walk to the Glacier Basin Trailhead in the middle of loop D, one of the many loops that comprise White River Campground.

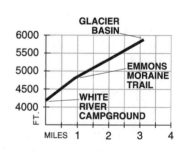

Parking & trailhead facilities: There are restrooms along loop C for you to use and a pay phone at the entrance.

Glacier Basin

Key points:

1.0	(1.7)	Emmons Moraine Trail junction.
3.5	(5.8)	Glacier Basin Camp.

The hike: Head west along the Glacier Basin Trail. Immediately after the trailhead, an informational billboard describes this and other hikes near White River Campground. From here, continue 1 mile through tranquil forest to the junction with the Emmons Moraine Trail. At this junction, stay to the right (west) along the main trail.

In about 0.1 mile, a small, bubbling falls crosses the path. The trail ascends gradually, but steadily for 2 miles. Only 0.5 mile from Glacier Basin Camp, the trail gets steeper. A sign marks your entrance into the camp.

The maintained trail ends soon after the camp, but a number of trails continue up the mountain. Just beyond the camp to the west is a small, marshy lake and the Inter River. A very steep path leads down the bank to the river below. The main trail, although unmaintained here, goes nearly to the mouth of the Inter River from the Inter Glacier. Camp Curtis and Camp Shurman, two possible base camps for the final ascent to the summit, sit toward the top of the Inter Glacier. Winthrop and Emmons Glaciers flank the Inter Glacier on either side.

When you have finished glacier spotting, turn around to follow the same path back to the White River Campground.

Options: The Emmons Moraine Trail proves a worthwhile side trip along this day hike. It ascends gradually along the Emmons Moraine, a collection of dirt and debris from glacial movement. The trail offers great views of the

Glacier Basin from Burroughs Mountain. JOHN CALDWELL PHOTO.

Emmons Glacier, and visitors may hear the crashing of falling rocks on ice. This trip adds 1 mile total to your hike, raising the total to 8 miles round trip. (See Hike 38: Emmons Moraine.)

Camping & services: If you want to car camp, you can stay at White River Campground, 5 miles past the White River Entrance Station. Campfires are allowed. The nearest place to obtain gas and supplies is Greenwater, which is north on Washington Highway 410.

For more information: Contact the White River Wilderness Information Center or the Sunrise Visitor Center (see Appendix A).

45 Northern Loop

Type of hike:	Loop; four-day backpack.
Total distance:	35.5 miles (59.2 kilometers).
Difficulty:	Strenuous.
Elevation gain:	[see elevation profile].
Best months:	Mid-July–September.
Maps:	USGS White River Basin; Trails Illustrated Mount Rainier National Park; Astronaut's Vista: Mount Rainier National Park, Washington; Earthwalk Press Hiking Map & Guide.
Starting point:	Sunrise complex.

Northern Loop

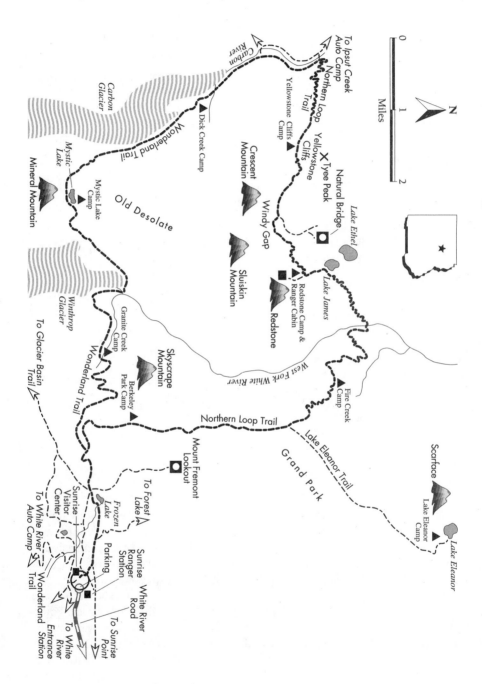

General description: A wondrous hike with intense ascents and descents and spectacular views of mountain meadows, massive parks, lakes, glaciers, wildlife, and Mount Rainier.

Finding the trailhead: From the White River Entrance Station, drive 13.8 miles west on White River Road to the Sunrise parking lot. Park and walk to the trailhead on the north end of the lot, to the right of the restrooms.

Parking and trailhead facilities: You should have no trouble finding a parking spot in the huge expanse of concrete except on sunny weekends. The Sunrise complex also has a variety for facilities, including running water, a cafeteria, restrooms, a gift shop, and a museum.

Key points:

0.1	(0.2)	Sourdough Ridge Nature Trail junction.
0.3	(0.5)	Sourdough Ridge Trail junction.
1.4	(2.2)	Frozen Lake/Five Trail intersection.
2.4	(3.8)	Northern Loop Trail junction.
3.9	(6.2)	Berkeley Camp.
6.9	(11.0)	Lake Eleanor Trail junction/Grand Park.
8.1	(13.0)	Fire Creek Camp Trail junction.
12.8	(20.5)	Lake James Trail junction.
13.4	(21.4)	Redstone Camp.
14.7	(23.5)	Windy Gap.
15.7	(25.1)	Independence Ridge Trail junction.
17.2	(27.5)	Yellowstone Cliffs Camp Trail junction.
20.1	(32.2)	Ipsut Creek Trail junction.
21.1	(34.8)	Wonderland Trail junction.
21.5	(34.4)	Carbon Glacier.
22.2	(35.5)	Dick Creek Camp.
25.6	(41.0)	Mystic Lake.
25.8	(41.3)	Mystic Lake Camp.
28.1	(45.0)	Winthrop Glacier.
31.1	(49.8)	Granite Creek Camp.
33.3	(53.3)	Northern Loop Trail junction.
34.4	(55.0)	Five Trail junction.
35.6	(57.0)	Sunrise complex.

The hike: Quite possibly our favorite backpacking trip in Mount Rainier National Park, the Northern Loop offers all anyone could want in the way of scenery without the drawbacks of more popular trails. From a massive expanse of mountain meadow to an even more massive expanse of nearby glaciers, this hike traverses nearly all of the climatic zones in the park. It also produced the greatest number of wildlife sightings for the authors.

To begin this hike, go to the northwestern part of the parking lot. Follow the wide trail that runs north beyond the restrooms. After about 0.1 mile, a map and display on the right (east) delineate some of the trails in the Sunrise area, including elevation charts and short descriptions. Continue 0.1 mile north of this sign to the Sourdough Ridge Nature Trail. Turn left (west) onto this trail. This wide, dusty path runs to and along Sourdough Ridge, giving you various opportunities to admire the awesome views on both sides.

Little Tahoma above the Wonderland Trail.

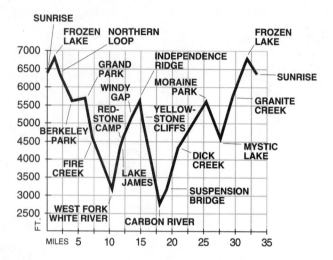

In 1.1 miles you descend from the ridge, only to rise again to a junction of five trails.

Follow the Wonderland Trail heading directly west. The trail goes downhill and toward a valley for 1.1 miles. At this point, the Northern Loop Trail splits right (north). Take this trail, entering the meadow below. This gap between Skyscrape Mountain to the west and Mount Fremont to the east is named Berkeley Park. Pink flowers line the creek that meanders beside you. If you look behind you (south), you can see Burroughs Mountain and Mount Rainier. Take your time appreciating the beauty of a subalpine meadow, because you soon leave it and enter the woods.

Continue to descend beyond the meadow and into a forested area. Berkeley Camp, 3.8 miles into the hike, is a possible camp for an overnight stay. The camp rests right next to the trail.

Continuing north on the main trail, the next 3 miles to Grand Park are divided into three sections. First, the trail climbs, then descends, and finally levels off for the final approach to Grand Park. The crest of the uphill gives you a nice view of Mount Rainier to the rear, so be sure to turn around for a look. The trail eventually leaves the sparse subalpine forest for an expanse of meadow. At the junction with the Lake Eleanor Trail, 6.9 miles from the trailhead, Grand Park is to the right (northeast); you cannot miss the massive plateau with numerous wildflowers directly in front of you.

If you do not plan to stay at Lake Eleanor (see Options), turn left (northwest) following the sign to Five Creek Camp. The trail quickly takes a downhill turn with switchbacks into forest for 1.2 miles. At this point, the trail forks. To the right (north) Fire Creek Camp is only 0.4 mile away. To the left (west) more than 2 miles of descending switchbacks leads to the West Fork of the White River. You may need to ford this river. Fed by the Winthrop Glacier, the West Fork of the White River is ridden with silt and debris. Do not count on this water as a good source from which to filter drinking water. Clearer streams can be found up the trail within 0.5 mile.

From the river valley, the trail once again starts up a steep incline. Many switchbacks through dense forest lead to a deceptive clearing. You may think that you have now reached Redstone Camp, but you must ascend a few more switchbacks first. About 5 miles from Fire Creek Camp, the trail forks. A sign is purposefully placed in the middle of the spur trail to discourage hikers, but the trail is by no means off limits. It leads to Lake James, a once popular fishing and recreational lake. If you would like to fish Lake James, turn right (north). The lake appears soon after leaving the main trail. If you plan on staying at Redstone Camp, stay to the left (south) and climb another 0.6 mile. The trail to Redstone Camp intersects to the left (east). Follow this trail 0.25 mile to the Redstone Ranger Cabin to learn more of the history of Lake James. Bulletins outside of the cabin offer historical accounts, and the location offers a look at Redstone Peak.

Continuing along the Northern Loop, 1.5 miles of uphill switchbacks through a forest and a pika-filled rockfield lead to Windy Gap. The trail crosses Van Horn Creek and threads through Windy Gap. Circumvented by Independence Ridge, Crescent Mountain, and Sluiskin Mountain, Windy Gap is a haven. Apparently cougars think so, too—we saw many cat prints in this area.

From the western part of Windy Gap, a possible side trip beckons to Independence Ridge and a natural land bridge (see Options). From here the trail runs flat and straight. It passes a small lake, a decent source of water, 0.1 mile beyond the Independence Ridge Trail. Another spur trail leaves the main trail 0.2 mile beyond the junction with the Independence Ridge Trail. This trail, destination Tyee Peak and the Yellowstone Cliffs, is unmaintained, so tread carefully if you choose to hike it.

From this spur, the trail begins to head downhill. Less than 1.5 miles from Windy Gap is the junction to Yellowstone Cliffs Camp. Towering above you and a meadow of flowers are the Yellowstone Cliffs, an impressive rock formation. The trail to Yellowstone Cliffs Camp, a very scenic place to stay, heads southeast for 0.2 mile. If you do not plan to stay here, keep to the right (west).

For nearly 3 miles, the trail heads dramatically downhill. Your feet will hurt and your knees will ache by the time you reach the junction with the trail to Ipsut Creek Campground. Stay to the left (south). You will find the next mile of flatness a relief. Three cool streams provide excellent water before you once again begin to ascend steeply.

About 1 mile beyond the trail to Ipsut Creek Campground, the trail joins the Wonderland Trail. To the right (west), a suspension bridge crosses the Carbon River. The Northern Loop Trail continues to the left (south). Less than 0.5 mile from the bridge, the trail provides a close-up view of the Carbon Glacier, a massive glacial formation blackened by rocks and debris. Mount Rainier rises imposingly above the glacier. The trail grows steeper and remains steep for the next 0.7 mile to Dick Creek Camp.

If the clanking of rocks falling from the glacier's face deters you from staying at Dick Creek Camp, bypass the camp, continuing south. The next 2 miles of ascent switche back and forth through a forest. The grade lessens when the path begins to run along Moraine Creek. Keep in mind that this is bear country. In fact, a fellow hiker told us that she has never come here without seeing a bear. When we were here, we saw a small black bear that was not easily deterred by loud voices, banging pots, and shrill singing.

Beyond the streambed, the trail passes a rock field, then a large mountain meadow. At this point you have only two small hills to climb before beginning your descent to Mystic Lake, 25.6 miles from the hike's beginning. The lake rests in a valley between Mineral Mountain and the appropriately named Old Desolate. The view is beautiful, but it cannot be seen from Mystic Lake Camp, 0.2 mile down the trail.

The next established camp, Granite Camp, is only 3 miles beyond Mystic Lake Camp, but in order to get there you must circumvent the Winthrop Glacier. An easy 1-mile descent skirts the Winthrop Glacier, leading to Winthrop Creek. Cross the prepared log to the other side.

You now begin to climb your final big hill. Hike 2 miles uphill with a few sporadic switchbacks to Granite Camp. These 2 miles run along the Winthrop Moraine, providing an excellent glimpse of the glacier, before turning west toward forest. More than 30 miles from the trailhead, Granite Camp is your last camping option. If you plan to pass the camp to finish the loop and go out for a burger, stay on the Wonderland Trail heading east through camp.

Less than 2 miles of nicely graded, long switchbacks lead to the highest point along the entire loop, a peak just below Skyscrape Mountain. From this peak you have great views in all directions, and you know that the worst is over. You can see the trail on which you started, and Sunrise seems deceptively close. The last 2.3 miles to Sunrise, however, are exhausting.

Options: The Lake Eleanor Trail makes a nice addition to the Northern Loop Trail. At the intersection with the Lake Eleanor Trail, turn right (northeast). The trail leads through Grand Park and descends to the lake. This option adds 6.6 miles to the total hiking distance and most likely another night's stay at Lake Eleanor Camp.

If you have the time and energy, you should also take the side trip along Independence Ridge to the natural bridge. Do not continue on the unmaintained trail beyond the spur trail to the natural bridge, but do descend to the natural bridge. The arching rocks are a wonder of nature. This side trip adds 1.8 miles to your hike.

Camping & services: There are several options for backcountry camps. Berkeley Camp has four sites, the first three clustered at the southern end of camp. To find site 4, you must walk farther north along the trail and a sign will point you there. Sites 3 and 4 are best for privacy, although site 4 is farther from water and the toilet.

Lake Eleanor Camp, 3 miles northeast of Grand Park, has three individual campsites and one group site. The camp was built on a very pretty lake that has reasonably good fishing. The tent sites leave something to be desired and the path back to Grand Park is rather steep, but the location is nice.

Fire Creek Camp, 1.6 miles beyond the Lake Eleanor Trail junction, has four mediocre sites with surprisingly good cooking areas.

Redstone Camp, a replacement for Lake James Camp while it is under repair, has two nice sites, although it offers little in the way of a view.

Yellowstone Cliffs Camp, on the other hand, has a fantastic view of, what else, the Yellowstone Cliffs. It also has two nice campsites, number 1 having the best view, and a close proximity to water.

Dick Creek Camp, one of our favorite backcountry camps, has two nice sites as well. Again, site 1 has an unbelievable view of the Carbon Glacier if you get there first. Dick Creek, its water source, is also only a short walk away.

Mystic Lake Camp is unfortunately located quite a distance from the lake. An established camp along the Wonderland Trail, this camp has a whopping five individual sites and two group sites, all with good tent sites but little privacy.

The two individual campsites and one group site at Granite Creek have no view but quite a bit of privacy. Granite Creek makes a nice water source.

For more information: Contact the White River Wilderness Information Center or the Sunrise Visitor Center (see Appendix A).

46 Lake Eleanor

Type of hike: Out-and-back; overnighter.
Total distance: 20.2 miles (33.7 kilometers).
Difficulty: Moderate.
Elevation gain: 1,800 feet round trip.
Best months: Mid-July–September.
Maps: USGS Sunrise; Trails Illustrated Mount Rainier National Park; Astronaut's Vista: Mount Rainier National Park, Washington; Earthwalk Press Hiking Map & Guide.
Starting point: Sunrise complex.

General description: A mild descent to a lovely mountain meadow brimming with wildflowers and clear streams, then a relatively flat hike through an expansive, and downhill meadow to a lake.

Finding the trailhead: From the White River Entrance Station, drive 13.8 miles west on White River Road to the Sunrise parking lot. Park and walk to the trailhead on the north end of the lot, to the right of the restrooms.

Parking & trailhead facilities: Even though the Sunrise complex offers a large parking lot, it fills beyond capacity on some sunny weekends. Visitors are turned away. Some circle the lot hoping for a vacancy. The Sunrise com-

Lake Eleanor

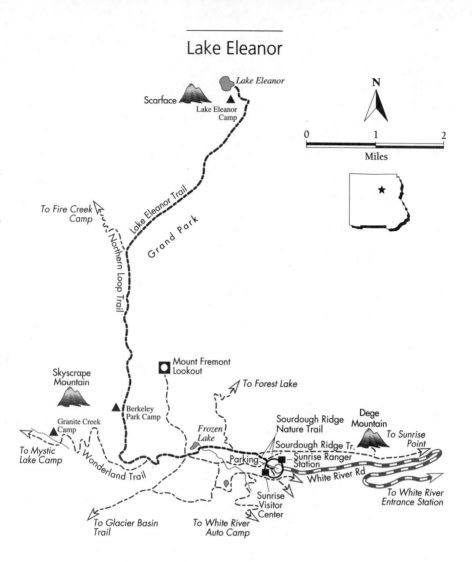

plex also has a variety of facilities, including running water, a cafeteria, restrooms, a gift shop, and a museum.

Key points:

0.1	(0.2)	Sourdough Ridge Nature Trail junction.
0.3	(0.5)	Sourdough Ridge Trail junction.
1.4	(2.2)	Frozen Lake/Five Trail intersection.
2.4	(3.8)	Northern Loop Trail junction.
3.9	(6.2)	Berkeley Camp.
6.9	(11.0)	Lake Eleanor Trail junction/Grand Park.
10.2	(16.8)	Lake Eleanor.

The hike: To begin this hike, go to the northwestern part of the parking lot. Follow the wide trail that runs north beyond the restrooms. After about 0.1

mile, a map and display on the right (east) delineate some of the trails in the Sunrise area, with elevation charts and short descriptions. Continue 0.1 mile north of this sign to the Sourdough Ridge Trail. Turn left (west) onto this trail. This wide, dusty path runs to and along Sourdough Ridge, giving you various opportunities to admire the awesome views on both sides. In 1.1 miles you descend from the ridge, only to rise again to a junction of five trails.

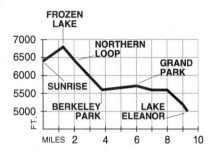

Follow the Wonderland Trail heading directly west. The trail goes downhill and toward a valley for 1.1 miles. At this point, the Northern Loop Trail splits right (north). Take this trail, entering the meadow below. This gap between Skyscrape Mountain to the west and Mount Fremont to the east is named Berkeley Park. Pink flowers line the creek that meanders beside you. If you look behind you (south), you can see Burroughs Mountain and Mount Rainier. Take your time appreciating the beauty of a subalpine meadow, because you soon leave it and enter the woods.

Continue to descend beyond the meadow and into a forested area. You reach Berkeley Camp 3.9 miles into the hike. Unless you plan to make this hike a multiple-nighter, bypass the camp, heading north toward Lake Eleanor.

Continue north on the main trail 3.0 miles to the Lake Eleanor Trail. The 3 miles is divided into three sections, first ascending, then descending, and finally leveling off for the final approach to Grand Park. The crest of the uphill gives you a nice view of Mount Rainier to the rear, so be sure to turn around at least once. The trail leaves the sparse subalpine forest and enters an expanse of meadow. At the junction with the Lake Eleanor Trail, 6.8 miles from the trailhead, Grand Park is to the right (northeast); you cannot miss the massive plateau with numerous wildflowers.

Aptly named, Grand Park is about 1.5 miles long and 0.5 mile wide, the largest area of flat ground on or around Mount Rainier. It is absolutely spectacular. Walk along the Lake Eleanor Trail about 1 mile, then turn around. Few places in Mount Rainier National Park offer such a majestic view of Mount Rainier.

The trail runs through Grand Park and descends steeply through woods. A little over 3 miles from the Lake Eleanor Trail junction, you reach the lake. Set up camp and fish to your heart's content (there are few restrictions on fishing in Mount Rainier National Park). This medium-sized lake is greenish and dense forest surrounds it, preventing remarkable views. From some spots along an unmaintained trail encircling the lake, however, you can catch a glimpse of Scarface (a rock formation) on the southwestern side of the lake. When you are ready to return to civilization, retrace your tracks to the Sunrise complex.

Camping & services: Lake Eleanor Camp has three mediocre individual sites and one nice group site. Of the three individual sites, number 2 has the nicest view. Fires are not permitted. The nearest place to obtain gas and supplies is Greenwater, north on Washington Highway 410.

For more information: Contact the White River Wilderness Information Center or the Sunrise Visitor Center (see Appendix A).

47 Summerland

Type of hike:	Out-and-back; day hike or overnighter.
Total distance:	8.4 miles (14 kilometers).
Difficulty:	Moderate.
Elevation gain:	2,000 feet.
Best months:	Mid-July–September.
Maps:	USGS White River Basin; Trails Illustrated Mount Rainier National Park; Astronaut's Vista: Mount Rainier National Park, Washington; Earthwalk Press Hiking Map & Guide.
Starting point:	Fryingpan Creek Trailhead.

General description: A moderate five-hour day hike to one of the most spectacular subalpine and alpine regions within the park.

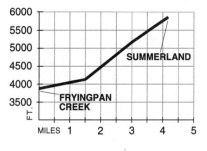

Finding the trailhead: From the White River Ranger Station, drive 2.8 miles west on White River Road. Adequate parking becomes visible just after you cross Fryingpan Creek. The trailhead is well-marked on the left (south) side of the road.

Parking & trailhead facilities: The Fryingpan Trailhead usually has enough parking for the many hikers except on sunny weekends. But it has no facilities. The White River Station Entrance has a line of toilets without plumbing. For running water, more toilets, and a picnic area, continue west on White River Road another 1.1 miles to the White River Picnic Area and Campground.

The hike: Heading south from Fryingpan Trailhead, the trail climbs gradually to moderately through woods. The path is straight, with only a gradual incline for the first 1.5 miles. The trail then steepens and starts to switchback. The southernmost end of two long switchbacks provides a good look at Fryingpan Creek below. The grade remains moderately steep for another mile, at which point you cross Fryingpan Creek.

Summerland

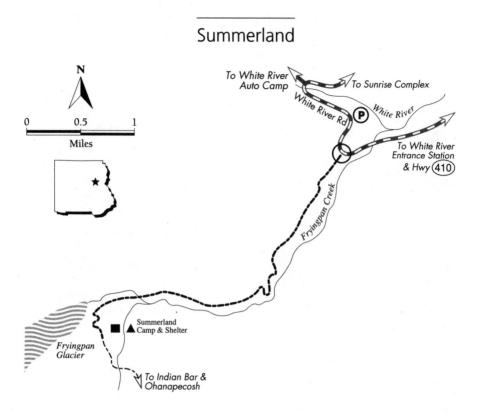

Just beyond the creek, a gap in the forest allows for a good glimpse of Mount Rainier. The trail then gets steeper. When the trail turns south, there is only 1 mile of switchbacks to go until you reach Summerland, 4.2 miles from the trailhead.

Summerland sits just below timberline, but it is well worth exploring farther along the trail into alpine regions. Less than 0.5 mile beyond Summerland, the terrain turns rocky with snowfields.

If you do not plan to stay at Summerland Camp, return to the trailhead. Otherwise, see the section below for a description of the camp.

Camping & services: Summerland Camp has five individual campsites and one group site. Although they are farther from the toilet than the other sites (except number 5, which has no view), we recommend camping at either site 3 or 4. They have the better views. The water source for all sites is a stream that runs south along the main trail.

If you want to car camp, you can stay at White River Campground, 5 miles past the White River Entrance Station. The nearest place to obtain gas and supplies is Greenwater, which is north on Washington Highway 410.

For more information: Contact the White River Wilderness Information Center or the Sunrise Visitor Center (see Appendix A).

Summerland.

48 Indian Bar

Type of hike: One way, with a vehicle shuttle; overnighter.
Total distance: 17.7 miles (28.2 kilometers).
Difficulty: Strenuous.
Elevation gain: 2,800 feet.
Best months: Late-July–September.
Maps: USGS White River Basin and Ohanapecosh Hot Springs; Trails Illustrated Mount Rainier National Park; Astronaut's Vista: Mount Rainier National Park, Washington; Earthwalk Press Hiking Map & Guide.
Starting point: Fryingpan Creek Trailhead.

General description: Trumpeted as one of the most spectacular hikes in Mount Rainier National Park, the trail from Sunrise to Ohanapecosh does not disappoint as an amazing overnight trip.

Finding the trailhead: As this hike requires a shuttle, you must first park a vehicle at the trail's end. From the Stevens Canyon Entrance Station, drive 0.8 mile south on Washington Highway 123. A pullout on the right (west) side of the road is the trail's end. Check the nearby trail signs to make sure that you have parked at the Laughingwater Trailhead.

To begin the hike, drive the second vehicle north on WA 123 to the junction with WA 410. Continue north on WA 410 about 1.9 miles and turn left (west) on White River Road. From the White River Station Entrance, continue 8.6 miles west on White River Road. Adequate parking becomes visible just after

Indian Bar

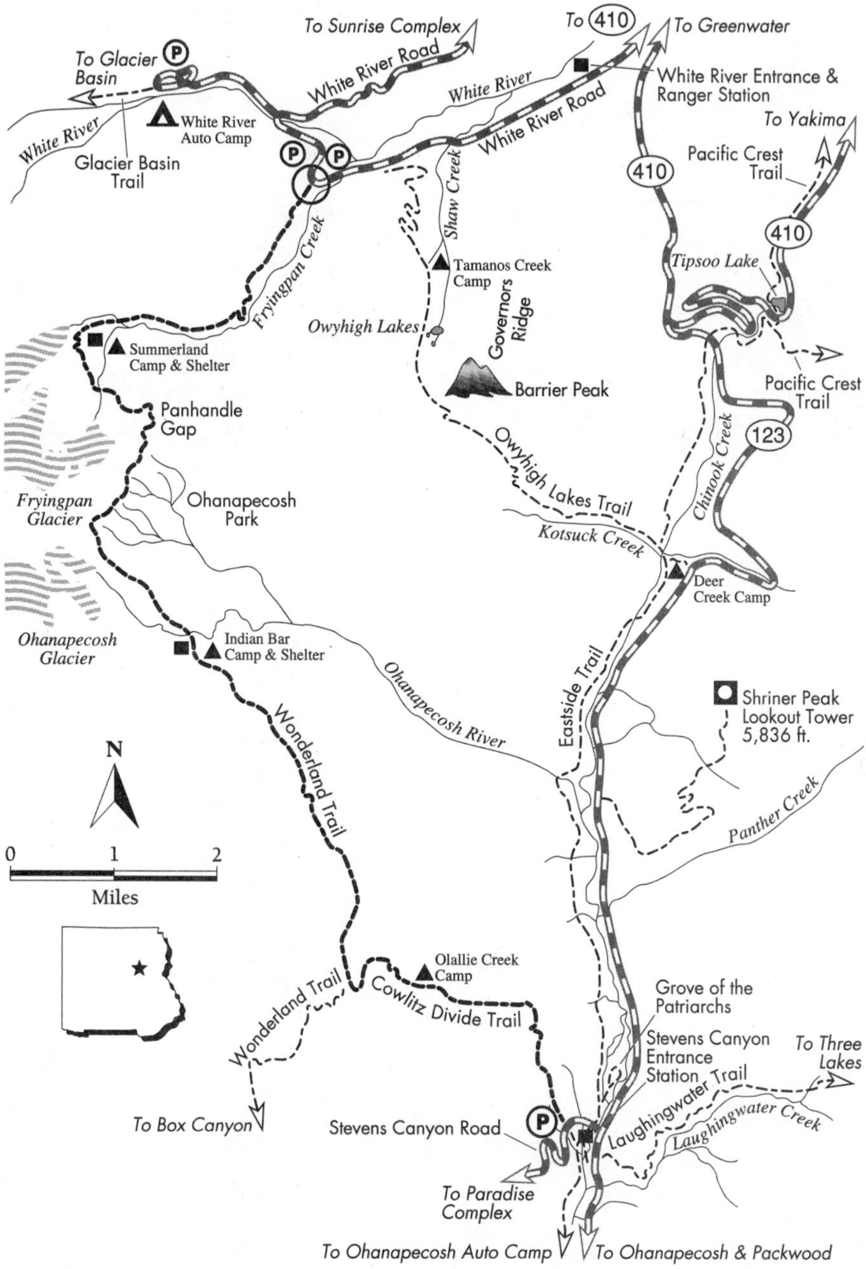

To Glacier Basin

To Sunrise Complex

To 410   To Greenwater

White River Road

White River

White River Auto Camp

White River Road

White River Entrance & Ranger Station

White River

Glacier Basin Trail

To Yakima

410

Pacific Crest Trail

410

Fryingpan Creek

Shaw Creek

Tamanos Creek Camp

Tipsoo Lake

Owyhigh Lakes

Governors Ridge

Summerland Camp & Shelter

Barrier Peak

Pacific Crest Trail

Panhandle Gap

123

Fryingpan Glacier

Ohanapecosh Park

Owyhigh Lakes Trail

Kotsuck Creek

Chinook Creek

Ohanapecosh Glacier

Indian Bar Camp & Shelter

Deer Creek Camp

Ohanapecosh River

Eastside Trail

Shriner Peak Lookout Tower 5,836 ft.

N

Wonderland Trail

Panther Creek

0   1   2

Miles

Olallie Creek Camp

Wonderland Trail

Cowlitz Divide Trail

Grove of the Patriarchs

Stevens Canyon Entrance Station

To Three Lakes

Laughingwater Trail

To Box Canyon

Stevens Canyon Road

P

Laughingwater Creek

To Paradise Complex

To Ohanapecosh Auto Camp   To Ohanapecosh & Packwood

Indian Bar.

you cross Fryingpan Creek. The trailhead is well-marked on the left (south) side of the road.

Parking & trailhead facilities: The Fryingpan Trailhead usually has enough parking for the many hikers except on sunny weekends. It has no facilities. The White River Station Entrance has a line of toilets. For running water, more toilets, and a picnic area, continue 1.1 miles west on White River Road to the White River Picnic Area and Campground.

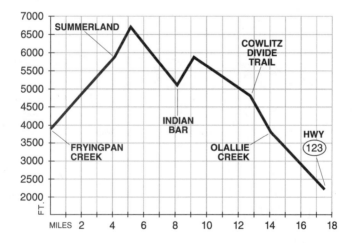

Key points:

4.2	(7.0)	Summerland.
8.2	(13.7)	Indian Bar.
12.8	(21.3)	Cowlitz Divide Trail junction.
14.1	(23.5)	Olallie Creek Camp.
17.1	(28.5)	Stevens Canyon Road.
17.3	(28.8)	Eastside Trail junction.
17.5	(29.2)	Silver Falls.
17.6	(29.3)	Laughingwater Trail junction.

The hike: Heading south from Fryingpan Trailhead, the trail climbs gradually to moderately through woods. A few switchbacks indicate that you are nearing the Fryingpan Creek crossing, about 2 miles into the hike. Just beyond the creek, a gap in the forest allows for a good glimpse of Mount Rainier. The trail then gets steeper. When the trail turns south, you have only 1 mile of switchbacks to go until you reach Summerland, 4.2 miles into the hike. From the Summerland area, standing in fields of wildflowers, you have a fantastic view of Mount Rainier and the alpine land leading up to it.

After crossing the creek that provides water for the Summerland campers, the trail leaves fields of subalpine flowers and crosses rock fields as it enters alpine terrain. The mountain looms over you as you pass an iceberg lake and Panhandle Gap, a saddle between two rocky rises. At this point you have reached the zenith of the hike.

In this area snow is a constant. Prepare to cross several steep and slippery snowfields even in the heat of late summer. After leaving the last snowfield, you have only 1.5 miles of hiking to reach Indian Bar. Descend along a ridge flanked by cliffs and falls on one side and a flowered valley on the other. A few switchbacks snake down to a mountain meadow covered with lupine and magenta paintbrush. You can see the Indian Bar Shelter across the meadow. If you are camping here, follow the sign that points left (east) to an available site. Otherwise, continue south along the main trail.

From Indian Bar, the trail heads uphill steadily. Be sure to turn around to enjoy another great view of Mount Rainier. The top of a nearby knoll makes for a great picture spot if the weather is nice. The descent from the top leads to a wooded ridge. Mount Rainier disappears. Follow this ridge 3 miles to a fork in the trail.

At the fork, head left (southeast) toward Olallie Camp and Ohanapecosh. After descending abruptly for 1.3 miles, you cross Olallie Creek. Immediately after the crossing, a trail spurs to the left (north). The wooden sign for the camp is camouflaged in the forest, so keep an eye out for it if you plan to stay there.

The main trail keeps descending steeply until highway noises indicate that you are approaching Stevens Canyon Road, 17.1 miles from the trailhead. Cross the road and look for the trail a bit to the right (west). You reach the intersection with the Eastside Trail only a bit away from the road. Rather than turning sharply left (north) onto the Eastside Trail, continue south toward Silver Falls.

Stay to the left as you approach the falls. Turn left to get onto the Silver Falls Trail, and cross the Ohanapecosh River to the left (east). Enjoy Silver Falls, then continue east about 0.1 mile. A sign points the way to the Laughingwater Trail and your car.

Camping & services: Summerland Camp has five individual campsites and one group site. Although they are farther from the toilet than the other sites (except number 5, which has no view), we recommend camping at either site 3 or 4. Both have the best views. The water source for all sites is a stream that runs south along the main trail.

Indian Bar has three lovely, private individual sites and one group site with bunks within the shelter.

For more information: Contact the White River Wilderness Information Center, the Sunrise Visitor Center, or the Ohanapecosh Visitor Center (see Appendix A).

49 Sunrise Rim

Type of hike: Loop; day hike or overnighter.
Total distance: 4 miles (7.8 kilometers).
Difficulty: Easy.
Elevation gain: 840 feet.
Best months: August–September.
Maps: USGS Sunrise and White River; Trails Illustrated Mount Rainier National Park; Astronaut's Vista: Mount Rainier National Park, Washington; Earthwalk Press Hiking Map & Guide.
Starting point: Sunrise complex.

General description: A loop past Shadow Lake, over the first hump of Burroughs Mountain, to an overlook of the Emmons Glacier.

Finding the trailhead: From the White River Entrance Station, drive 13.8 miles west on White River Road to the Sunrise parking lot. Park and walk to the trailhead on the north end of the lot, to the right of the restrooms.

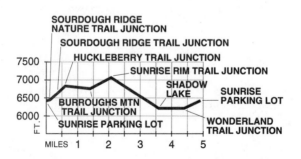

Sunrise Rim

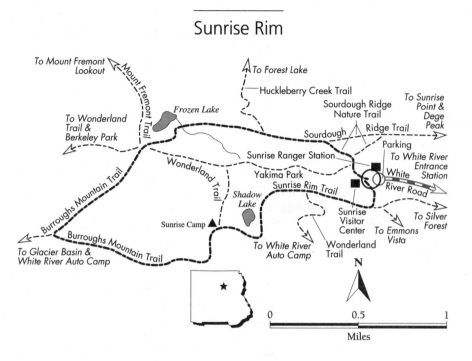

Parking & trailhead facilities: You should have no trouble finding a parking spot unless it is a sunny weekend, in which case you might have to choose an alternate hike. A number of facilities are located at the Sunrise complex, such as restrooms, a pay phone, a restaurant, a museum, and a gift shop.

Key points:

0.1	(0.2)	Junction with Sourdough Ridge Nature Trail.
0.3	(0.5)	Junction with Sourdough Ridge Trail.
0.6	(1.0)	Junction with Huckleberry Creek Trail.
1.4	(2.2)	Junction with Burroughs Mountain Trail.
2.1	(3.4)	First hump of Burroughs Mountain.
3.4	(5.4)	Sunrise Camp/Junction with Sunrise Rim Trail.
3.6	(5.8)	Shadow Lake.
4.4	(7.0)	Junction with Wonderland Trail.
4.9	(7.8)	Sunrise parking lot.

The hike: Great for kids and adults alike, this hike explores the scenic area around the Sunrise complex. You walk along Sourdough Ridge, climb to the first hump of Burroughs Mountain, and look over the Emmons Glacier. It is rare to cover such a wide range of landscapes and see such incredible views in such a short hike.

Walk up the paved path to the right (east) of the restrooms until you see a dirt trail on your right heading north. Get on the trail and walk up it until you come to the junction with the Sourdough Ridge Nature Trail. Turn left (northwest) onto the Sourdough Ridge Nature Trail and walk 0.2 mile to the Sourdough Ridge Trail. Then, turn left (west) onto the Sourdough Ridge Trail.

While you are walking along this trail, you can see the Cascades to your right and on really clear days you can even see Mount Baker. Mount Rainier also looks magnificent from Sourdough Ridge. You will walk a total of 0.3 mile along the ridge, 0.6 mile from the Sunrise complex, to the Huckleberry Creek Trail on your right, heading northwest. Stay to the left and on the Sourdough Ridge Trail for another 0.8 mile to the junction with Burroughs Mountain Trail. Directly before the junction, you pass Frozen Lake to your right (north). As the signs tell you, Frozen Lake is a domestic water supply; the National Park Service has fenced in the lake to avoid possible human contamination. The fence is not very aesthetically pleasing, but it is a necessity.

Once you have reached the five-trail junction, take the Burroughs Mountain Trail, which heads southwest. Steep snowfields cover this trail into August in most years. Sturdy boots and an ice axe are recommended. The trail up to the first hump of Burroughs Mountain gains about 200 feet and travels through alpine terrain. The vegetation in this area is very fragile and susceptible to human impact. Please stay on the trail to avoid damaging the delicate ecosystem.

From Burroughs Mountain, you can see Old Desolate to the northwest and Berkeley Park to the north. Old Desolate is a barren plateau that sticks out among forested hills. It is quite a contrast to the bright wildflowers that fill Berkeley Park.

When you reach the first hump of Burroughs Mountain, 0.7 mile from Frozen Lake, turn left (east). To the south is the Emmons Glacier, the largest glacier in the contiguous United States. A better view of the glacier comes from the glacier overlook, 1.1 miles away. It is all downhill to the overlook and to Sunrise Camp.

You can see all of the Emmons Glacier and the beginning of the White River from the glacial overlook. Goat Island Mountain towers above both of these natural wonders. The White River originates from the Emmons Glacier and is filled with sediment and glacial flour deposited from the glacier. Notice that there are several pools in the valley below. These pools appear sea-foam green due to the large concentration of sediment suspended in their waters. The sun reflects light off of the cloudy waters to produce this gorgeous color. It is amazing to imagine that the Emmons Glacier once filled the valley below. Global warming has reduced the glacier to its present size, but all glaciers in the park are presently advancing.

From the glacial overlook, continue heading downhill to Sunrise Camp, until you intersect with the Sunrise Rim Trail. To your left, an administrative road heads north and passes Sunrise Camp. Continue going east, but on the Sunrise Rim Trail instead of the Burroughs Mountain Trail.

After hiking 0.2 mile east on the Sunrise Rim Trail, a total of 3.6 miles into your hike, Shadow Lake appears to the left. Previous hikers have greatly damaged the area around Shadow Lake, the water source for Sunrise Camp. Again, please stay on the trail to reduce your personal impact on the lake.

The remainder of the loop travels through the subalpine meadows of Yakima Park. In July and early August, Yakima Park is filled with a variety of wildflowers. At times, you can see Goat Island Mountain and the Emmons

Glacier from the trail. The trail is flat until you intersect with the Wonderland Trail and then it travels gradually uphill all the way to the Sunrise parking lot.

Options: This hike has a myriad of options. At almost every trail junction, there is a desirable option. We recommend taking the Huckleberry Creek Trail to Forest Lake, a total of 2.6 miles out of your way. Another short side trip is to the Mount Fremont Lookout. At the Burroughs Mountain Trail junction, you come to the Mount Fremont Trail. This side trip is also a total of 2.6 miles long.

Camping & services: If you want to car camp, you can stay at the White River Campground, 5 miles past the White River Entrance Station. Unlike backcountry campsites, campfires are allowed. The nearest place to obtain gas and supplies is Greenwater, which is north on Washington Highway 410.

If you want to stay in the backcountry, you can stay at Sunrise Camp. There are eight sites available. None of the sites are very private, but number 8 is the most secluded. Try to snag sites 5 or 6; they have a great view of Shadow Lake.

For more information: Contact the White River Wilderness Information Center or Sunrise Visitor Center (see Appendix A).

Carbon River

Carbon River, tucked away in the northwestern corner of Mount Rainier National Park, is the closest section to the Seattle and Tacoma area. Even so, actually getting to the trailheads in Carbon River can involve traveling slowly on winding, dirt roads. The area contains Mount Rainier's only rain forest, rich in old-growth trees and a product of abundant rainfall and mild weather.

The Carbon River also originates here. The actual origin of the Carbon River is located at the end of the Carbon Glacier, which extends to a lower elevation than any other glacier in the contiguous United States. Carbon River Road was recently washed out by the river, but has since been restored and is scheduled to open in early 1999. Even so, the road may wash out again due to the unpredictability of glacial outburst floods.

50 Windy Gap

Type of hike: Out-and-back; day hike or overnighter.
Total distance: 11.2 miles (18.7 kilometers).
Difficulty: Strenuous.
Elevation gain: 3,450 feet.
Best months: Mid-July–September.
Maps: USGS Carbon River and Sunrise; Trails Illustrated Mount Rainier National Park; Astronaut's Vista: Mount Rainier National Park, Washington; Earthwalk Press Hiking Map & Guide.
Starting point: Ipsut Creek Campground.

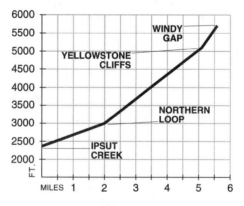

General description: A long, steep climb to impressive rock formations and a meadowed pass.

Windy Gap

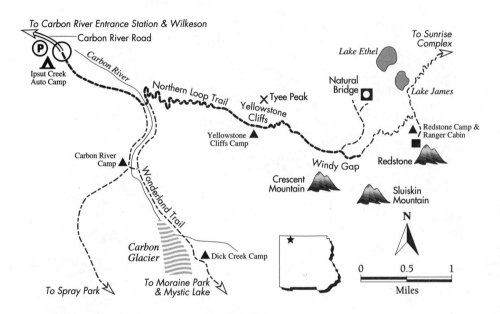

Finding the trailhead: From the Carbon River Entrance Station, drive 5 miles east on Carbon River Road. Ipsut Creek Campground marks the end of the 5 miles, the end of the road, and the trailhead.

Parking & trailhead facilities: If the many spaces at Ipsut Creek Campground are full, you can park along the road wherever "no parking" signs do not prohibit doing so. Toilets are also provided for your convenience.

Key points:

1.7	(3.3)	Junction with trail across Carbon River.
2.0	(3.7)	Northern Loop Trail junction.
5.1	(8.5)	Yellowstone Cliffs.
5.6	(9.3)	Independence Ridge Trail/Windy Gap.

The hike: Although it offers little in the way of views of Mount Rainier, the hike to Windy Gap increases elevation dramatically, ending in lovely high mountain meadows. From Ipsut Creek Campground, follow the Wonderland Trail bound southeast. The trail ascends very gently for the first 1.7 miles and crosses the Carbon River, at which point you reach the junction to the Northern Loop Trail.

Cross the silty waters of the Carbon River to the east bank. This crossing frequently washes out and sometimes remains so for weeks at a time. If fording the Carbon River seems too dangerous, you must follow the Wonderland Trail (southeast) for another mile, cross the Carbon River over the suspension bridge, then follow the Northern Loop Trail north 1 mile to reach

Windy Gap.

the spot where you would have otherwise crossed. Stay to the left (north) at the junction just beyond the Carbon River, heading toward Yellowstone Cliffs and Windy Gap. The trail now takes a turn toward the sky. In only 3 miles, it climbs more than 3,000 feet, making this a long and very steep hill. There is no view along the climb, save the foliage of the tall trees and low bushes, to distract you from the effort.

When the trees open up to reveal a steep mountain meadow covered with a variety of wildflowers, you know that you are near Yellowstone Cliffs. Almost immediately after entering the meadow, the trail forks. To your right (south), a small trail descends to Yellowstone Cliffs Camp. To your left (northeast), the main trail ascends toward Windy Gap. As you continue to switchback through fields of flowers, look to the north to admire Yellowstone Cliffs, a columned rock formation topped by Tyee Peak.

The switchbacks soon end in a subalpine clearing between two mountains and a ridge. About 0.5 mile beyond the junction to Yellowstone Cliffs Camp, an unmaintained trail spurs to the left (north). If you want to explore Yellowstone Cliffs, this trail bends southward, nearing Tyee Peak. Tread lightly, though: The subalpine meadow is fragile and susceptible to damage.

Back on the Northern Loop Trail, you enter Windy Gap less than 1 mile beyond the unmaintained spur trail. Nestled between Sluiskin Mountain and Independence Ridge, Windy Gap is a green meadow strewn with boulders. As you reach Windy Gap, you also come to the intersection with the Independence Ridge Trail, 5.6 miles into the hike. (See Options for more details about possible side trips from this point.) A clear stream, perfect for filtering water, bisects the gap. A great view can be had of the northeastern section of the park.

If you do not plan on camping at either Redstone or Yellowstone Cliffs Camp, retrace your footsteps back to Ipsut Creek Campground.

Options: If you have the time and energy, you should take the side trip along Independence Ridge to the natural bridge. Do not continue on the unmaintained trail beyond the spur trail to the natural bridge, but do descend to the natural bridge. The arching rocks are a wonder of nature. Only 0.9 mile to the natural bridge, this side trip adds 1.8 miles to your hike.

If you would like to fish at Lake James or stay at Redstone Camp, you should continue east along the Northern Loop Trail. The trail leads down Windy Gap, into a boulder field and through a forest to Redstone Camp, 0.7 mile east of Windy Gap. To find Lake James, bypass the trail to Redstone Camp and hike another 1.3 miles. A mileage sign in the middle of the trail attempts to dissuade of people from going to this area. Overuse in the 1970s led to the destruction of the land around Lake James, but recent efforts at recovery are proving successful. You can still fish at Lake James and the lake beyond it, Lake Ethel, but please avoid straying from the path. Take the trail to the left (northwest) and you encouter Lake James in less than 0.2 mile. If you stay at Redstone Camp, you add 2.6 miles of trail to your hike. If you go to Lake James to fish, you add 4 miles.

Camping & services: Yellowstone Cliffs Camp has a fantastic view of, what else, Yellowstone Cliffs. It also has two nice campsites, number 1 having the better view, and a close proximity to water.

Redstone Camp, a replacement for Lake James Camp while it is being repaired, has two nice sites, although it offers little in the way of a view, no food storage pole, and a short trek to water.

Ipsut Creek Campground has a picnic area, toilets, and camping areas. The nearest gas station is in Wilkeson, 17 miles north of the Carbon River Entrance Station on Washington Highway 165. For more extensive services, go to Buckley or Enumclaw, both north of Wilkeson on WA 165.

For more information: Contact the Wilkeson Wilderness Information Center (see Appendix A).

51 Carbon Glacier and Moraine

Type of hike: Out-and-back; day hike or overnighter.
Total distance: 8.2 miles (13.7 kilometers).
Difficulty: Moderate.
Elevation gain: 1,200 feet.
Best months: Mid-July–September.
Maps: USGS Carbon River; Trails Illustrated Mount Rainier National Park; Astronaut's Vista: Mount Rainier National Park, Washington; Earthwalk Press Hiking Map & Guide.
Starting point: Ipsut Creek Campground.

General description: A moderate ascent to the foot of the Carbon Glacier, the lowest elevation glacier in the contiguous states.

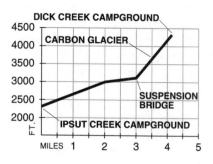

Finding the trailhead: From the Carbon River Entrance Station, drive 5 miles east on Carbon River Road. Ipsut Creek Campground marks the end of the 5 miles, the end of the road, and the trailhead.

Parking & trailhead facilities: If the many spaces at Ipsut Creek Campground are full, you can park along the road wherever "no parking" signs do not prohibit doing so. The campground has toilets for your convenience.

Key points:
2.0	(3.3)	Northern Loop Trail junction.
3.0	(5.0)	Second junction/Carbon River Camp.
3.4	(5.7)	Carbon Glacier.
4.1	(6.8)	Dick Creek Camp.

Carbon Glacier and Moraine

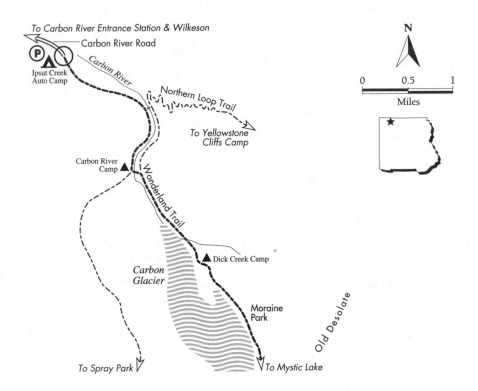

The hike: Follow the Wonderland Trail heading southeast from the end of Carbon River Road. A spur trail almost immediately intersects to the right (west). This trail leads to a small falls on Ipsut Creek. Visit the falls if you want. Otherwise, continue southeast on the Wonderland Trail. For the first 3 miles of the hike, the trail is very wide and gradually uphill. At the 2-mile point, the Northern Loop Trail leads to the left (east) across the Carbon River. To cross the river on a suspension bridge, rather than the prepared logs at this crossing, stay to the right (south) along the Wonderland Trail.

About 1 mile beyond that junction, 3 miles into the hike, the trail forks. Carbon River Camp is 0.1 mile before this junction. If you do not plan to camp here, follow the Wonderland Trail east across the suspension bridge over the Carbon River. This bridge offers a fantastic view above the Carbon River. Its source, the massive, black Carbon Glacier, rests only 0.4 mile upstream. On the other side of the Carbon River, stay to the right (south) ascending toward the glacier and Dick Creek. The easy grade gives way to a steep pitch. The trees open up to reveal the Carbon Glacier with Mount Rainier towering above. Rubble and debris from the glacier carving the earth litter the blue ice of the Carbon Glacier. Do not be surprised to hear the echoing crashes of falling rocks.

Suspension bridge over the Carbon River.

For the next 0.7 mile, climb steeply parallel to the Carbon Glacier to Dick Creek Camp. If you plan on camping, Dick Creek Camp has a spectacular view and nice sites. If you do not, spend some time here anyway, admiring the Northern Crags over the Carbon Glacier. The main trail leads right by camp. If you have time, we strongly recommend venturing to Moraine Park. (See Options.) If not, follow the same trail back to Ipsut Campground.

Options: From Dick Creek Camp, the next 2 miles of trail climb steadily, switching back and forth through a forest. The grade lessens when the path begins to run along Moraine Creek. You enter Moraine Park, a boulder-strewn meadow. Keep in mind that this is bear country. In fact, a fellow hiker said that she has not come to this area without seeing a bear. When we were here, we came across a small black bear that was not easily deterred by loud voices, banging pots, and shrill singing. Beyond the streambed, you come to a rock field, then a larger mountain meadow. You can see Mount

Rainier above the wildflowers. From here, you can either move on to Mystic Lake or return the way you came. The path to Moraine Park increases your total mileage by 5 miles round trip.

Camping & services: If you plan to backpack, you have two options in the way of camps: Carbon River and Dick Creek. We suggest camping at Dick Creek Camp. The sites are few (two), but it has an amazing view of the Carbon Glacier and a great water source (Dick Creek).

Ipsut Creek Campground has a picnic area, toilets, and camping areas. The nearest gas station is in Wilkeson, 17 miles north of the Carbon River Entrance Station on Washington Highway 165. For more extensive services, go to Buckley or Enumclaw, both north of Wilkeson on WA 165.

For more information: Contact the Wilkeson Wilderness Information Center (see Appendix A).

52 Mystic Lake

Type of hike: Out-and-back; day hike or overnighter.
Total distance: 15 miles (23.3 kilometers).
Difficulty: Strenuous.
Elevation gain: 3,900 feet.
Best months: Mid-July–September.
Maps: USGS Carbon River and Sunrise; Trails Illustrated Mount Rainier National Park; Astronaut's Vista: Mount Rainier National Park, Washington; Earthwalk Press Hiking Map & Guide.
Starting point: Ipsut Creek Campground.

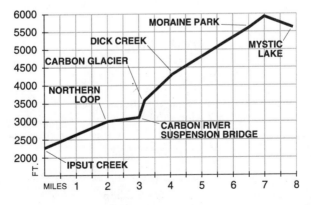

General description: A difficult ascent around a glacier to a high mountain meadow and finally to Mystic Lake.

Mystic Lake

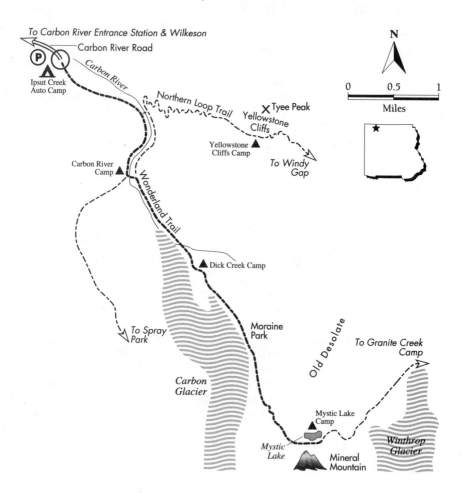

Finding the trailhead: From the Carbon River Entrance Station, drive 5 miles east on Carbon River Road. Ipsut Creek Campground marks the end of the 5 miles, the end of the road, and the trailhead.

Parking & trailhead facilities: If the many spaces at Ipsut Creek Campground are full, you can park along the road wherever "no parking" signs do not prohibit doing so. The campground has toilets for your convenience.

Key points:

2.0	(3.3)	Northern Loop Trail junction.
3.0	(5.0)	Second junction/Carbon River Camp.
3.4	(5.7)	Carbon Glacier.
4.1	(6.8)	Dick Creek Camp.
6.6	(11.0)	Moraine Park.
7.5	(12.5)	Mystic Lake.

Carbon Glacier.

The hike: Follow the Wonderland Trail heading southeast from the end of Carbon River Road. A spur trail almost immediately intersects to the right (west). This trail leads to a small falls on Ipsut Creek. Visit the falls if you want. Otherwise, continue southeast on the Wonderland Trail. For the first

3 miles of the hike, the trail is very wide and gradually uphill. At the 2-mile point, the Northern Loop Trail leads to the left (east) across the Carbon River. To cross the river on a suspension bridge, rather than the prepared logs of this crossing, stay to the right (south) along the Wonderland Trail.

About 1 mile beyond that junction, 3 miles into the hike, the trail forks. Carbon River Camp is 0.1 mile before this junction. If you do not plan to camp here, follow the Wonderland Trail east across the suspension bridge over the Carbon River. This bridge offers a fantastic view high above the Carbon River. Its source, the massive, black Carbon Glacier, rests only 0.4 mile upstream. On the other side of the Carbon River, stay to the right (south), ascending toward the glacier and Dick Creek. The easy grade gives way to a steep pitch. The trees open up to reveal the Carbon Glacier with Mount Rainier towering above. Rubble and debris from the glacier carving the earth litter the blue ice of the Carbon Glacier. Do not be surprised to hear the echoing crashes of falling rocks.

For the next 0.7 mile, the trail climbs steeply parallel to the Carbon Glacier to Dick Creek Camp. If you plan on camping, Dick Creek Camp has a spectacular view and nice sites. If you do not, spend some time here anyway, admiring the Northern Crags over the Carbon Clacier. The main trail leads through camp. The next 2 miles of trail climb steadily, switching back and forth through a forest. The grade lessens when the path begins to run along Moraine Creek. Keep in mind that this is bear country. In fact, a fellow hiker said that she has not come to this area without seeing a bear. When we were here, we came across a small black bear that was not easily deterred by loud voices, banging pots, and shrill singing.

Beyond the streambed, you come to a rock field, then a large mountain meadow. At this point, you have only two small hills to climb before beginning your descent to Mystic Lake. The lake rests in a valley between Mineral Mountain and the appropriately named Old Desolate. The view at the lake is beautiful, but it cannot be seen from Mystic Lake Camp, 0.2 mile down the trail. You can either stay at this camp or return to Ipsut Creek Campground.

Camping & services: You can stay at one of three backcountry camps along the way: Carbon River, Dick Creek, or Mystic Lake. We recommend either Dick Creek or Mystic Lake. Dick Creek Camp, one of our favorite backcountry camps, has two nice sites. Site 1 has an unbelievable view of the Carbon Glacier. Dick Creek, its water source, is also only a short walk away.

Mystic Lake Camp is unfortunately located quite a distance from the lake. An established camp along the Wonderland Trail, this camp has a whopping seven individual sites and two group sites, all with good tent sites but little privacy. Two flimsy food storage poles offer little protection from a bear that apparently frequents this camp. Use the poles to protect your food from the mice and chipmunks, which are more of a nuisance.

For more information: Contact the Wilkeson Wilderness Information Center (see Appendix A).

53 Green Lake

Type of hike: Out-and-back; day hike.
Total distance: 3.6 miles (6 kilometers).
Difficulty: Moderate.
Elevation gain: 1,000 feet.
Best months: May–September.
Maps: USGS Carbon River; Trails Illustrated Mount Rainier National Park; Astronaut's Vista: Mount Rainier National Park, Washington; Earthwalk Press Hiking Map & Guide.
Starting point: Green Lake Trailhead.

General description: A moderate, two-hour hike past a waterfall to a small, quaint lake in the northwestern region of the park.

Finding the trailhead: From the Carbon River Entrance Station, drive 3 miles east on Carbon River Road. The Green Lake Trailhead is well marked by Ranger Creek to the right (south) and a small parking lot to the left (north).

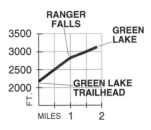

Parking & trailhead facilities: The Green Lake Trailhead has few available spaces. Cars often line the road, parked on either side. It offers no services.

Green Lake.

Green Lake

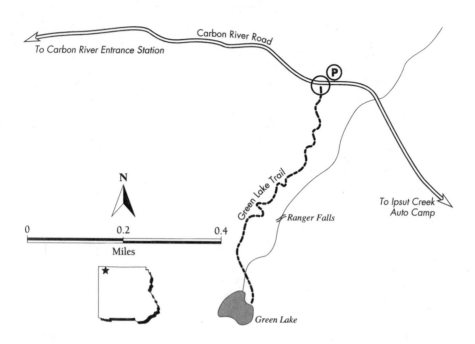

Key points:

1.0	(1.7)	Ranger Falls.
1.5	(2.5)	Ranger Creek crossing.
1.8	(3.0)	Green Lake.

The hike: The hike to Green Lake attracts many late spring hikers because the snow clears earlier on this trail than most others in the park. Its traffic may lessen as the other trails open, but its charm does not.

Dense, green rain forest and the gurgling sound of streams surround you as you ascend this moderate hill. After only 1 mile, the gurgling becomes churning. A very short jaunt to the left (east) leads you to a close-up view of Ranger Falls, and the right takes you to Green Lake.

Only 0.5 mile beyond Ranger Falls on the way to Green Lake, you must cross Ranger Creek. No fording is necessary, but the log bridge with only wire for a grip gets a bit slippery when wet, so cross carefully.

Less than 0.3 mile beyond the bridge, you come upon Green Lake. One glance, and the inspiration for the name becomes apparent. Surrounded by evergreens, the water reflects their emerald hue. The surrounding mountains shelter the water, keeping it placid. From a small clearing at the trail's end, a nice view of Tolmie Peak can be seen across the lake. No trails run around the lake for further exploration, but the small clearing is a good place to picnic or just rest before descending along the same path.

Option: If you would rather not hike the full 3.6 miles round trip, turning back at Ranger Falls shortens the hike to only 2 miles round trip, and the falls still make the effort worthwhile.

Camping & services: You can car camp at Ipsut Creek Campground, 2 miles east of the Green Lake Trailhead on Carbon River Road. A pay phone and restrooms are provided at the Carbon River Entrance Station. You can also find restrooms at Ipsut Creek Campground.

For more information: Contact the Wilkeson Wilderness Information Center (see Appendix A).

54 Paul Peak Trail

> **Type of hike:** Out-and-back; day hike.
> **Total distance:** 8 miles (13 kilometers).
> **Difficulty:** Moderate.
> **Elevation gain:** 1,820 feet.
> **Best months:** May–October.
> **Maps:** USGS Golden Lakes; Trails Illustrated Mount Rainier National Park; Astronaut's Vista: Mount Rainier National Park, Washington, Earthwalk Press Hiking Map & Guide.
> **Starting point:** Paul Peak Trailhead.

General description: A relatively short descent along the side of Paul Peak to the Wonderland Trail and the Mowich River.

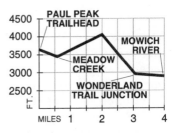

Finding the trailhead: From Wilkeson, stay on Washington Highway 165 for 9 miles until the road forks. Stay to the right (south) at this fork, the way to Mowich Lake. After 3.2 miles, the road turns into a well-maintained dirt road, although it can be very slippery and downright dangerous when muddy. Follow this road for another 8.8 miles to the Paul Peak Trailhead on the right (south) side of the road. There is a fee station at the trailhead; make sure to pay the entrance fee before heading off on your trip.

Parking & trailhead facilities: There is a restroom at the trailhead and a small parking lot.

Key points:

0.6	(1.0)	Meadow Creek.
3.1	(5.0)	Junction with the Wonderland Trail.
4.0	(6.5)	North Mowich River.

Paul Peak Trail

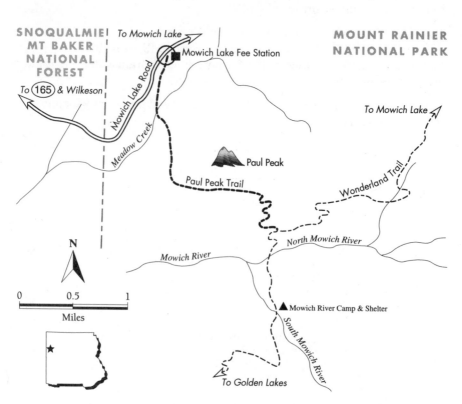

The hike: The Paul Peak Trail is one of the few park trails that is completely snow free in May. For this reason, the traffic on this trail is commonly heavy in May and dwindles further into the summer. The trail takes you over a pleasant creek and through a beautiful forest, and the Mowich River offers a destination worth the distance.

The first 0.6 mile of the trail is steep down to Meadow Creek. At the bottom of the hill, a wide sturdy bridge crosses the clear waters of Meadow Creek. Although it is early on in the hike, it is worth spending a little time at Meadow Creek, which originates from Eunice Lake.

After Meadow Creek, the trail gradually climbs uphill for the next 2 miles through the forest. On a foggy morning, the hazy sunlight shines through the trees and makes the forest seem eerie, even magical.

After about 2.5 miles, you will arrive at another set of downhill switchbacks that drop to the Wonderland Trail. They are relatively steep at points, probably because they cover a little over 1,000 feet in only 1 mile.

At the junction with the Wonderland Trail, go right (south) and continue on the Wonderland Trail 0.9 mile to the North Mowich River. After enjoying the river's environs, turn around and retrace your steps to the trailhead. Be sure to leave plenty of time for the 1 mile climb from the Wonderland Trail junction.

Bridge over Meadow Creek.

Options: If it is at least mid-July, or later you can hike from the Paul Peak Trailhead to Mowich Lake. At the junction with the Wonderland Trail, go left (northwest) for 3.2 miles to Mowich Lake. This one-way hike would be a total of 6.3 miles long and would require a two-car shuttle.

Camping & services: To extend this hike into an overnighter, consider staying at Mowich River Camp. You can also camp at Mowich Lake Campground the night before you head out, if you want to get an early start. Campfires are prohibited at this campground. The nearest place to get gas and supplies is Wilkeson on Washington Highway 165.

For more information: Contact the Wilkeson Wilderness Information Center in Wilkeson (see Appendix A).

55 Tolmie Peak

Type of hike: Out-and-back; day hike.
Total distance: 6.5 miles (10.8 kilometers).
Difficulty: Moderate.
Elevation gain: 1,020 feet.
Best months: Mid-July–September.
Maps: USGS Carbon River; Trails Illustrated Mount Rainier National Park; Astronaut's Vista: Mount Rainier National Park, Washington; Earthwalk Press Hiking Map & Guide.
Starting point: Mowich Lake Campground.

General description: A very popular half-day hike through forest and meadow to a fire lookout atop Tolmie Peak with a spectacular view of the northwestern side of Mount Rainier.

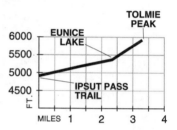

Finding the trailhead: From Wilkeson, drive 9 miles south on Washington Highway 165. Where Carbon River Road joins in, stay to the right on WA 165. The pavement ends 3.2 miles beyond the intersection. You have to drive along a dirt road for 8.8 miles to reach the park boundary, and another 5.3 miles to Mowich Lake Campground, which has a small parking lot. Many trails originate here; the trail to Tolmie Peak (Wonderland Trail) will be to your immediate left.

Key points:
1.3 (2.2) Ipsut Pass Trail junction.
2.2 (3.7) Eunice Lake.
3.1 (5.2) Tolmie Peak Lookout.
3.2 (5.3) Tolmie Peak.

The hike: The hike to Tolmie Peak is one of the most popular in the park for many reasons. You do not have to pass through an entrance station to reach the trailhead, but be certain that you pay the required amount at the fee station, 11 miles after the intersection with Carbon River Road. The hike is not too long, nor too rigorous, and the rewards are immense. The view of Mount Rainier from Tolmie Peak is absolutely breathtaking.

From Mowich Lake Campground, follow the trail to the left heading north. The trail hugs the west side of Mowich Lake for about 0.5 mile before leaving the lake side and heading northwest. After reaching the top of a small hill, continue another 0.5 mile on flat terrain to the junction with the Tolmie Peak Trail. At the junction turn left (west).

After turning, you immediately begin to descend steeply. At the bottom of this hill, about 2 miles into the hike, the trail forks. The trail to the left is an unmaintained social trail created by those eager to see a rather unimpressive

Tolmie Peak

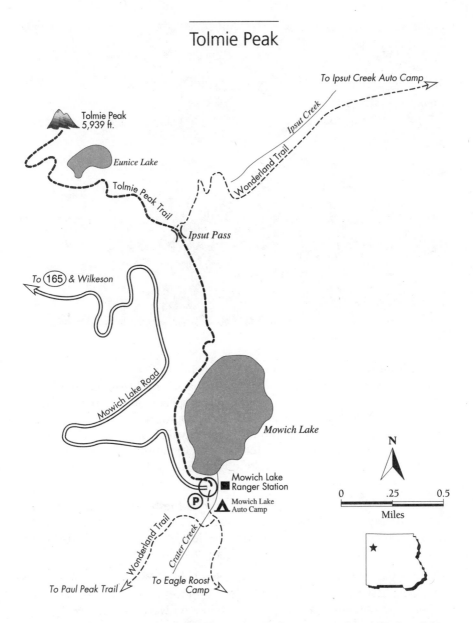

waterfall only a few paces off the beaten path. Stay to the right (north) to continue the journey to Eunice Lake and Tolmie Peak.

At this point, the trail begins a steep climb through via switchbacks. In mid-July, as you approach Eunice Lake you step into a field blanketed by avalanche lilies. The lake's aqua waters are surrounded by jutting peaks and subalpine forest.

A sign points the way to Tolmie Peak, with only 0.8 mile remaining of the 3.1 miles total to the lookout. Stay to the left (west) on the marked trail around the lake. Those who have ventured off have spoiled the land, killing the fragile meadow plants and creating an array of ugly paths to the lake.

View of Mount Rainier from Tolmie Peak.

The trail reaches the northwestern part of the lake in 0.2 mile. It then begins to ascend by means of long switchbacks until reaching the Tolmie Peak Lookout. The view from the lookout is spectacular. To the north, you see an expanse of rolling mountains. To the south, however, you see one of the best panoramic views of Mount Rainier available in the park.

The more adventurous can carefully walk the unmaintained trail along a ridge for 0.1 mile to the true Tolmie Peak. The trail is not steep, but it is rocky and a bit tricky at points.

Options: Rather than hiking all the way to the top of Tolmie Peak, you could go only as far as Eunice Lake. This option would cut 2 miles off the total distance. Eunice Lake is absolutely delightful, and the fields of avalanche lilies present in July are amazing.

Camping & services: For no fee, Mowich Lake Campground offers campsites on a first-come, first-served basis. Campfires are prohibited. The nearest place to obtain gas and supplies is Wilkeson North on WA 165.

For more information: Contact the Wilkeson Wilderness Information Center (see Appendix A).

56 Mother Mountain

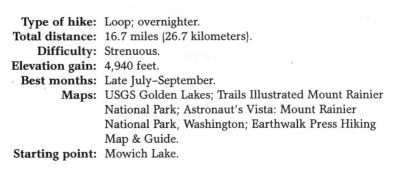

Type of hike: Loop; overnighter.
Total distance: 16.7 miles (26.7 kilometers).
Difficulty: Strenuous.
Elevation gain: 4,940 feet.
Best months: Late July–September.
Maps: USGS Golden Lakes; Trails Illustrated Mount Rainier National Park; Astronaut's Vista: Mount Rainier National Park, Washington; Earthwalk Press Hiking Map & Guide.
Starting point: Mowich Lake.

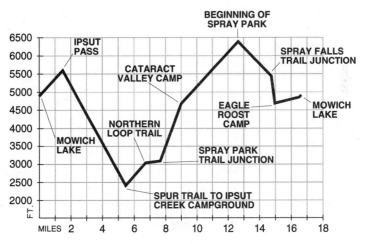

General description: A strenuous loop through the scenic meadows of Spray Park and Seattle Park and around massive Mother Mountain.

Finding the trailhead: From Wilkeson, drive 9 miles south on Washington Highway 165 to where the road forks. Stay to the right (south) at this fork, the way to Mowich Lake. After 3.2 miles, the road turns into a well-maintained dirt road, although it can be slippery when muddy. Follow this road another 8.8 miles to the Paul Peak Trailhead on the right (south) side of the road. Pause here to pay the entrance fee at the fee station. Then continue south and east another 5.3 miles to Mowich Lake (a total of 26.3 miles from Wilkeson).

Parking & trailhead facilities: There are restrooms at Mowich Lake, but they get pretty rancid from excessive use. The parking lot is fairly big, although on weekends you might have to park along the road.

Key points:
1.5   (2.4)   Ipsut Pass.
5.1   (8.2)   Junction with spur trail to Ipsut Creek Campground.

Mother Mountain

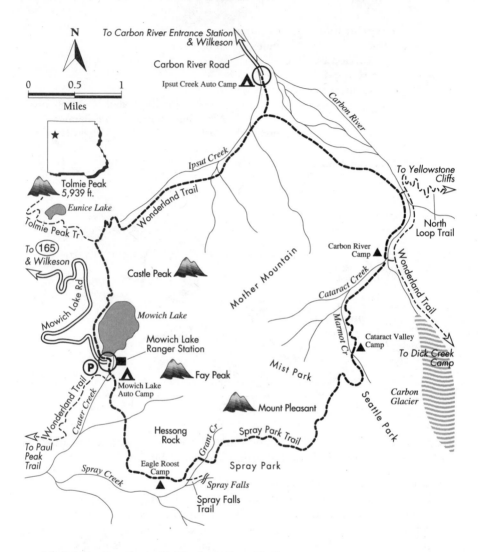

6.8 (10.9) Junction with Northern Loop Trail.
7.7 (12.3) Junction with Spray Park Trail.
9.0 (14.4) Cataract Valley Camp.
12.7 (20.3) The beginning of Spray Park.
14.8 (23.7) Junction with Spray Falls Trail.
15.0 (24.0) Eagle Roost Camp.
16.5 (26.4) Junction with Wonderland Trail.
16.7 (26.7) Mowich Lake.

The hike: Named for the impressive mountain it encircles, this loop affords
excellent views of Mount Rainier and travels through Spray Park and Seattle

Mount Rainier from Spray Park.

Park. Note that the second day of your hike contains most of the scenery and uphill hiking. There is one difficult hill, from the Spray Park Trail junction to Spray Park; break it up by staying at Cataract Valley Camp the first night.

From the Mowich Lake parking lot, go to the Wonderland Trail that runs along the west side of Mowich Lake. There are several paths down to this trail, but the only trail that runs north-south along Mowich Lake is the Wonderland Trail. Head north on the Wonderland Trail. The first 0.5 mile continues along Mowich Lake and then slopes gently uphill to the top of Ipsut Pass. Just before the top of Ipsut Pass, the Tolmie Peak Trail splits left (west). Stay right (north) traveling on the Wonderland Trail.

The first 0.5 mile of the descent down Ipsut Pass is very steep and open. If it is a hot day, be sure to drink plenty of water and be thankful you are not going the other direction! You can see Castle Peak to your right (east) towering above the valley. After 0.5 mile of steep downhill, the trail levels out a little and heads into the forest, but it is still downhill for the next 3.1 miles. You will cross several clear streams on the descent, in case you need to filter water.

The next 2.6 miles to the Spray Park Trail climb, easily along the Carbon River, whose waters run brown from an abundance of glacier silt. Do not try to filter this water, it will ruin your filter. If it is a necessity, let the silt settle in a container before filtering. The trail is lined with bushes, and in August the thimbleberries are ripe for the picking. You can see the north side of Mother Mountain at times, but the south side is much more impressive.

At the junction with the Spray Park Trail head west (right), unless you are taking the option to the Carbon Glacier. (See Options.) Steep switchbacks lead to Cataract Valley Camp, 1.2 miles from the Spray Park Trail junction and 8.8 miles into the hike. Keep in mind you have to gain 1,600 feet before reaching camp. If you are a berry lover, this trail to Cataract Camp is often lined with salmonberries and blueberries in August.

On the second day, you will continue up the hill, gaining another 1,700 feet. The trail travels through forest at first, but when the trail opens up you know you are in Seattle Park. Even though you only travel through a corner of Seattle Park, the green grass of Seattle Park is breathtaking, as are the charming little streams that wind through the meadows. From Seattle Park, you can see Mother Mountain's jagged peaks.

Continuing uphill, you come to several snowfields. How many snow-fields you encounter depends on the time of year, although at least one lingers here all year. Flags, painted rocks, and cairns help you through the snowfields, but we recommend not attempting this hike until August unless you have well-tuned navigational skills. Later on in the season, it is easier to find your way, but people often get temporarily lost, especially if it is foggy.

When you start heading downhill, you have entered Spray Park. Mount Rainier towers majestically above, with Tillicum Point jutting out its side. Marmots and lupine fill the meadows of Spray Park. As you head downhill, you will see Hessong Rock and Mount Pleasant in front of you.

It is downhill to the end of Spray Park, with more downhill to the junction with Spray Falls Trail, 14.8 miles into the hike. Take the side trip to Spray Falls when you reach this junction. (See Options.) From the Spray Falls junction, it's only 1.9 miles to the Mowich Lake parking lot and the end of the loop. A viewpoint from Eagle Cliff, which has a great view of the North Mowich Glacier, is located 0.4 mile after the junction with the Spray Falls Trail. This home stretch takes you over gentle rolling hills, a relief after the previous severe elevation gains and losses.

Options: Some hikers prefer to do this loop counterclockwise, which means climbing the steep side of Ipsut Pass (a 3,000-foot climb). Weather may dictate which direction to hike the loop—go counterclockwise if the day you start on is clear and the following day is forecast to be cloudy. This way you will not miss the spectacular scenery in Spray Park.

A side trip to the Carbon Glacier is well worth the trip. It is only 1 mile round trip from the junction with the Spray Park Trail. (See Hike 51: Carbon Glacier and Moraine.) The side trip to Spray Falls, only 0.1 mile one way from the junction with the main trail, is also worthwhile.

Camping & services: Both backcountry camps, Carbon River Camp and Cataract Valley Camp, allow stoves only, as is the case in all backcountry camps. You can stay at either Carbon River Camp or Cataract Valley Camp depending on their availability and your itinerary.

Carbon River Camp has four individual sites, and the park service is in the process of adding a group site. The first two sites have excellent tent sites but are not very private. On the other hand, sites 3 and 4 are more secluded with slanted tent sites, site 4 being the most remote. The water source for this camp is Cataract Creek, a good 0.1 mile from all the sites.

Cataract Valley Camp has seven individual sites and a group site for parties with more than five people. The most reliable water source is located in the center of the camp. There are normally two small streams in early summer, but one dries up later on in the season. Sites 3, 4, and 5 are located in the center of camp, all very flat and all relatively spacious. The group site is much bigger and has the same attractive qualities. Sites 6 and 7 are tucked away at the end of camp next to a rock field. The tent site at site 6 is definitely lacking, but 7 is very flat and spacious. Sites 1 and 2 are at the beginning of camp next to the outhouse. Avoid site 1 if possible, but site 2 can fit one tent without too much difficulty. The nearest place to obtain gas and supplies is Wilkeson north on WA 165.

For more information: Contact the Wilkeson Wilderness Information Center in Wilkeson (see Appendix A).

57 Yellowstone Cliffs

Type of hike: Out-and-back; day hike or overnighter.
Total distance: 10.2 miles (16.7 kilometers).
Difficulty: Strenuous.
Elevation gain: 2,950 feet.
Best months: Mid-July–September.
Maps: USGS Carbon River and Sunrise; Trails Illustrated Mount Rainier National Park; Astronaut's Vista: Mount Rainier National Park, Washington; Earthwalk Press Hiking Map & Guide.
Starting point: Ipsut Creek Campground.

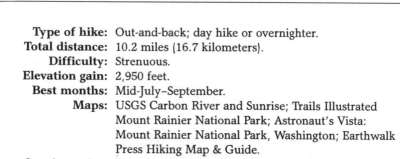

General description: A long, steep climb to impressive rock formations and a meadowed pass.

Finding the trailhead: From the Carbon River Entrance Station, drive 5 miles east on Carbon River Road. Ipsut Creek Campground marks the end of the 5 miles, the end of the road, and the trailhead.

Yellowstone Cliffs

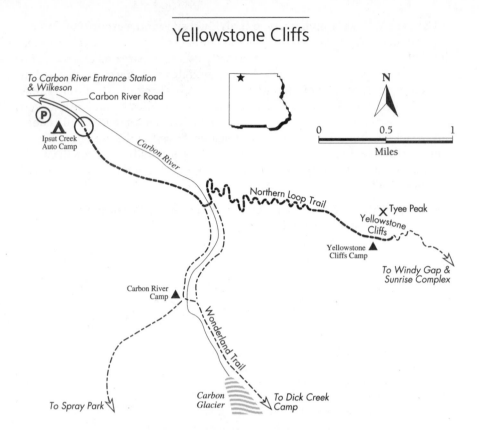

Parking & trailhead facilities: If the many spaces at Ipsut Creek Campground are full, you can park along the road wherever "no parking" signs do not prohibit doing so. Toilets are also provided for your convenience.

Key points:

1.7	(3.3)	Junction with trail across Carbon River.
2.0	(3.7)	Northern Loop Trail junction.
5.1	(8.5)	Yellowstone Cliffs.

The hike: Although it offers little in the way of views of Mount Rainier, the hike to Yellowstone Cliffs increases elevation dramatically, resulting in lovely high mountain meadows. From Ipsut Creek Campground, follow the Wonderland Trail southeast. The trail ascends very gently for the first 1.7 miles, at which point you reach the junction to the Northern Loop Trail.

Cross the silty waters of the Carbon River to the east bank. This crossing frequently washes out, and sometimes remains so for weeks at a time. If fording the Carbon River seems too dangerous, you must follow the Wonderland Trail (southeast) for another mile, cross the Carbon River over the suspension bridge, then follow the Northern Loop Trail north for 1 mile to reach the spot where you would have otherwise crossed. Stay to the left (north) at the junction just beyond the Carbon River, heading toward

Yellowstone Cliffs.

Yellowstone Cliffs and Windy Gap. The trail now takes a turn toward the sky. In only 3 miles, you ascend more than 3,000 feet, making this a long and very steep hill. There is no view, save the foliage of the tall trees and low bushes, to relieve the tedium of the climb.

When the trees open up to reveal a steep mountain meadow covered with a variety of wildflowers, you know that Yellowstone Cliffs are near. Almost immediately after entering the meadow, the trail forks. To your right (south), a small trail descends to Yellowstone Cliffs Camp. If you plan to stay here, descend the 0.2 mile to a small creek, two campsites, and a brilliant view of the cliffs above.

To your left (northeast), the main trail ascends toward Windy Gap, an option as a day hike. (See Options.) As you continue to switchback through fields of flowers, look north to admire Yellowstone Cliffs, a columned rock formation topped by Tyee Peak.

Options: Adding less than 2 miles round trip, Windy Gap is a marvelous side trip along the Yellowstone Cliffs hike. Nestled between Sluiskin Mountain and Independence Ridge, Windy Gap is a green meadow strewn with boulders. As you reach Windy Gap, you also come to the intersection with the Independence Ridge Trail, 5.6 miles into the hike. A clear stream, perfect for filtering water, bisects the gap. A great view can be had of the northeastern section of the park and beyond.

If you have the time and energy, you should take the side trip along Independence Ridge to the natural bridge. Do not continue on the unmaintained trail beyond the spur trail to the natural bridge, but do descend to the natural bridge. The arching rocks are a wonder of nature. Only 0.9 mile to the natural bridge, this side trip adds 1.8 miles to your hike.

Camping & services: Yellowstone Cliffs Camp has a fantastic view of Yellowstone Cliffs. It also has two nice campsites, number 1 having the better view, and a close proximity to water.

Ipsut Creek Campground has a picnic area and toilets. The nearest gas station is in Wilkeson, 17 miles north of the Carbon River Entrance Station on Washington Highway 165. For more extensive services, go to Buckley or Enumclaw, both north of Wilkeson on WA 165.

For more information: Contact the Wilkeson Wilderness Information Center (see Appendix A).

58 Spray Park

Type of hike:	Out-and-back; day hike.
Total distance:	8 miles (12.8 kilometers).
Difficulty:	Easy.
Elevation gain:	1,929 feet round trip.
Best months:	Late July–September.
Maps:	USGS Golden Lakes; Trails Illustrated Mount Rainier National Park; Astronaut's Vista: Mount Rainier National Park, Washington; Earthwalk Press Hiking Map & Guide.
Starting point:	Mowich Lake.

General description: A short hike to the top of Spray Park with excellent views of Mount Rainier and Mother Mountain.

Finding the trailhead: From Wilkeson, drive 9 miles south on Washington Highway 165 until the road forks. Stay to the right (south) at this fork, the way to Mowich Lake. After 3.2 miles, the road turns into a well-maintained dirt road, although it can be very slippery when muddy. Follow this road for another 8.8 miles to the Paul Peak Trailhead on the right (south) side of the road. Pause to pay the entrance fee at the fee station here. Then continue south and east another 5.3 miles to Mowich Lake, a total of 26.3 miles from Wilkeson.

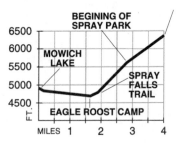

Parking & trailhead facilities: There are restrooms at Mowich Lake, but they get pretty rancid from excessive use. The parking lot is fairly big, although on weekends you might have to park along the road.

Key points:

0.2	(0.3)	Junction with the Spray Park Trail.
1.7	(2.7)	Junction with spur trail to Eagle Roost Camp.
1.9	(3.0)	Spray Falls Trail junction.
2.8	(4.5)	The beginning of Spray Park.
4.0	(6.4)	The end of Spray Park.

The hike: The Spray Park Trail is very popular and rightfully so considering the amazing views of Mount Rainier available from Spray Park. You can also see Mother Mountain, Mount Pleasant, and Hessong Rock. Hoary marmots and lupine fill the rocky meadows of Spray Park. The first 1.9 miles of the trail dip and climb over rolling hills, and then it is uphill all the way to the end of Spray Park.

Head to the south end of the Mowich Lake parking lot, past the restrooms and campground to the trailhead. Head south on the Wonderland Trail and travel downhill for 0.2 mile to the next junction. Go left (southeast) where the Spray Park Trail forks off from the Wonderland Trail. There is a short spur trail about a mile from the junction that leads to a viewpoint over Eagle Cliff, a total of 1.5 miles into your hike. You can see the North Mowich Glacier clearly from the viewpoint.

When you have traveled 1.7 miles total, you will see the signs for Eagle Roost Camp, which is less than 0.1 mile away and south of the Spray Park Trail. Just 0.2 mile beyond Eagle Roost Camp is the junction with the Spray Falls Trail. This is a worthy option. (See Options.) If you choose not to see Spray Falls, stay left and head northeast up the trail. There is no official beginning for Spray Park, but it probably starts when the forest thins and Hessong Rock appears to the north of the trail.

Spray Park continues for 1.2 miles to its highest point before the trail starts descending into Seattle Park. There is a permanent snowfield at this point, but how many snowfields you encounter depends on the time of year. Flags, painted rocks, and cairns help you through the snowfields, but we recommend not attempting this hike until August unless you have well-tuned navigational skills. Later on in the season, it is easier to find your way, but people often get temporarily lost, especially in the fog. You can travel as far into Spray Park as you desire and then head back the way you came.

Options: Take the side trip to Spray Falls. Spray Falls is only a short 0.1 mile up the Spray Falls Trail, and the falls are fascinating. At the junction with the Spray Falls Trail, go right (east) and follow the trail to the falls.

Camping & services: You can stay at Eagle Roost Camp. The camp only allows stoves, as in all backcountry campgrounds. There are seven sites and one pit toilet. Sites 2 and 3 have a nice view of the North Mowich Glacier, but the rest of the sites are tucked away in the forest. The only water source is Granite Creek, a little more than 0.1 mile from the camp.

You can also stay at Mowich Lake Campground. For no fee, this campground offers campsites on a first come, first served basis. Campfires are prohibited at this campground. The nearest place to obtain gas and supplies is Wilkeson north on WA 165.

For more information: Contact the Wilkeson Wilderness Information Center in Wilkeson (see Appendix A).

59 Spray Falls

<table>
<tr><td align="right">Type of hike:</td><td>Out-and-back; day hike or overnighter.</td></tr>
<tr><td align="right">Total distance:</td><td>4 miles (6.4 kilometers).</td></tr>
<tr><td align="right">Difficulty:</td><td>Easy.</td></tr>
<tr><td align="right">Elevation gain:</td><td>Minimal.</td></tr>
<tr><td align="right">Best months:</td><td>Early July–September.</td></tr>
<tr><td align="right">Maps:</td><td>USGS Golden Lakes; Trails Illustrated Mount Rainier National Park; Astronaut's Vista: Mount Rainier National Park, Washington; Earthwalk Press Hiking Map & Guide.</td></tr>
<tr><td align="right">Starting point:</td><td>Mowich Lake parking lot.</td></tr>
</table>

MOWICH LAKE — SPRAY FALLS elevation profile: 5000, 4500 FT.; MILES 1 2

General description: A short, relatively flat hike through forest to the striking Spray Falls.

Finding the trailhead: From Wilkeson, drive 9 miles south on Washington Highway 165 until the road forks. Stay to the right (south) at this fork, the way to Mowich Lake. After 3.2 miles, the road turns into a well-maintained dirt road, although it can be very slippery when muddy. Follow this road for another 8.8 miles to the Paul Peak Trailhead on the right (south) side of the road. Pause here to pay the entrance fee at the fee station. Then continue south and east 5.3 miles to Mowich Lake, a total of 26.3 miles from Wilkeson.

Parking & trailhead facilities: There are restrooms at Mowich Lake. The parking lot is fairly big, but on sunny weekends you might have to park along the road.

Key points:
0.2	(0.3)	Junction with Spray Park Trail.
1.8	(2.9)	Junction with spur trail to Eagle Roost Camp.
1.9	(3.0)	Spray Falls Trail junction.
2.0	(3.2)	Spray Creek/View of Spray Falls.

The hike: This hike has no significant elevation gain, but trundles over rolling hills all the way to Spray Falls. The well-maintained, heavily used trail winds through beautiful forest. Expect to see many other park visitors; please reduce your impact by staying on the trail.

Head to the south end of Mowich Lake, past the restrooms and Mowich Lake Campground to the Wonderland Trail. Go south on the Wonderland

Spray Falls

Trail for a little over 0.2 mile to the junction with the Spray Park Trail. Go left (southeast) when the Spray Park Trail forks off from the Wonderland Trail. There is a short spur trail 1.3 miles from the junction that leads to an overlook from Eagle Cliff, a total of 1.5 miles into your hike. You can see the North Mowich Glacier clearly from the lookout.

When you have traveled 1.9 miles total, you will see the signs for Eagle Roost Camp. Eagle Roost Camp is less than 0.1 mile away and northwest of the Spray Park Trail. A bit beyond Eagle Roost Camp is the junction with the Spray Falls Trail. Go right (southeast) onto the Spray Falls Trail. The Spray Falls Trail goes 0.1 mile to Spray Creek and Spray Falls.

The falls drop roughly 160 feet down. At the top of the falls, the water sprays off the mossy rocks leaving the air misty and cool. Lewis and yellow monkeyflowers line Spray Creek to add to the beauty of this natural wonder.

Options: You can hike further on up to Spray Park, which begins only 0.9 mile from the junction with the Spray Falls Trail. This will make your trip roughly 2 to 2.5 miles longer depending how far you decide to hike up Spray Park. (See Hike 58: Spray Park.)

Camping & services: Eagle Roost Camp allows only stoves, as in all backcountry campgrounds. There are seven sites and one pit toilet. Sites 2 and 3 have a nice view, but the rest of the sites are tucked away in the forest. The only water source is Granite Creek, a little more than 0.1 mile from camp.

Spray Falls. PHOTO BY MARIKA ENGELHARDT.

You can also stay at the Mowich Lake Campground. Campfires are prohibited. The nearest place to obtain gas and supplies is Wilkeson on WA 165.

For more information: Contact the Wilkeson Wilderness Information Center in Wilkeson (see Appendix A).

The Wonderland Trail

Food Cache System:

As you can imagine, carrying all your supplies for a nearly 90-mile hike could be rather overwhelming. For just this reason, the National Park Service has devised a food cache system that allows you to store your food at various intervals throughout your hike. You can store food caches at the Longmire Wilderness Information Center, Sunrise Visitor Center, White River Wilderness Information Center, Ohanapecosh Ranger Station, or Mowich Ranger Station. The guidelines for this system are listed below, but be aware that changes often occur in the procedure. It is always a good idea to send away for additional information or to check out the Mount Rainier website. (See Appendix A.) Also, if you are a late or early season hiker, some of these stations may be closed.

- All caches must be packed in rodent-proof containers (sealed hard plastic preferred).

- All caches must be dropped off or sent to the Longmire Wilderness Information Center, Sunrise Visitor Center, White River Ranger Station, Ohanapecosh Wilderness Information Center, or the Mowich Ranger Station only and will not be transported form one area to another by park staff.

- Fuel may not be mailed or shipped to the park, nor may it be included in any food cache. Carry enough fuel for your hike with you.

- Longmire and Sunrise are near the Wonderland Trail for easy cache pickup. Ohanapecosh and White River are not along the Wonderland Trail and require a side trip. However, before mid-June and after early September, White River or Ohanapecosh may be your only options on the east side of the park.

- Use the U.S. Post Office or UPS to ship your package. Allow at least two weeks delivery time.

- All caches must have the following information printed outside, separate from the shipping label:
  FOOD CACHE FOR: (YOUR NAME)
  FOR PICKUP AT: (NAME OF CACHE STATION)
  FOR PICKUP ON: (DATE)

60 Wonderland Trail

Type of hike:	Loop; extended backpack.
Total distance:	87.2 miles (139.5 kilometers).
Difficulty:	Strenuous.
Elevation gain:	(See elevation chart)
Best months:	Mid-July–September.
Maps:	USGS Maps Golden Lakes, Mount Rainier East, Mount Rainier West, Chinook Pass, White River, Sunrise, Mowich Lake, and Mount Wow; Trails Illustrated Mount Rainier National Park; Astronaut's Vista: Mount Rainier National Park; Washington, Earthwalk Press Hiking Map & Guide.
Starting point:	Paul Peak Trailhead.

General description: A spectacular loop, just over 90 miles, that completely encircles Mount Rainier, presenting a challenge to the ablest hiker and a comprehensive taste of Mount Rainier.

Finding the trailhead: From Wilkeson, drive 9 miles south on Washington Highway 165 until the road forks. Stay to the left (south) at this fork, the way to Mowich Lake. After 3.2 miles, the road turns into a well-maintained dirt road, although it can be very slippery when muddy. Follow this road for another 8.8 miles to the Paul Peak Trailhead on the right (south) side of the road. Pause here to pay the entrance fee at the fee station. Then continue 5.3 miles south and east to Mowich Lake, a total of 26.3 miles from Wilkeson.

Parking & trailhead facilities: There are restrooms at Mowich Lake, but they get pretty rancid from excessive use. Although there is a big parking lot, you might have to park along the road on a sunny weekend.

Key points:

1.5	(2.4)	Ipsut Pass.
5.1	(8.2)	Junction with spur trail to Ipsut Creek Campground.
6.8	(10.9)	Junction with Northern Loop Trail.
7.7	(12.3)	Junction with Spray Park Trail.
8.1	(6.5)	Carbon Glacier.
8.8	(14.1)	Dick Creek Camp.
11.5	(18.4)	Moraine Park.
12.0	(19.2)	Mystic Lake.
12.6	(20.2)	Mystic Lake Camp.
17.5	(28.0)	Granite Creek Camp.
20.2	(32.3)	Northern Loop Trail junction.
20.9	(33.4)	Frozen Lake.
21.8	(34.9)	Sunrise Camp.
25.2	(40.2)	White River Campground.
26.2	(41.9)	White River Road.
26.8	(42.9)	Wonderland Trail junction.
27.8	(44.5)	Fryingpan Creek Trail junction.

Wonderland Trail

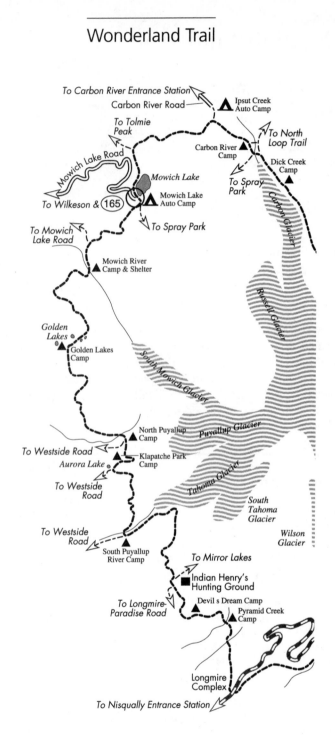

Wonderland Trail

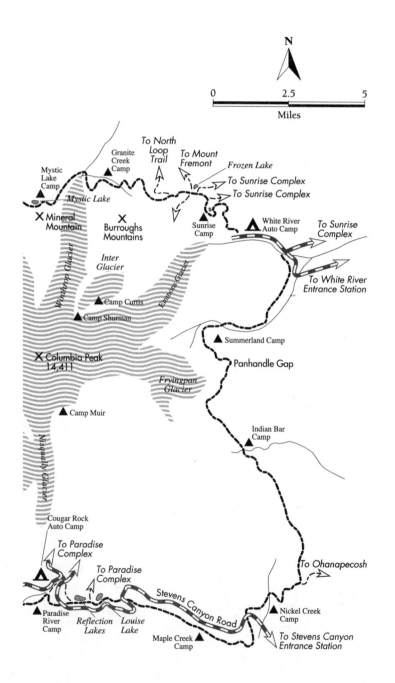

N

0   2.5   5
Miles

To North Loop Trail

Granite Creek Camp

To Mount Fremont

Frozen Lake

Mystic Lake Camp

To Sunrise Complex

To Sunrise Complex

Mystic Lake

X Mineral Mountain

X Burroughs Mountains

Sunrise Camp

White River Auto Camp

To Sunrise Complex

Winthrop Glacier

Inter Glacier

Emmons Glacier

To White River Entrance Station

Camp Curtis

Camp Shurman

Summerland Camp

Panhandle Gap

X Columbia Peak 14,411

Fryingpan Glacier

Camp Muir

Indian Bar Camp

Nisqually Glacier

Cougar Rock Auto Camp

To Paradise Complex

To Ohanapecosh

To Paradise Complex

Stevens Canyon Road

Paradise River Camp

Reflection Lakes

Louise Lake

Nickel Creek Camp

Maple Creek Camp

To Stevens Canyon Entrance Station

31.9 (51.0)   Summerland.
33.3 (58.2)   Panhandle Gap.
36.4 (58.2)   Indian Bar.
41.1 (65.8)   Cowlitz Divide Trail.
43.2 (69.1)   Nickel Creek Camp.
44.1 (70.6)   Box Canyon Trail.
45.5 (72.8)   Stevens Creek Trail.
46.5 (74.4)   Maple Creek Camp.
49.2 (78.7)   Stevens Canyon Road.
50.3 (80.5)   Louise Lake.
50.5 (80.8)   Lakes Trail.
50.6 (81.0)   Stevens Canyon Road/Reflection Lakes.
52.5 (84.0)   Junction with Narada Falls Trail.
53.2 (85.1)   Paradise Camp.
54.0 (86.4)   Carter Falls.
55.1 (88.2)   Longmire-Paradise Road.
56.6 (90.6)   Spur trail to Longmire complex.
58.4 (93.4)   Junction with Rampart Ridge Trail.
59.4 (95.0)   Kautz Creek.
60.1 (96.2)   Pyramid Creek Camp.
62.4 (99.8)   Devil's Dream Camp.
63.5(101.6)   Kautz Creek Trail junction.
67.0(107.2)   Suspension bridge over Tahoma Creek.
67.3(107.7)   Emerald Ridge.
68.9(110.2)   Junction with South Puyallup Trail.
72.1(115.4)   St. Andrew's Lake.
72.9(116.6)   Klapatche Park Camp.
75.7(121.1)   Junction with North Puyallup Trail.
80.7(129.1)   Golden Lakes.
86.8(138.9)   South Mowich Camp.
87.7(140.3)   Junction with Paul Peak Trail.
90.9(145.4)   Mowich Lake.

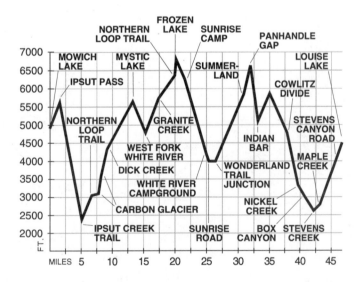

The hike: From the Mowich Lake parking lot, go to the Wonderland Trail that runs along the west side of Mowich Lake. There are several paths down to this trail, but the only trail that runs north-south along Mowich Lake is the Wonderland Trail. Head north on the Wonderland Trail. The first 0.5 mile continues along Mowich Lake and then slopes gently uphill to the top of Ipsut Pass. Near the top of Ipsut Pass, the Tolmie Peak Trail splits left (west). Stay right (north), traveling on the Wonderland Trail.

The first 0.5 mile down Ipsut Pass is very steep and open. If it is a hot day, be sure to drink plenty of water and be thankful you are not going the other direction! You can see Castle Peak to your right (east) towering above the valley. After 0.5 mile of steep downhill, the trail levels out a little and heads into the forest, but it is still downhill for the next 3.1 miles to the spur trail to Ipsut Creek Campground. You will cross several clear streams on the descent, in case you need to filter water.

The next 2.6 miles to the Spray Park Trail climb gently along the Carbon River, which runs brown from an abundance of glacial silt. Do not try to filter this water; it will ruin your filter. You can see the north side of Mother Mountain when the trail opens up. You come to the junction with the North Loop Trail, 1.7 miles from the spur trail to Ipsut Creek Campground, but stay to the right and on the Wonderland Trail. The trail is lined with bushes, and in August the thimbleberries are ripe for the picking. Continue to the junction with Spray Park Trail, 7.7 miles into your hike.

If you do not plan to camp at Carbon River Camp, 0.1 mile north, follow the Wonderland Trail east across the suspension bridge over the Carbon River. This bridge offers a fantastic view high above the Carbon River. Its source, the massive, black Carbon Glacier, rests only 0.4 mile upstream. On the other side of the Carbon River, stay to the right (south), ascending toward the glacier and Dick Creek. The easy grade gives way to a steep pitch. The trees open up to reveal the Carbon Glacier with Mount Rainier towering above. Rubble and debris from the glacier carving the earth litter the blue ice of the Carbon Gla-

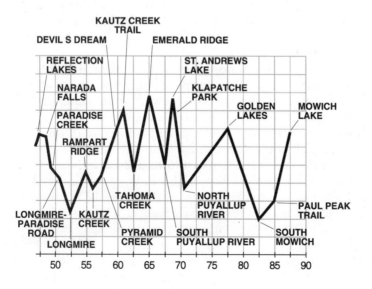

cier. Do not be surprised to hear the echoing crashes of falling rocks.

For the next 0.7 mile, the trail climbs steeply, parallel to the Carbon Glacier, to Dick Creek Camp. If you plan on camping, Dick Creek Camp has a spectacular view and nice sites. If you do not, spend some time here anyway, admiring the Northern Crags over the Carbon Glacier. The main trail leads through camp. The next 2 miles of trail climb through forest, switching back and forth. The grade lessens when the path begins to run along Moraine Creek. Keep in mind that this is bear country. In fact, a fellow hiker said that she has not come here without seeing a bear. When we were here, we came across a small black bear that was not easily deterred by loud voices, banging pots, and shrill singing.

Beyond the streambed, you come to a rock field, then a large mountain meadow. At this point you have only two small hills to climb before beginning the descent to Mystic Lake, 13.4 miles from the hike's start. The lake rests in a valley between Mineral Mountain and the appropriately named Old Desolate. The view is beautiful, but it cannot be seen from Mystic Lake Camp 0.2 mile down the trail.

The next established camp, Granite Camp, is only 4.9 miles beyond Mystic Lake Camp, but in order to get there you must circumvent the Winthrop Glacier. An easy 2 mile descent skirts the Winthrop Glacier, leading to Winthrop Creek. Cross the prepared log to the other side.

You now begin to climb your final big hill before reaching the Sunrise area. Hike 2 miles uphill with a few sporadic switchbacks uphill to Granite Creek Camp. These 2 miles run along the Winthrop Moraine, providing an excellent glimpse of the glacier, before turning west toward forest. About 17 miles from the trailhead, Granite Camp is a good camping option. If you plan to bypass the camp, stay on the Wonderland Trail heading east through camp.

Less than 2 miles of nicely graded, long switchbacks lead to a peak just below Skyscrape Mountain. From this peak you have great views in all directions. From this point, the trail drops, skirting around the southern edge of Berkeley Park to the Northern Loop Trail junction, 20.2 miles into the Wonderland Trail. After a 0.7 mile ascent leads Frozen Lake, the point at which five trails intersect.

If you do not desire to go to the Sunrise complex, take the trail that heads southeast, toward Sunrise Camp. Head downhill until you come to a junction. The trail heading east, to your left, is somewhat of an administrative road. Instead of taking this road to the Sunrise Complex, head right (south) and travel until you come to Sunrise Camp. From Sunrise Camp, you must take the Sunrise Rim Trail to the Wonderland Trail. The Sunrise Rim Trail begins to the south of the camp, heading east toward Shadow Lake.

More than 3 miles of steep, downhill switchbacks bring you to the popular White River Campground. You have now reached one of the breaks in the Wonderland Trail. Follow the small paved road to where it intersects with White River Road. Turn right (southeast) onto White River Road. You must hike along this road for 0.4 mile before it once again meets up with a maintained trail. On the right (south) side of White River Road, look for a sign for the Wonderland Trail, opposite a small pullout on the north side of the road. Take this trail heading southeast into forest. This trail continues downhill 1 mile before intersecting with the Fryingpan Creek Trail. At this intersection, stay to the right (south), following the Wonderland Trail.

Heading south from the Fryingpan Creek Trail junction, the trail climbs gradually through woods. A few switchbacks indicate that you are nearing the Fryingpan Creek crossing. Just beyond the creek, you enter a gap in the forest that allows for a good glimpse of Mount Rainier. The trail then gets steeper. When the trail turns south, you have only 1 mile of switchbacks to go until you reach Summerland, 31.9 miles into the hike. In the Summerland area, you stand in fields of wildflowers with a fantastic view of Mount Rainier and the alpine land leading up to it.

After crossing the creek that provides water for the Summerland campers, the fields of subalpine flowers turn into rock fields as you enter alpine terrain. The mountain looms over you as you pass an iceberg lake and Panhandle Gap, a saddle between two rocky rises. At this point you have reached the apex of the entire length of the Wonderland Trail.

In this area snow is a constant. Prepare to cross several steep and slippery snowfields even in the heat of late summer. Route-finding in this area may be very difficult in bad weather. After leaving the last snowfield, you have about 1 mile of hiking before you reach Indian Bar, 33.2 miles into your hike. Descend along a ridge flanked by cliffs and falls on one side and a flowered valley on the other. A few switchbacks lead down to a mountain meadow covered with lupine and magenta paintbrush. The Indian Bar Shelter is across the meadow. If you are camping here, follow the sign that points left (east) to an available site. Otherwise, continue south along the main trail.

From Indian Bar, the trail climbs steadily, gaining 1,000 feet to the top of a small hill. Make sure you look behind you, because you once again have a great view of Mount Rainier. The top of the knoll makes for a good picture spot if the weather is nice. The descent from the top leads to a wooded ridge, eclipsing Mount Rainier. Walk along this ridge 3 miles to a fork in the trail.

At the fork, head right (southwest) toward Nickel Creek. Bloodthirsty mosquitoes frequent the snowfields in this area in midsummer, so come prepared for the onslaught. Soon after taking the Wonderland Trail toward Nickel Creek, you leave the snowfields, descending quickly along steep switchbacks. The trail flattens as you approach Nickel Creek Camp, 2 miles beyond the intersection to the Cowlitz Divide Trail. If you do not plan to stay here, follow the Wonderland Trail around the camp. You cross a small stream before crossing Nickel Creek along a prepared log. Only 0.9 mile more of gradual descent, and you come to Box Canyon, 44.1 miles from Mowich Lake.

Stay to the right (northwest) along the small Box Canyon Loop. Years of glacial erosion have smoothed the surfaces of these rocks. Plants struggle to survive. You soon come to the bridge over the Cowlitz River. Water churns below. The trail almost immediately forks beyond the bridge. Stay to the right (southwest) along the Wonderland Trail. The trail ascends a bit before crossing Stevens Canyon Road over a tunnel. Less than 1 mile from the road crossing, you come to the Stevens Creek Trail junction. Stay to the left (west), once again along the Wonderland Trail. Cross the bridge where Stevens Creek churns over gray, black, and turquoise boulders.

Another mile of hiking on relatively flat terrain brings you to Maple Creek Camp. Reaching Maple Creek Camp, 46.5 miles from where you began, means that you have almost traveled halfway around the Wonderland Trail. Unless you want to explore campsites or use the pit toilet, stay to the right (northwest) toward a deceptively narrow part of the trail. The trail, however, will widen and cross a stream along a small log. While crossing, look up and to your left to see Maple Falls, which you may find difficult to spot as a result of its distance from the path.

Sylvia Falls, less than 1 mile beyond Maple Falls, is obscured by large trees, but what is visible remains engaging. It appears as though the water shoots directly out of the land from no source. A small clearing that looks out upon Sylvia Falls makes a nice, cool lunch spot for summer hikers.

A gradual ascent begins here and continues 1 mile to Martha Falls, the most impressive of the five falls on this stretch, if just for its size. The gradual ascent soon becomes a steep ascent for 0.7 mile of switchbacks. The sound of cars tells you that you have neared Stevens Canyon Road. The trail continues directly across Stevens Canyon Road.

The ascent continues for 1.1 miles to Louise Lake. The trail, however, becomes dangerously narrow and obscured by brush, so tread carefully. If you would like a closer look, choose the marked and maintained trail to the lake. After the lake, the main trail widens, a sign of more frequent usage. A more gradual ascent heads to the junction with the Lakes Trail. Turn left (south) to once more encounter Stevens Canyon Road in 0.1 mile. The trail's end, Reflection Lakes, can be seen up the road to your right (west) only 0.1 mile away.

When you reach Reflection Lakes, the trail ends and you must hike 0.1 mile along the road until the trail resumes on the west side of the lakes. Stay on the trail until you cross Stevens Canyon Road and are on the Wonderland Trail again. The trail slopes down and then slightly up to the beginning of a set of downhill switchbacks. It is 1.3 miles from Stevens Canyon Road to the junction with Narada Falls Trail. We recommend hiking the 0.1 mile to Narada Falls before continuing on the Wonderland Trail. Go right if you chose to look at the falls or go left if you are too tired or in a hurry. Head west on the Wonderland Trail. You can hear the Paradise River flowing directly to your right and you soon cross it. Before you reach the Paradise River, pass Paradise River Camp on your left, which is 0.7 mile from the junction with the Narada Falls Trail.

Three bridges take you over the relatively calm forks of the Paradise River. About 0.5 mile from here is Madcap Falls, where Tatoosh Creek flows into the Paradise River. Instead of dropping straight down, Madcap Falls flows at somewhat of a diagonal. The water gushes over the rocks to create a white wonder that is breathtaking.

Carter Falls is 0.2 mile after Madcap Falls. A sign reaffirms that the gorgeous waters you see dropping straight down are in fact Carter Falls. You might come upon a number of people here, considering the close proximity to Cougar Rock Campground.

The next 1.1 miles are a pleasant walk along the Paradise River, despite some metal drain pipes and power lines along the trail. Then, a set of bridges crosses the Nisqually River. The waters of the Nisqually River originate from active glaciers that deposit silt and grind glacial flour into the river—making the water extraordinarily muddy.

After you cross the bridges, climb up to Longmire-Paradise Road. The Wonderland Trail continues to your left (southwest) is next to a sign indicating you have 1.6 miles to Longmire. In 0.1 mile, you come to another junction. The trail to your right (north) goes to Cougar Rock Campground, and the horse ford for the Nisqually River is to the left. Continue heading southwest on the Wonderland Trail until you reach a junction, 56.6 miles into your hike. If you need or desire to go to the Longmire complex, go left (west). If not, go right (north). You will cross Longmire-Paradise Road 0.1 mile after this junction. The Wonderland Trail continues on the other side of the road, heading north up to Rampart Ridge.

You are about to begin the part of the Wonderland Trail coined "the pie crust" due to the extreme elevation changes. Be prepared for steep ups and downs. After traveling for 1.6 miles from Longmire-Paradise Road, you come to the junction with the Van Trump Park Trail heading east. Stay to the left heading north and you will come to the junction with the Rampart Ridge Trail in just 0.2 mile. The next mile to Kautz Creek is relatively level and a break from the uphill. During a hot spell, the waters of Kautz Creek can rise high enough to make a ford necessary. Be prepared and bring high-traction footwear.

On the other side of Kautz Creek, the trail ascends to Pyramid Creek Camp, 0.7 mile away, and continues to steeply ascend all the way to Devil's Dream Camp. The trail takes you through dense forest for the whole 2.3 miles. From Pyramid Peak to Devil's Dream Canyon, after Devil's Dream Camp, the trail continues uphill, but it is not as steep. You pass Squaw Lake about 0.3 mile from Devil's Dream Camp. The Kautz Creek Trail junction, in the center of Indian Henry's Hunting Ground, is 0.8 mile away. Iron Mountain and Copper Mountain are visible to the right of the trail as you head toward Indian Henry's Hunting Ground.

Indian Henry's Hunting Ground is filled with lupine and a variety of other colorful flowers in August. On a clear day, you have fantastic views of the southwest side of Mount Rainier and Pyramid Peak. A ranger station appears to the right of the trail nestled in the meadow just before you come to the Kautz Creek Trail on your left. The trail is relatively level as it travels through Indian Henry's Hunting Ground. Pass the Mirror Lakes Trail 0.2 mile after you pass the Kautz Creek Trail. If you have the time and energy, consider the option to Mirror Lakes. (See Options.)

After you pass the Mirror Lakes Trail, the trail begins to descend to Tahoma

Creek. This part of the trail has steep switchbacks and travels through pleasant forest to the suspension bridge, 1.5 miles from the Kautz Creek Trail. From the suspension bridge, there is an amazing view of Tahoma Creek. If it is not too windy, take the time to look up the creek. Tahoma Creek continually experiences glacial outburst floods. If you hear a loud, roaring sound, immediately head to higher ground.

Just after you cross the suspension bridge, look for a sign for Tahoma Creek Trail on the right heading west. The Tahoma Creek Trail connects with Westside Road in 2.1 miles. As the sign indicates, the trail is not recommended for use. The Wonderland Trail takes off uphill at this point and travels up steep switchbacks until it leaves the forest. Hike over the South Tahoma Moraine and head up to Emerald Ridge, which is 2.3 miles from Tahoma Creek and 67.3 miles into the hike.

The top of Emerald Ridge is an emerald green meadow filled with wildflowers in mid-July. The scent of lupine wafts on the breeze. A plethora of hoary marmots live in the meadows. Do not feed these wild animals; they need to remain self-sufficient to survive in their natural habitat. It is also illegal to feed the wildlife in Mount Rainier National Park. The trail along the north side of Emerald Ridge has washed out many times, hiking a steep, unstable ledge. Be very careful. Take the new trail that crosses the ridge diagnally.

The Tahoma Glacier and its moraine are directly to the left (north). If you look up at Mount Rainier, you will see the top of Tahoma Glacier, accompanied by the South Tahoma Glacier on its south side. Between the two glaciers rests Glacier Island. Often, mountain goats can be seen grazing on Glacier Island, a green haven in a sea of glaciers. If you look closely, you can see fields of lupine.

From the top of the ridge, it is 1.6 miles down rocky trail to the intersection with South Puyallup Trail. The trail travels along the edge of Emerald Ridge; it can be dangerous. This part of the trail has a fabulous view of the Tahoma Glacier and Moraine. At the South Puyallup Trail junction, the South Puyallup Trail heads left (west) toward South Puyallup Camp, 0.1 mile away. The Wonderland Trail is to the right. Cross the silty waters of South Puyallup River soon after the intersection and start heading uphill. The trail is extremely steep and brushy for the next 2.2 miles to St. Andrews Park.

The meadows of St. Andrew's Park are beautiful. In mid-July, avalanche lilies, lupine, and magenta paintbrush fill the meadows with their splendor, and Mount Rainier towers above it all. Hike through the colorful meadows and pass over a rocky ridge to St. Andrews Lake.

Previous hikers have greatly impacted the lake by creating numerous social trails along the fragile banks of this subalpine lake. Minimize your impact by admiring the lake from the designated trail. You can also see a west-side climbing route that many climbers have used to attempt the summit. Fortunately, the trails do not entirely take away from the beauty of the deep blue waters of St. Andrews Lake.

As much as you will hate leaving St. Andrews Lake, Klapatche Park Camp is only 0.8 mile away and just as amazing. The trail slopes downhill the rest of the way. Beautiful wildflowers fill the meadows of Klapatche Park and surround Aurora Lake in mid-July. Aurora Lake is only a shallow pool of snowmelt but looks astonishing with Mount Rainier towering above it. If you are staying at Klapatche Park Camp, it is located at the south end of the lake. You are now 72.9 miles into your hike with only 18 miles left to go.

The descent from Klapatche Ridge is long, steep, and brushy. Watch your step; the trail has an unstable ledge that drops straight off. You have a great view of Mount Rainier, Tokaloo Spire, and the Puyallup Glacier on a clear day from the ridge.

At the bottom of Klapatche Ridge, you come to the North Puyallup Trail next to the group/horse site of North Puyallup Camp. If you have the time and energy, take the option to Klapatche Ridge. (See Options.) Otherwise, cross the North Puyallup River via a prepared log. As you cross the river, make sure to look down at the raging white waters of the North Puyallup River and up at the Puyallup Glacier. Soon after you cross this river, you come to the individual sites of North Puyallup Camp. The trail descends slightly before it resumes climbing for the next 4 miles to Sunset Park. At the edge of Sunset Park, the hillside is filled with ghost trees, the eerie remains of a fire many years before. Magenta paintbrushes and avalanche lilies fill the meadows of the park in mid-July.

A 0.5-mile descent from Sunset Park brings you to Golden Lakes Camp and the Golden Lakes Ranger Station to the left, 80.7 miles into your hike and only 10.2 miles to the final destination. Wildflowers, such as shooting stars and avalanche lilies, line the lakeshore. You can filter water here, but the water is thick with bugs and dirt. A mile from Golden Lakes Camp, you reach the top of a ridge covered in beargrass and Columbia lilies in mid-July. Hike over the ridge and begin the descent down steep switchbacks to the Mowich River. The next 5.1 miles are all downhill with no water source.

When you reach the South Mowich River, it is only 4.1 miles to Mowich Lake. The area around the South Mowich River is scattered with debris and crushed trees from previous glacial outburst floods due to the ever-changing south fork of the Mowich River. When we hiked this trail, one of the three bridges over the South Mowich River was washed out, which it apparently does several times a year. Be aware that it is a tricky ford and glacial boulders in the river are a possible hazard. It is a good idea to call ahead to the Wilkeson Wilderness Information Center to find out if the bridge is down so you can prepare accordingly, but understand that it might be washed out regardless due to the unpredictability of the washouts.

After crossing the South Mowich River via three bridges, you come to Mowich Camp and the South Mowich Shelter. Hike through lush forest to the North Mowich River, which you cross via two bridges, and start climbing to Mowich Lake. The next 3.6 miles of trail are very steep ascending through old-growth forest. When you reach the junction with Spray Park Trail, you know you only have 0.2 mile left to go!

Options: Side Trip 1: The detour to Mirror Lakes is a total of 1.4 miles long out and back. Before you take this option, be aware that these lakes are not very big. It is a very enjoyable side trip through flower-filled meadows. Go right (northeast) on Mirror Lakes Trail for 0.7 mile to the lakes. Follow the Mirror Lakes Trail to its end, where there is a great view of Pyramid Peak and Mount Rainier.

Side Trip 2: Another option is Denman Falls. At the west end of Aurora Lake, the St. Andrews Trail splits west from the Wonderland Trail. It plummets 2.5 miles down steep switchbacks to Westside Road. The Denman Falls Trail begins on the other side of the road and a few steps north. Denman Falls is 0.2 mile from Westside Road and has two overlooks. The first trail that forks off from the Denman Falls Trail leads to the overlook above the falls, and the second trail takes you below the falls.

Side Trip 3: Klapatche Point offers a vantage beyond the park's western boundary. From the junction with the North Puyallup Trail, go west along the side of the group/horse site of North Puyallup Camp. The trail is flat all the way to Westside Road. An abundance of berries lines the trail, and bear scat is everywhere. At the end of the North Puyallup Trail, about 2.4 miles from North Puyallup Camp, is Klapatche Point. Enjoy the view, and then hike back to the Wonderland Trail.

Camping & services: Fires are not permitted in any backcountry camps. Here is a list of camps along the Wonderland Trail. Depending on how you decide to take on the Wonderland Trail and availability of sites, you will choose from these options:

Carbon River Camp: There are four individual sites. The first two have excellent tent sites but are not very private. Sites 3 and 4 are more secluded with slanted tent sites, 4 being the most remote. The water source for this camp is Cataract Creek, a good 0.1 mile from all the sites. The National Park Service is in the process of adding a campsite here.

Dick Creek Camp: One of our favorite backcountry camps, it two nice sites as well. Site 1 has an unbelievable view of the Carbon Glacier. Dick Creek, the water source, is only a short walk away.

Mystic Lake Camp: Unfortunately, this camp is located quite a distance from the lake. An established camp along the Wonderland Trail, it has a whopping seven individual sites and two group sites, all with good tent sites but little privacy. Two flimsy food storage poles offer little protection from a bear that frequents this camp.

Granite Creek Creek: The two individual campsites and one group site at Granite Creek have no view but quite a bit of privacy. Granite Creek makes a nice water source.

Sunrise Camp: There are eight sites available. None of the sites are very private, but site 8 is the most secluded. Try to snag site 5 or 6 for a great view of Shadow Lake.

Summerland Camp: It has five individual campsites and one group site. We recommend camping at either site 3 or 4, even though they are farther from the toilet than the other sites (except site 5 which has no view). Both have the best views. The water source for all sites is a stream south along the main trail.

Indian Bar Camp: It has three lovely, private individual sites and one group site with bunks within the shelter.

Nickel Creek Camp: A large, flat area for camping includes three individual campsites and one large group camp. Nickel Creek provides a good water source.

Maple Creek Camp: There are four individual sites and one group site, which is situated very near the pit toilet. The National Park Service is currently establishing another camp here. Take site 4 for the privacy and view, although it is farthest from water and the toilet.

Paradise River Camp: Its three individual sites and one group site are small and flat. Site 2 is the most secluded, but it overlooks site 1. Site 3 is nearest to the toilets and directly off the spur trail. The Paradise River is the water source for this backcountry camp.

Pyramid Creek Camp: The camp only has two sites, but the National Park Service is currently adding another. It has a pit toilet, and its water source is Pyramid Creek, less than 0.1 mile north on the Wonderland Trail. Both sites are flat and nice, site 2 being more private and more spacious.

Devil's Dream Camp: The campsites here are nothing to dream about, but seven individual sites and the group site are very nice and flat. Sites 5 and 6 offer the most privacy. There are two pit toilets, and the camp is often filled with Wonderland Trail hikers. Be careful when you use the toilet near site 4 because it is likely that the residents at site 4 can see you! All of the other sites are next to the trail, spacious, and flat. Usually the water source for Devil's Dream Camp is near site 1, but it often dries up in late summer. If this is the case, you will have to hike about 0.25 mile to Squaw Lake or to the creek directly after Squaw Lake, depending on where you prefer to obtain your water.

South Puyallup Camp: There are four individual sites at South Puyallup Camp and one group site. Site 1 is probably the best campsite. It is private, with a close water source. Be forewarned that the toilet is 0.1 mile from all the campsites. Site 2 also has its own water source with good tent sites. Sites 3 and 4 have just been improved, and if seclusion is your primary concern, site 4 is your best bet.

Klapatche Park: The campsites here spoil you. There are four individual sites. The toilet is near all the sites, although the food storage pole is too close. Site 1 is closest to the lake and has an incomparable view. Watching the sun rise and reflect Mount Rainier in Aurora Lake will take your breath away. You cannot see Mount Rainier clearly from any of the other sites, but the view down the north side of Klapatche Ridge from sites 2, 3, and 4 is also very pleasant.

North Puyallup Camp: The camp is along the North Puyallup River, although you do not see the river from any of the sites. The camp, tucked away in the forest, has three individual sites and one group/horse site. Each site is flat, but all are small and directly next to the trail. The group/horse site is rather spacious and open, but still near the trail. The group/horse site is separate from the three individual sites and located across the footbridge over the North Puyallup River.

Golden Lakes: There are five individual campsites and one group site. The camp also has a food storage pole to hang your food. Sites 1, 2, and 3 are near the toilets and far away from water. The group site and sites 4 and 5 are near the lake. You have a fantastic view at site 5, as well as a close water source. The group site is closest to the lake, and site 4 is on top of the ridge and looks down into the valley on the other side of the lakes.

Mowich Camp: This camp has four individual sites and a group site. (The South Mowich Shelter is considered one of the individual sites.) Sites 3 and 4 are closer to the South Mowich River, while sites 1 and 2, along with the group site, are crunched together and near the trail. There is an outhouse.

For more information: Contact the Wilkeson Wilderness Information Center, the Longmire Wilderness Information Center, or the White River Wilderness Information Center Whanapecosh Visitor Center (see Appendix A).

Appendix A: For More Information

For a great summary of basic facts on visiting Mount Rainier, call the 24-hour information number 360-569-2211) and ask for a free copy of *Tahoma News—Visitor Guide to Mount Rainier*, a newspaper published by The Northwest Interpretive Association. Visitors also receive a copy of this publication at the entrance station. It contains a list of commercial services available in the park, updates on park road construction, campground information, regulations and safety tips, a list of events, and lots more useful information. The *Tahoma News* will answer most of your questions about park services.

If you have access to the Internet, the Mount Rainier website, www.nps.gov/mora, is a wealth of information. Updated almost daily, this website can probably answer any question you have about Mount Rainier. The site contains information on wilderness permits, explicit camping options, trailside campsites and their elevations, and the information found in the newspaper.

Associations: Hiking and Conservation

Longmire Wilderness Information Center; (360) 569-2211 ext. 3317.
Longmire Museum; (360) 569-2211 ext. 3314.

Both associations are located in the Longmire Historic District, along Longmire-Paradise Road. From the Nisqually Entrance Station, drive 6.7 miles east to the Longmire complex. (See Planning Your Trip for directions to the Nisqually Entrance Station.) The Longmire Wilderness Information Center issues permits primarily for backpacking and has rangers equipped to help with any questions you might have. The Longmire Museum offers a range of information, such as natural history, cultural history, backpacking, hiking, and trail conditions.

Food Cache Shipping Address:

Mount Rainier National Park
Longmire Wilderness Information Center
General Delivery
Longmire, WA 98397

Paradise Ranger Station; (360) 569-2315.
From the Nisqually Entrance Station, drive 15.9 miles east on Longmire-Paradise Road to the turnoff for Ohanapecosh. (See Planning Your Trip for directions to the Nisqually Entrance Station.) Stay to the left and head 2.2 miles up to the Paradise complex. The Paradise Ranger Station mainly issues climbing permits for routes starting from Paradise, but you can obtain backcountry permits and information here as well. This ranger station is open only in the summer.

White River Wilderness Information Center; (360) 829-5127.
The White River Wilderness Information Center is located next to the White River Entrance Station. (See Planning Your Trip for directions to the White River Entrance Station.) This center issues permits primarily for backpacking and north-side climbing routes. The center is open from late May through summer.

Mowich Ranger Station; (360) 829-2127.
The Mowich Ranger Station is on the west side of Mowich Lake. From Wilkeson, drive 9 miles south on Washington Highway 165 to where the road forks. Stay to the right (south) at this fork, the way to Mowich Lake. After 3.2 miles, the road turns into a well-maintained dirt road, although it can be slippery when muddy. Follow this road for another 8.8 miles to the Paul Peak Trailhead on the right (south) side of the road. Pause at the fee station here and pay the park entrance fee. Then continue south and east 5.3 miles to Mowich Lake, a total of 26.3 miles from Wilkeson.

Food Cache Shipping Address:

Mount Rainier National Park
Carbon River Wilderness Information Center
Star Route
Carbonado, WA 98323

Wilkeson Wilderness Information Center; (360) 829-5127.
Drive to Wilkeson on Washington Highway 165. The Wilkeson Wilderness Information Center is located in the center of Wilkeson, in a red caboose next to the town library. This center is open from mid-May through the end of summer. Staff issues permits primarily for backpacking and north-side climbing routes.

Sunrise Visitor Center; (360) 663-2425.
From the White River Entrance Station, drive 13.8 miles west on White River Road to the Sunrise complex. (See Planning Your Trip for directions to the White River Entrance Station.) The Sunrise Visitor Center opens in early July, about the time White River Road opens, and stays open throughout the summer.

Food Cache Shipping Address: (for either the Sunrise Visitor Center or the White River Ranger Station)

Mount Rainier National Park
Sunrise Ranger Station or White River Ranger Station
70002 Highway 410 East
Enumclaw, WA 98022

Ohanapecosh Visitor Center; (360) 569-2211 ext. 2353.
From the Stevens Canyon Entrance Station, drive 1.8 miles south on Washington Highway 123 to the turnoff for Ohanapecosh Campground. (See Planning Your Trip for directions to the Stevens Canyon Entrance Station.) The road forks just after you turn in; go right (north) and drive until the

Ohanapecosh Visitor Center appears directly in front of you. If possible, plan on getting your permit from one of the main locations listed above. In some cases, you can also get permits at the Ohanapecosh Visitor Center, but the rangers stationed here have other responsibilities and may not be available. This center provides a variety of exhibits and information about Mount Rainier National Park. It opens late May and stays open throughout the summer.

Ohanapecosh Visitor Center; (360) 569-2211 ext. 2353.
From the Stevens Canyon Entrance Station, drive south 1.8 miles on Washington Highway 123 to the turnoff for Ohanapecosh Campground. (See Planning Your Trip for directions to the Stevens Canyon Entrance Station.) The road forks just after you turn in; go left (south) and drive until the Ohanapecosh Ranger Station appears directly in front of you.

Food Cache Shipping Address:

Mount Rainier National Park
Ohanapecosh Ranger Station
208 Ohanapecosh
Packwood, WA 98361

National Park Inn; (360) 569-2275.

Paradise Inn; (360) 569-2275.

Ohanapecosh Campground Reservations; (800) 365-CAMP.

Where to Get Weather Information
The optimal place to obtain weather information is Mount Rainier's website, www.nps.gov/mora. If you do not have access to the Internet, you can call the 24-hour information number, 360-569-2211, or one of the associations listed above.

Where to Get Maps
There are a variety of maps for Mount Rainier, but in preparing this book, we used Trails Illustrated Maps, Earthwalk Press Maps, and U.S. Geological Survey quadrangles. You can get these maps at park visitor centers or sport stores around the park. You can usually special order any USGS quad from your local sport store, or you can order them directly from the USGS at the following address:

Map Distribution
U.S. Geological Survey
Box 25286, Federal Center
Denver, CO 80225

Appendix B: Further Reading

A variety of literature addresses Mount Rainier's rich history, geological and human. Listed below is a short list of informational books that you might consider reading about Mount Rainier National Park, as well as a list of how-to books and picture books about Mount Rainier. The following books are all available through Falcon Publishing. Order toll-free by calling 800-582-2665.

Bear Aware
By Bill Schneider

Rainier Panorama
By Will Landon

Mount Rainier Pocket Portfolio
By Ron Warfield

Mount Rainier Postcard Book
By Sierra Press

Avalanche Aware
By John Moynier

Backpacking Tips
By Bill Schneider, Russ Schneider, and others
Illustrated by Todd Telander

Reading Weather
By Jim Woodmencey
Illustrated by Todd Telander

A Field Guide to Scats & Tracks of the Rocky Mountains
By James Halfpenny, Ph.D.
Illustrated by Todd Telander

Wild Country Companion
By Will Harmon

Mountain Lion Alert
By Steven Torres

Leave No Trace
By Will Harmon

Wilderness First Aid
By Gilbert Preston, M.D.

Wilderness Survival
By Suzanne Swedo

Washington Wildlife Viewing Guide
By Joe La Tourrette

The Rocky Mountain Berry Book
By Bob Krumm

Western Trees
By Maggie Stuckey and George Palmer
Illustrated by Keith Bowers

Wayside Wildflowers of the Pacific Northwest
By Dr. Lee Stickler

Adventure Guide to Mount Rainier
By Jeff Smoot

The Northwest Interpretive Association also offers educational publications on Mount Rainier. You can order any of the following books by calling 360-569-2211 ext. 3320, or writing to: Northwest Interpretive Association (NWIA), Longmire, Washington 98397.

Where the Waters Begin: The Traditional Nisqually Indian History of Mount Rainier
By Celia S. Carpenter

Island in the Sky: Pioneering Accounts of Mount Rainier, 1833-1894
By Paul Schullery

The Geological Story of Mount Rainier
By Dwight R. Crandall

A Visitor's Guide to Mount Rainier Glaciers
By C. Driedger

Mount Rainier: The Story Behind the Scenery
By Ray "Skip" Snow

Appendix C: Hiker's Checklist

HIKING EQUIPMENT: Equipment does not have to be new or fancy (or expensive), but make sure you test everything before you leave home.

Equipment Checklist for Day Hiking (* = optional)

- [ ] Day pack or fanny pack
- [ ] Water bottles
- [ ] First-aid kit
- [ ] Survival kit
- [ ] Compass
- [ ] Maps
- [ ] Toilet trowel
- [ ] Toilet paper
- [ ] Sunscreen and lip lotion
- [ ] Binoculars*
- [ ] Camera and extra film*
- [ ] Flashlight and extra batteries
- [ ] Pocketknife
- [ ] Sunglasses

Added Equipment for Overnight Trips

- [ ] Tent and waterproof fly
- [ ] Sleeping bag (rated 20 degrees F or warmer) and stuffsack
- [ ] Sleeping pad
- [ ] Cooking pots and potholder
- [ ] More water bottles
- [ ] Full-size backpack
- [ ] Cup, bowl, and eating utensils
- [ ] Lightweight camp stove and adequate fuel
- [ ] Garbage sacks
- [ ] Zip-locked bags
- [ ] Stuffsacks*
- [ ] Paper towels*
- [ ] Nylon cord (50 ft.)
- [ ] Small towel
- [ ] Personal toilet kit
- [ ] Notebook and pencil*

CLOTHING: In general, strive for natural fibers such as cotton and wool, and "earth tones" instead of bright colors. Dig around in the closet for something "dull." Your wilderness partners will appreciate it. Try out the clothing before leaving home to make sure everything fits loosely with no chafing. In particular, make sure your boots are broken in, lest they break you on the first day of the hike.

Clothing for Day Hiking

- ☐ Large-brimmed hat or cap
- ☐ Sturdy hiking boots
- ☐ Light, natural fiber socks
- ☐ Lightweight hiking shorts or long pants
- ☐ Long-sleeved shirt
- ☐ Lightweight, windproof coat
- ☐ Rain gear
- ☐ Mittens or gloves

Additional Clothing for Overnight Trips

- ☐ Warm hat (stocking cap)
- ☐ Long underwear
- ☐ Water-resistant, windproof wilderness coat
- ☐ Sweater and/or insulated vest
- ☐ Long pants
- ☐ One pair of socks for each day, plus one extra pair
- ☐ Underwear
- ☐ Extra shirts
- ☐ Sandals or lightweight shoes for wearing in camp

FOOD: For day hiking, bring high-energy snacks for lunching along the way. For overnight trips, bring enough food, including high-energy snacks for lunching during the day, but don't overburden yourself with too much food. Plan meals carefully, bringing just enough food, plus some emergency rations. Freeze-dried foods are the lightest and safest in bear country, but expensive and not really necessary. Don't forget hot and cold drinks.

About the Authors

Hiking along the Pacific Crest Trail. Photo by John Caldwell

Heidi Schneider and Mary Skjelset make up the youngest author team to ever write a FalconGuide. Heidi has hiked extensively throughout the West with her family since high school and is currently attending Lewis and Clark College in Portland, Oregon. Mary also lives in Portland, where she studies political science at Reed College. When not writing or studying, she enjoys hiking, of course, and camping, skiing, dance, and soccer. They hiked all the trails of Mount Rainier National Park during the summer of 1998.

FALCON GUIDES® Leading the Way™

FALCONGUIDES® are available for where-to-go hiking, mountain biking, rock climbing, walking, scenic driving, fishing, rockhounding, paddling, birding, wildlife viewing, and camping. We also have FalconGuides on essential outdoor skills and subjects and field identification. The following titles are currently available, but this list grows every year. For a free catalog with a complete list of titles, call FALCON toll-free at 1-800-582-2665.

HIKING GUIDES:

State-specific guides to Alaska, Arizona, California, Colorado, Florida, Georgia, Idaho, Maine, Michigan, Minnesota, Montana, Nevada, New Hampshire, New Mexico, New York, North Carolina, Oregon, Pennsylvania, South Carolina, Tennessee, Texas, Utah, Vermont, Virginia, Washington, and Wyoming.

Regional guides to Arizona's Cactus Country, the Beartooths, Best Hikes Along the Continental Divide, Big Bend, Bob Marshall Country, California's Desert Parks, Canyonlands & Arches, Carlsbad Caverns & Guadalupe Mtns., Columbia River Gorge, Glacier & Waterton Lakes, Grand Canyon, Grand Staircase-Escalante/Glen Canyon, Great Basin, Hot Springs of the Pacific Northwest, North Cascades, Northern Arizona, Olympic Natl. Park, Oregon's Eagle Cap Wilderness, Oregon's Mount Hood/Badger Creek, Oregon's Three Sisters Country, Shenandoah, South Dakota's Black Hills Country, Southern New England, Utah's Summits, Wyoming's Cloud Peak Wilderness, Wyoming's Wind River Range, Yellowstone, and Zion & Bryce Canyon. Also: Exploring Canyonlands & Arches, Exploring Hawaii's Parklands, and Best Hikes Along the Continental Divide.

Best Easy Day Hikes to the Beartooths, Canyonlands & Arches, Cape Cod, Colorado Springs, Glacier & Waterton Lakes, Glen Canyon, Grand Canyon, Grand Teton, Grand Staircase-Escalante & the Glen Canyon Region, Olympics, Lake Tahoe, Mount St. Helens, North Cascades, Salt Lake City, Shenandoah, and Yellowstone.

MOUNTAIN BIKING GUIDES:

Arizona, Colorado, Georgia, New Mexico, New York, Northern New England, Oregon, South Carolina, Mountain Biking Southern California, Southern New England, Utah, Wisconsin, and Wyoming.

Local mountain biking guides to Bend, Boise, Chequamegon, Chico, Colorado Springs Denver-Boulder, Durango, Flagstaff & Sedona, Helena, Moab, Utah's St. George/Cedar City Area, White Mountains (West), and Fat Trax Bozeman.

WILDLIFE VIEWING GUIDES:

Alaska, Arizona, California, Colorado, Florida, Idaho, Indiana, Iowa, Kentucky, Massachusetts, Montana, Nebraska, Nevada, New Hampshire, New Jersey, New Mexico, New York, North Carolina, North Dakota, Ohio, Oregon, Puerto Rico and the Virgin Islands, Tennessee, Texas, Utah, Vermont, Virginia, Washington, West Virginia, and Wisconsin.

SCENIC DRIVING:

Alaska/Yukon, Arizona, Beartooth Highway, California, Colorado, Florida, Georgia, Hawaii, Idaho, Michigan, Minnesota, Montana, New England, New Mexico, North Carolina, Pennsylvania, Oregon, Ozarks, Texas, Utah, Washington, Wisconsin, Wyoming, and Yellowstone & Grand Teton. Plus, Back Country Byways, Scenic Byways East, Scenic Byways Far West, and Scenic Byways Rocky Mountains.

Historic trail driving guides to California's Gold Rush Country, Lewis and Clark Trail, the Pony Express Trail, and the Oregon Trail.

■ *To order any of these books, check with your local bookseller or call FALCON® at **1-800-582-2665**.*
Visit us on the world wide web at:
www.FalconOutdoors.com

FALCON®

FALCONGUIDES® Leading the Way™

FALCONGUIDES® are available for where-to-go hiking, mountain biking, rock climbing, walking, scenic driving, fishing, rockhounding, paddling, birding, wildlife viewing, and camping. We also have FalconGuides on essential outdoor skills and subjects and field identification. The following titles are currently available, but this list grows every year. For a free catalog with a complete list of titles, call FALCON toll-free at 1-800-582-2665.

MOUNTAIN BIKING GUIDES

Mountain Biking Arizona
Mountain Biking Colorado
Mountain Biking Georgia
Mountain Biking New Mexico
Mountain Biking New York
Mountain Biking Northern New England
Mountain Biking Oregon
Mountain Biking South Carolina
Mountain Biking Southern California
Mountain Biking Southern New England
Mountain Biking Utah
Mountain Biking Wisconsin
Mountain Biking Wyoming

LOCAL CYCLING SERIES

Fat Trax Bozeman
Mountain Biking Bend
Mountain Biking Boise
Mountain Biking Chequamegon
Mountain Biking Chico
Mountain Biking Colorado Springs
Mountain Biking Denver/Boulder
Mountain Biking Durango
Mountain Biking Flagstaff and Sedona
Mountain Biking Helena
Mountain Biking Moab
Mountain Biking Utah's St. George/Cedar City Area
Mountain Biking the White Mountains (West)

■ *To order any of these books, check with your local bookseller*
*or call FALCON® at **1-800-582-2665**.*
Visit us on the world wide web at:
www.FalconOutdoors.com

FALCON®

FALCONGUIDES® Leading the Way™

WILDLIFE VIEWING GUIDES

Alaska Wildlife Viewing Guide
Arizona Wildlife Viewing Guide
California Wildlife Viewing Guide
Colorado Wildlife Viewing Guide
Florida Wildlife Viewing Guide
Indiana Wildlife Vewing Guide
Iowa Wildlife Viewing Guide
Kentucky Wildlife Viewing Guide
Massachusetts Wildlife Viewing Guide
Montana Wildlife Viewing Guide
Nebraska Wildlife Viewing Guide
Nevada Wildlife Viewing Guide
New Hampshire Wildlife Viewing Guide
New Jersey Wildlife Viewing Guide
New Mexico Wildlife Viewing Guide
New York Wildlife Viewing Guide
North Carolina Wildlife Viewing Guide
North Dakota Wildlife Viewing Guide
Ohio Wildlife Viewing Guide
Oregon Wildlife Viewing Guide
Puerto Rico and the Virgin Islands WVG
Tennessee Wildlife Viewing Guide
Texas Wildlife Viewing Guide
Utah Wildlife Viewing Guide
Vermont Wildlife Viewing Guide
Virginia Wildlife Viewing Guide
Washington Wildlife Viewing Guide
West Virginia Wildlife Viewing Guide
Wisconsin Wildlife Viewing Guide

HISTORIC TRAIL GUIDES

Traveling California's Gold Rush Country
Traveling the Lewis & Clark Trail
Traveling the Oregon Trail
Traveler's Guide to the Pony Express Trail

SCENIC DRIVING GUIDES

Scenic Driving Alaska and the Yukon
Scenic Driving Arizona
Scenic Driving the Beartooth Highway
Scenic Driving California
Scenic Driving Colorado
Scenic Driving Florida
Scenic Driving Georgia
Scenic Driving Hawaii
Scenic Driving Idaho
Scenic Driving Michigan
Scenic Driving Minnesota
Scenic Driving Montana
Scenic Driving New England
Scenic Driving New Mexico
Scenic Driving North Carolina
Scenic Driving Oregon
Scenic Driving the Ozarks including the
   Ouchita Mountains
Scenic Driving Pennsylvania
Scenic Driving Texas
Scenic Driving Utah
Scenic Driving Washington
Scenic Driving Wisconsin
Scenic Driving Wyoming
Scenic Driving Yellowstone & Grand Teton
   National Parks
Back Country Byways
Scenic Byways East
Scenic Byways Farwest
Scenic Byways Rocky Mountains

■ *To order any of these books, check with your local bookseller*
or call FALCON® at 1-800-582-2665.
Visit us on the world wide web at:
www.FalconOutdoors.com

FALCON®

FALCON GUIDES® Leading the Way™

HIKING GUIDES

Best Hikes Along the Continental Divide
Hiking Alaska
Hiking Arizona
Hiking Arizona's Cactus Country
Hiking the Beartooths
Hiking Big Bend National Park
Hiking the Bob Marshall Country
Hiking California
Hiking California's Desert Parks
Hiking Carlsbad Caverns
    and Guadalupe Mtns. National Parks
Hiking Colorado
Hiking Colorado, Vol. II
Hiking Colorado's Summits
Hiking Colorado's Weminuche Wilderness
Hiking the Columbia River Gorge
Hiking Florida
Hiking Georgia
Hiking Glacier & Waterton Lakes National Parks
Hiking Grand Canyon National Park
Hiking Grand Staircase-Escalante/Glen Canyon
Hiking Grand Teton National Park
Hiking Great Basin National Park
Hiking Hot Springs in the Pacific Northwest
Hiking Idaho
Hiking Maine
Hiking Michigan
Hiking Minnesota
Hiking Montana
Hiking Mount Rainier National Park
Hiking Mount St. Helens
Hiking Nevada

Hiking New Hampshire
Hiking New Mexico
Hiking New York
Hiking the North Cascades
Hiking Northern Arizona
Hiking Olympic National Park
Hiking Oregon
Hiking Oregon's Eagle Cap Wilderness
Hiking Oregon's Mount Hood/Badger Creek
Hiking Oregon's Three Sisters Country
Hiking Pennsylvania
Hiking Shenandoah
Hiking the Sierra Nevada
Hiking South Carolina
Hiking South Dakota's Black Hills Country
Hiking Southern New England
Hiking Tennessee
Hiking Texas
Hiking Utah
Hiking Utah's Summits
Hiking Vermont
Hiking Virginia
Hiking Washington
Hiking Wisconsin
Hiking Wyoming
Hiking Wyoming's Cloud Peak Wilderness
Hiking Wyoming's Wind River Range
Hiking Yellowstone National Park
Hiking Zion & Bryce Canyon National Parks
Wild Montana
Wild Country Companion
Wild Utah

■ *To order any of these books, check with your local bookseller*
or call FALCON® at 1-800-582-2665.
Visit us on the world wide web at:
www.FalconOutdoors.com

FALCON®

FALCON GUIDES® Leading the Way

FIELD GUIDES
Bitterroot: Montana State Flower
Canyon Country Wildflowers
Central Rocky Mountains
　Wildflowers
Great Lakes Berry Book
New England Berry Book
Ozark Wildflowers
Pacific Northwest Berry Book
Plants of Arizona
Rare Plants of Colorado
Rocky Mountain Berry Book
Scats & Tracks of the Pacific
　Coast States
Scats & Tracks of the
　Rocky Mountains
Southern Rocky Mountain
　Wildflowers
Tallgrass Prairie Wildflowers
Western Trees
Wildflowers of Southwestern
　Utah
Willow Bark and Rosehips

FISHING GUIDES
Fishing Alaska
Fishing the Beartooths
Fishing Florida
Fishing Glacier National Park
Fishing Maine
Fishing Montana
Fishing Wyoming
Fishing Yellowstone
　National Park

ROCKHOUNDING GUIDES
Rockhounding Arizona
Rockhounding California
Rockhounding Colorado
Rockhounding Montana
Rockhounding Nevada
Rockhound's Guide to New
　Mexico
Rockhounding Texas
Rockhounding Utah
Rockhounding Wyoming

MORE GUIDEBOOKS
Backcountry Horseman's
　Guide to Washington
Camping California's
　National Forests
Exploring Canyonlands &
　Arches National Parks
Exploring Hawaii's Parklands
Exploring Mount Helena
Exploring Southern California
　Beaches
Recreation Guide to WA
　National Forests
Touring California & Nevada
　Hot Springs
Touring Colorado Hot Springs
Touring Montana & Wyoming
　Hot Springs
Trail Riding Western
　Montana
Wild Country Companion
Wilderness Directory
Wild Montana
Wild Utah

BIRDING GUIDES
Birding Minnesota
Birding Montana
Birding Northern California
Birding Texas
Birding Utah

PADDLING GUIDES
Floater's Guide to Colorado
Paddling Minnesota
Paddling Montana
Paddling Okefenokee
Paddling Oregon
Paddling Yellowstone & Grand
　Teton National Parks

HOW-TO GUIDES
Avalanche Aware
Backpacking Tips
Bear Aware
Desert Hiking Tips
Hiking with Dogs
Leave No Trace
Mountain Lion Alert
Reading Weather
Route Finding
Using GPS
Wilderness First Aid
Wilderness Survival

WALKING
Walking Colorado Springs
Walking Denver
Walking Portland
Walking St. Louis
Walking Virginia Beach

■ *To order any of these books, check with your local bookseller*
or call FALCON ® at 1-800-582-2665.
Visit us on the world wide web at:
www.FalconOutdoors.com

FALCON®

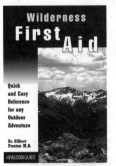

WILDERNESS FIRST AID

By Dr. Gilbert Preston M.D.

Enjoy the outdoors and face the inherent risks with confidence. By reading this easy-to-follow first-aid text, all outdoor enthusiasts can pack a little extra peace of mind on their next adventure. *Wilderness First Aid* offers expert medical advice for dealing with outdoor emergencies beyond the reach of 911. It easily fits in most backcountry first-aid kits.

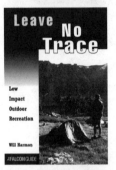

LEAVE NO TRACE

By Will Harmon

The concept of "leave no trace" seems simple, but it actually gets fairly complicated. This handy quick-reference guidebook includes all the newest information on this growing and all-important subject. This book is written to help the outdoor enthusiast make the hundreds of decisions necessary to protect the natural landscape and still have an enjoyable wilderness experience. Part of the proceeds from the sale of this book go to continue leave-no-trace education efforts. The Official Manual of American Hiking Society.

BEAR AWARE

By Bill Schneider

Hiking in bear country can be very safe if hikers follow the guidelines summarized in this small, "packable" book. Extensively reviewed by bear experts, the book contains the latest information on the intriguing science of bear-human interactions. *Bear Aware* can not only make your hike safer, but it can help you avoid the fear of bears that can take the edge off your trip.

MOUNTAIN LION ALERT

By Steve Torres

Recent mountain lion attacks have received national attention. Although infrequent, lion attacks raise concern for public safety. *Mountain Lion Alert* contains helpful advice for mountain bikers, trail runners, horse riders, pet owners, and suburban landowners on how to reduce the chances of mountain lion-human conflicts.

Also Available

Wilderness Survival • Reading Weather • Backpacking Tips • Climbing Safely •
Avalanche Aware • Desert Hiking Tips • Hiking with Dogs • Using GPS •
Route Finding • Wild Country Companion

To order check with your local bookseller or
call FALCON® at **1-800-582-2665.**
www.FalconOutdoors.com